Volume Seven

AMERICAN TRIBAL RELIGIONS

a monograph series,
published by the
University of Nebraska Press

Karl W. Luckert, General Editor

Department of Religious Studies
Southwest Missouri State University

published in collaboration
with LUFA-type and
the Museum of Northern Arizona

The UPWARD MOVING and EMERGENCE WAY

The Gishin Biye' Version

Father Berard Haile, O.F.M.

Karl W. Luckert, Editor

Navajo Orthography by
Irvy W. Goossen

University of Nebraska Press

Lincoln and London

In the interest of timeliness and economy, this work was printed directly from camera-ready copy provided by the General Editor.

Library of Congress Cataloging in Publication Data

Main entry under title:

The Upward moving and emergence way.

    (American tribal religions ; v. 7)
    1. Navaho Indians—Religion and mythology. 2. Navaho Indians—Rites and ceremonies. 3. Indians of North America—Southwest, New—Religion and mythology. 4. Indians of North America—Southwest, New—Rites and ceremonies. I. Begay, Gishin. II. Haile, Berard, 1874–1961. III. Luckert, Karl W., 1934–   . IV. Goossen, Irvy W. Series.
E99.N3U76   299'.78   81–7441
ISBN 0–8032–2320–X (cloth)
ISBN 0–8032–7212–X (paper)

Contents

(v)

Editor's Introduction

During the summer of 1979 a very rough typescript, without title page but containing extensive corrections in the hand of Father Berard, was delivered to the University of Arizona Library for safekeeping. When this editor was asked to identify the document for proper cataloguing, it was found that the text somewhat resembled, but also significantly departed from, the Mary C. Wheelwright publication of Father Berard's *haneełnéehee (Emergence Myth According to the Hanelth-nayhe or Upward-reaching Rite*. Santa Fe, 1949). There had to be a final draft of this work somewhere. Copies of the suspected typescript were subsequently found in the Wheelwright Museum at Santa Fe and in the Museum of Northern Arizona. Sincere thanks are extended to these institutions for having provided ready access to their materials. I also thank the Franciscan Missionary Union, Cincinnati, for granting permission to publish the original version in the American Tribal Religions series.

The Father Berard version of Upward-moving or Emergence Way *(haneełnéehee)*, which Mary Wheelwright published in her book, is very abbreviated and stripped of many of its original Navajo character-istics. In her preface she informs us that Father Berard had remarked to her that the text "was far too long and involved." She also tells that "he read and approved of this version." There is no reason at all to doubt these statements, or even the good intentions of Miss Wheel-wright. Nor are there any real grounds on which to suspect that Father Berard did not in some sense mean what he said. The fact remains, the Upward-moving or Emergence Way, which Father Berard recorded in 1908, is still not available in its full form to students of Navajo tradition.

Father Berard seems to have acceded to the rewritten Wheelwright version of the text. What other options did he have after he was already indebted to her for a typing job? But in response to this situation his cofratres remember him as having said: "It was not a good manuscript, anyhow."

As for Father Berard's dissatisfaction with his original manuscript, his reasons are not difficult to perceive. The recording of this text had been done rather early in his career. The typescript bears on its last page the date 1908. In comparison with many later and completely bilinguial texts, this one might indeed be evaluated as less expert. In addition, the structure of the long narrative leaves something to be desired. For the first seven world levels the informant proceeded in a reasonably disciplined manner. But then, the "eighth speech" gets associated with an unexpected world-level color (Chapter 3), and the next world level is no longer identifiable by number (Chapter 4). It seems as though the narrator got into a hurry to get to world-level eleven (Chapter 5). After all, the events that took place there have become most important for our present existence, on the twelfth level.

Thus, it seems as though the Father's relative newness to the field, plus this stretch of narrational irregularities between the seventh and eleventh world levels, disturbed his extra-orderly mind to the point that he aired his feelings in a polite "sour grapes" remark—"it was not a good one, anyhow." Notwithstanding all of this, in his Introduction to another Emergence tradition (published as ATR Vol. 6) Father Berard referred to the present version as being more detailed and in some ways "told better."

Regardless of how one finally arranges this mythic narrative, the major problem with it is its confused subdivision of at least the third major underworld. So, for instance, level eight should still be part of the Red Underworld, but it is identified as being yellow. Apparently, Father Berard tried to accomplish an association between it and the Red Underworld; he distinguished it from the next mentioned level by putting the latter into a separate chapter under the heading "Blue World" (Chapter 4). All would have been well, had not the latter world level been described specifically as "white yellowish." Such a color code, obviously, lifts the earlier plain "yellow" level out of the Red Underworld, together with the similar next "white yellowish" level, into an overall Yellow Underworld. But in the cosmography of *haneełnéehee* there is no place for a Yellow Underworld. The next major division of world levels is supposed to be blue.

A logical solution to this difficulty might begin with recognizing the fact that the structure of the narrative begins to waver at level eight, precisely at the color-boundary to another major subdivision. Perhaps at this point in his arithmetic and geometry the narrator changed from counting levels or "realms" to counting boundaries or "breakthroughs into next higher realms." The constant emphasis in the plot on upward moving can conceivably force this change. In a state of being overpowered by the plot, the narrator might simply have abandoned numbering his world levels and hurried to his intermediary goal at world-level eleven. He knew that the last step of upward moving, from there, brought the people into their present realm.

Be that as it may, the only editorial solution to these problems remains the one which Father Berard himself has chosen, namely, to present each of these two yellow(ish) world levels separately, as Chapters Three and Four.

But then, a little ways into Chapter Four, the original typescript can no longer be followed. Father Berard appears to have overlooked the break at which his informant suddenly jumped to level eleven. In the present volume this break shall be marked as the beginning of Chapter Five. The entire prehuman and formative drama of sexuality, separation, reunion, flood, and escape was acted out at this level. There the prehuman people lived, fought, and were reconciled before they moved upward to discover our present world and to establish these and other life patterns there.

The original typescript is entitled "Creation and Emergence Myth of the Navajo, According to the *haneełnéehee* Moving-up Rite." The actual name of the ceremonial Father Berard has translated variously as Moving-up-, Upward-moving-, Upward-reaching-, and Emergence-way. (See especially his discussion in *American Anthropologist*, Vol. 44, 1942, pp. 407ff.) Shortened in accordance with these options, his title translates thus into "Creation and Emergence Myth of the Emergence Rite." The redundancy of the first "emergence" suggests that its author regarded this text as an emergence myth first, and as a chantway myth only second. This then suggests an additional reason why Father Berard might have despaired about the poorly structured "emergence sequence."

The interest of Westerners in cosmogonies notwithstanding, the *haneełnéehee* myth was never told to enlighten curious listeners about human origins in general. It was narrated specifically to get into focus the process by which "downward illness" and the corresponding "upwardness of healing power" were brought into the proximity of humankind. This myth was told not to satisfy an intellectual curiosity about the origin of things, but rather to substantiate Navajo soteriology and medicinal knowledge. And this process of substantiation had to be accomplished in the context of Pueblo Indian cosmography into which some ancestral Athapascan hunter bands happened to have migrated a few centuries ago. Very early, it seems, certain Navajo shamans must have recognized how "emergence power" proved especially effective among patients who, like they themselves, were caught up in the agricultural ideology of the Pueblo Indian Southwest—namely, among people who in this relatively advanced and complicated cosmography felt "low down" or "down under." *Haneełnéehee* brings people up from below. It rescues them from drowning in the flood and from dying downward in that direction. It lifts them onto the now sunlit surface of the twelfth world level.

The association of death with "being down there" has for the Navajos in itself been an inheritance from Pueblo (i.e., Middle American) thought. The original Navajo counterpart to the Pueblo "down under" had earlier been their home of departed ancestors, somewhere "up north" in the direction from which ancestral Navajos had formerly migrated. Thus, not only the healing process of upward emergence, but also the very diagnosis of certain illnesses in association with "down there," presented themselves to Navajo shamanic practitioners as new challenges. We must view the history of a people's religion always in the context of real life. The real animal world of Navajo hunters used to be "out there," while to Pueblo Indian farmers the mystery of plant growth was constantly being revealed from "down there." This, in a nutshell, states the difference to which Navajo shamans had to adapt when they began to infiltrate and to mingle with cultured natives of the Southwest.

With this revised perspective on what is essential in Upward-moving Way mythology, the occasional fuzziness in numerical sequence and color pattern seems suddenly less tragic. Numerous passages, which under the original perspective seemed to imply memory lapses on the part of the narrator—for instance, passages which digress from a mythic event to a detail in ceremonial practice—can no longer be evaluated as flaws of the narrative. Sentences of this sort, some of which Father Berard enclosed apologetically in brackets, could thus be liberated by the editor into equality with the remainder of the narrative. A ceremonial myth is told as theory of healing practices. Religiously and medicinally speaking, it is the human realm with its riddles of suffering, existence, and death which stands in need of explanation and of justification. The divine era of mythic causes and realms has been, and continues to exist, in its own right. And the fact that the prehuman realms and events can be talked about by Navajo professionals in magnificently structured narratives is in itself the proof of their validity. The daily lives of the Navajos, and the ordinary world in which they survive, are far less structured and predictable than the narrational theories known by healer priests. It is from the orderliness of mythology, therefore, that hope does flow into the present.

Among his many wonderfully disorganized notes Father Berard has left us a diagram, several yards long, brush-drawn, and untitled, on newsprint material. I owe its discovery to Bernard Fontana and Phyllis Ball of the University of Arizona. At the time when I copied it into my notebook, its significance for the present *haneełnéehee* myth was not yet fully apparent. But now this sketch can be added as further evidence of Father Berard's continued interest in *haneełnéehee*. What the present text leaves ambiguous or untold, concerning the sequence of realms and events, is presented in this diagram as a complete cosmographic system. Unfortunately, we have not yet been able to learn when the Father obtained these data or which informant provided them.

The "Speeches" or World Levels in this diagram indicate twelve underworlds in three major divisions. This would render the current Navajo realm as World Level Thirteen. Such numbering suggests a different informant for the diagram than for the text. On the other hand, the same narrator may simply have confused the world levels with breakthroughs—a confusion which plagues the text as well. The fact, that the third and twelfth realms show no names of inhabitants, reveals a preoccupation with numbering. Notwithstanding such numerical difficulties, the drawing tells much about the Puebloized Navajo anthropogony and about the conceptualization of epistemology in the green and growing world.

This diagram literally reaches from mythic cosmography and mythic history up into the present. It does so precisely in the manner in which the myth explains the ascent of the people to the present world level, namely, by way of a reed. Through the stem of a reed the first people escaped the flood, and by doing so they, at one and the same time, "grew up to" and were "born into" the realm in which we find their kind now. But what happened to the reed after the people had come out from it? The diagram is not quite clear about this. Either that same reed, or another one which grew next to it, continued growing as the very *haneełnéehee* tradition itself. As other ceremonials are branching off from this "Emergence Way stem," the entire repertoire of Navajo ceremonials seems to be accounted for. Indeed, from the point of view of an Upward-moving or Emergence Way singer, his chantway *is* Navajo ceremonialism.

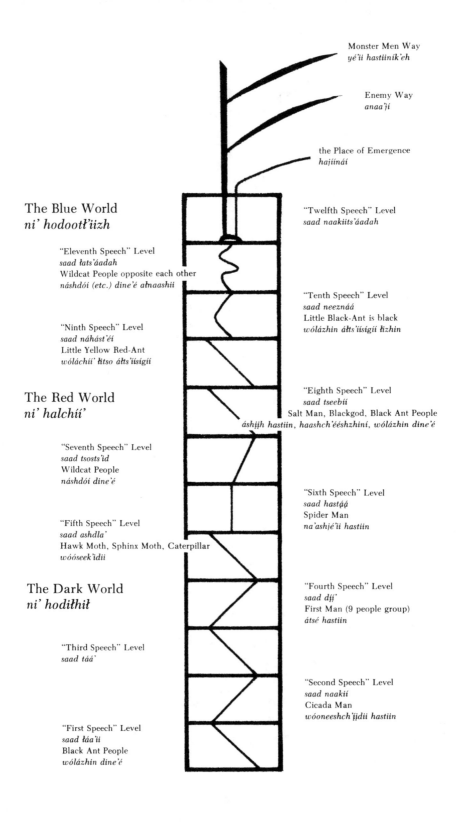

Monster Men Way
yé'ii hastiiník'eh

Enemy Way
anaa'jí

the Place of Emergence
hajíínái

The Blue World
ni' hodootł'iizh

"Twelfth Speech" Level
saad naakiits'áadah

"Eleventh Speech" Level
saad łats'áadah
Wildcat People opposite each other
náshdói (etc.) dine'é ałnaashii

"Tenth Speech" Level
saad neeznáá
Little Black-Ant is black
wólázhin áłts'íísígíí łizhin

"Ninth Speech" Level
saad náhást'éí
Little Yellow Red-Ant
wóláchíí' łitso áłts'íísígíí

The Red World
ni' halchíí'

"Eighth Speech" Level
saad tseebíí
Salt Man, Blackgod, Black Ant People
áshįįh hastiin, haashch'ééshzhiní, wólázhin dine'é

"Seventh Speech" Level
saad tsosts'id
Wildcat People
náshdói dine'é

"Sixth Speech" Level
saad hastą́ą́
Spider Man
na'ashjé'ii hastiin

"Fifth Speech" Level
saad ashdla'
Hawk Moth, Sphinx Moth, Caterpillar
wóóseek'idii

The Dark World
ni' hodiłhił

"Fourth Speech" Level
saad dį́į́'
First Man (9 people group)
átsé hastiin

"Third Speech" Level
saad táá'

"Second Speech" Level
saad naakii
Cicada Man
wóoneeshch'įįdii hastiin

"First Speech" Level
saad łáa'ii
Black Ant People
wólázhin dine'é

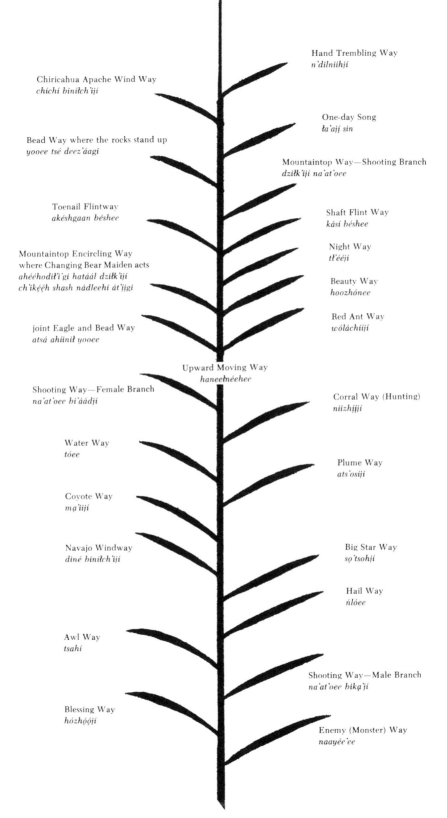

Hand Trembling Way
n'dilniihjí

Chiricahua Apache Wind Way
chichí binítch'ijí

One-day Song
ła'ąjí sin

Bead Way where the rocks stand up
yooee tsé deez'áagi

Mountaintop Way—Shooting Branch
dziłk'ijí na'at'oee

Toenail Flintway
akéshgaan béshee

Shaft Flint Way
kásí béshee

Night Way
tł'ééjí

Mountaintop Encircling Way
where Changing Bear Maiden acts
ahééhodił'i'gi hatáál dziłk'ijí
ch'ikę́ę́h shash nádleehí át'įigi

Beauty Way
hoozhónee

Red Ant Way
wóláchíijí

joint Eagle and Bead Way
atsá ahíinił yooee

Upward Moving Way
haneełnéehee

Shooting Way—Female Branch
na'at'oee bi'áádjí

Corral Way (Hunting)
niizhíjí

Water Way
tóee

Plume Way
ats'osíjí

Coyote Way
mą'iijí

Navajo Windway
diné binítch'ijí

Big Star Way
sǫ'tsohjí

Hail Way
níłóee

Awl Way
tsahí

Shooting Way—Male Branch
na'at'oee biką'jí

Blessing Way
hózhǫ́ǫ́jí

Enemy (Monster) Way
naayée'ee

At the same time, it is generally also believed that Navajo ceremonials have all grown from the stem of Blessingway. That, of course,
constitutes a statement of faith spoken from the point of view of
Blessingway singers. Long Mustache, when he explained to Father
Berard how Blessingway controls the other chantways, elaborated that
it "is representative for them, it is the spinal column of songs"
(Wyman, *Blessingway*. Tucson, 1970, p.5). Frank Mitchell explained
how Blessingway can be used to renew or "sharpen" other chantways
the powers of which had become weak or "dull." "Blessingway is the
root of the whole thing; it supports all ceremonials" (Mitchell, *Navajo
Blessingway Singer*. Tucson, 1978, p.227).

All these claims, of course, do not tell the history of Navajo ceremonialism in objective patterns of causality and temporal sequence.
What has been claimed concerning the centrality of Blessingway has
also been claimed, as we have seen, in regard to Upward-moving Way.
In fact, it can be claimed for all ceremonials the origin myth of which
begins with an account of the emergence. This, of course, excludes
certain hunting and curing traditions which still function in the
hunters' world of Athapascan ancestry from the north.

In a strict historical sense, the reed in our Upward-moving Way
diagram is not a "family tree" of ceremonials. Nevertheless, it
represents a most significant moment in the history of Navajo thought.
Navajo hunter shamans, at the moment of its conception, have begun
to function within the cosmology of Pueblo planters, and they have
succeeded in grafting many of their Athapascan ceremonial elements so
that they could watch them grow as branches from that magnificent
reed of emergence. This Navajoized mythical reed not only gave them
equal status with other advanced people in the Southwest—people
who also believed that they had emerged from the earth—it also gave
them an intellectual tradition and identity. The reed in this diagram
represents Navajo ceremonialism in its totality. A semblance of the
passageway, a means through which the first people were born into
this world, continues thus to grow and to sprout new means of
healing—that is, ways of rebirth, health, and re-creation. To use
categories from the general history of religions, the "tree of life"
continued growing as a "tree of knowledge" in promise of more life.

What shall one make then of the claims of singers concerning the
centrality of their own healing methods and specialties? They are all
correct. They are not speaking objectively about a reed "over there"
which grew and was observed in measurable time. Measured time is a
control-oriented abstraction by means of which outsiders and modern
men relativize their gods. It has therefore no place in the present
religious context.

The reed of Navajo ceremonialism stands as a living plant, growing from its roots from down in a deeper world. Inside the stem of their reed, Navajo singers continued climbing. Ordinary people on the twelfth surface knew nothing about the nature of this continuing "reed of knowledge" in the stem of which their singers continued to climb.

Navajo singers kept climbing in the stem of their growing tradition. Along the way, as some of them surpassed and climbed past their colleagues in other chantways, they saw the latter (in relative motion) extending outward as stationary branches. Without themselves remaining on the stem and aiming for the growing tip, how else could these singers achieve excellence in their specialties? Then, encouraged by many prayers and chants which resounded from within this stem of Navajo ceremonial tradition, surely, the gods themselves took notice of the human predicament. And in keeping with their divine compassion and grace, the gods entrusted their priestly devotees with ever larger combinations of song ceremonials. Upward-moving or Emergence Way, presented in this volume, is one of these divine trusts.

In addition to the persons and institutions already mentioned above in the Introduction, the editor wishes to express his appreciation to Susan McGreevey, director of the Wheelwright Museum, and to Katherine Bartlett, director of archives at the Museum of Northern Arizona, for help rendered. Irvy Goossen has rewritten Navajo words in contemporary orthography, Ursula Luckert has set type, and Nancy Holman has assisted in reading proofs. The sketches of sandpaintings and other items in the manuscript were adapted to the format of this book and redrawn by the editor. Presumably, the first sketches on which Father Berard based his manuscript drawings were done by *Gishin Biye'*.

PART ONE:

UPWARD MOVING
AND EMERGENCE WAY

THEORY AND MYTH

1

The Dark Underworld

WORLD-LEVEL OF THE FIRST SPEECH

In the Dark Underworld, they say, there were no birds, no trees, no stones, no men like here. The Ant (and Beetle) People only lived there, they say. The Small Yellow Black-Ants were there, and the Yellow Beetles, and the Large Black-Ants, and the Stag Beetle, and the Black Large Black-Ants, and the Large Dark Red-Ants, and the Red Ants proper, and the Spider Ant, and the Beet Beetle. These nine peoples lived there, they say.

In the east they had four dwellings, one built above the other. In the south, in the west and north, in each direction, there were four of these dwellings built, one upon the other. Their dwellings were round with slight depressions in the center, much resembling anthills.

The Small Yellow Black-Ant was chief in the east; Stag Beetle was chief of the south; Dark Red-Ant was chief in the west; and Red Ant was chief of the north. These four spoke one and the same language. The chief of the east spoke, and the chiefs of the south, west, and north repeated his words without difference in speech. Hence this place is known as First Speech (*saad ła'i*).

The chiefs discussed the subject of leaving the place and of how it might be accomplished. Accordingly, they decided that four chambers (should) be built in the center of the world, one above the other. They then built one chamber, and upon this a second, third, and fourth one. And when these were ready they entered them and passed on to the next chamber which is *saad naaki*, the Second Speech World-Level.

WORLD-LEVEL OF THE SECOND SPEECH

Here they remarked to the others: "Now then, we have accomplished this much, it is your turn to devise some means for further action." For this reason, in council, we see that the headchiefs call on others to express their opinion after they themselves have spoken. Thereupon the others made four roads leading to each of the cardinal points until they reached the end of the world. But they found that in this manner they would not arrive at the next (higher world-level). Thus at present, there are roads leading east, south, west and north. "These roads do not lead to a definite place," said they, "and yet we cannot (remain and) live here." But it so happened that the Beet Beetle[1] had forgotten his pots and mentioned this fact to the others. "Why not return and get them?" said the Spider Ant to him. Therefore these two returned to the first world. And that accounts for the forgetfulness, particularly among old people. The Beet Beetle thus carried his pots with him to the second world-level.

This second world, too, was void of stone and stick and vegetation. It was merely a world, round like the first, though somewhat larger in size. It was here that the travellers met two old persons, the Locust People, of whom one was male, the other female. And looking this world over they found no exit from it, and owing to its barrenness they did not wish to remain. They had gone east and south, west and north, until they had reached its limits, and had again found that it was not possible for them to leave in this manner. They discussed the matter four times—something like four days long, for at that time there was neither sun nor light, and consequently no days. Therefore we say "something like four days."

They were camped, one in the east, another in the south, a third in the west, and the fourth in the north round about the Locust People. The chief of the east spoke, and he of the south, west, and north each spoke in succession of ways and means to leave this place. "What do I hear, my Grandchildren!" said the Locust Man. "You will leave? If so, I will join you and also leave, my Grandchildren!" Thus they started upward together, and entered the third chamber (or world-level).

WORLD-LEVEL OF THE THIRD SPEECH

That, too, was a barren spot, devoid of stone, stick, or grass. Again they travelled to the cardinal points until they reached its limits. They found it larger than the previous world, yet not fit to live in. Again, therefore, the chiefs discussed ways and means of leaving it—(and so the third world-level was named) Third Speech (*saad táá'*). "That's right, my Grandchildren," said the Locust Man, "do talk this matter over." But the chiefs resented this remark and refused to discuss the matter any further. The others therefore held council (among themselves).

---

[1] The Navajo, *ásaa' neiyéhí*, designating the beet beetle, literally means "pot carrier." This explains the reference to pots.

Now the first or chief speaker (of the east) felt slighted because the Locust Man had interfered with the discussion, and the others felt likewise. "What is the use of us speaking anyway," said one, "we ought to step aside and never be heard again!" "No," said another, "that will never do. It is but a small matter, at any rate." "True, but others should not open their mouths while elders are speaking. This cannot be! Let the chiefs be heard for all!" In this manner they disagreed. Some advised to drop the matter while others insisted that a definite decision be reached in favor of the chiefs. This latter opinion finally prevailed, so that the chiefs were asked to voice the opinion for all as they had done heretofore. To this the chiefs consented and then all travelled to the fourth world. We see this done even now. Whenever the subchiefs have vainly endeavored to reach a decision in any matter, it is submitted to the headchiefs for final settlement.

WORLD-LEVEL OF THE FOURTH SPEECH

They found *saad dįį'*, this Fourth Speech world to be larger than any of those they had left. Its appearance was different. It was inherited by people. Like the other world(-levels), its color was black. And here the rite of *haneełnéehee*, of Moving-upward, has its origin, they say. The place was inhabited by some old people. There was First Man *(átsé hastiin)* and First Woman *(átsé asdzá)* and (another) First Man and First Woman. These four lived there, they say. There was also First-Made *(átsé hazlį́į')* and Second-Made, also First Boy *(átsé ashkii)* and First Girl *(átsé at'ééd)*, and First Scolder *(átsé hashké)* and Coyote. These nine people lived here, just as there were nine peoples on the first world(-level). In the Witchcraft legend the Blackgod, or Firegod, is mentioned as the tenth person. First Man possessed white shell, turquoise, abalone, jet, and red-white stone. These were his wealth, they say.

First Man *(átsé hastiin)* now took a piece of white shell, the size of a woman's comb, and placed it in the east, and a piece of turquoise of the same size and placed it in the south, and a piece of abalone of the same size and placed it in the west, and a piece of jet of the same size and placed it in the north. Into the white shell in the east he put white mirage; into the turquoise in the south he put blue mirage; into the abalone in the west he put yellow mirage; and into the jet in the north he put dark mirage. Accordingly, in the east arose a cloud, as it were— a column of white. In the west (arose) a similar one of a yellow color. These ascended gradually, spreading light over the earth. And when they would reach the zenith, that would correspond to our midday. That was the first form of light. Likewise in the south where the turquoise, and in the north where the jet had been placed, columns of blue and black, respectively, arose which caused darkness to fall on the place. That (darkness) resembled our night here. And the people then retired.

Again First Man took a small piece of white shell and placed it in the east, and a turquoise in the south, and an abalone shell in the west, and jet in the north, and finally a small red-white stone in the center. He then breathed on the white shell in the east. It expanded, and from its center arose a pillar of white. First Woman also went to the turquoise in the south, breathing on it, which caused the turquoise to expand and send forth a pillar of blue. In turn the (other) First Man proceeded west and breathed on the abalone shell there, causing it to expand and send forth a pillar of yellow. And when the (other) First Woman went north and breathed on the jet there, it expanded likewise and sent forth its pillar of black. First Man now breathed on the red-white stone in the center, and this, too, expanded and sent forth a pillar of various colors. Thus, there were four columns, one at each cardinal point. And one (a fifth one, was) in the center. The column or pillar in the east was called Folding Dawn, that of the south was called Folding Skyblue, that of the west Folding Twilight, and that of the north Folding Darkness.

Meanwhile, Coyote approached the pillar in the east and turned white, he approached the pillar in the south and turned blue, he approached the pillar of the west and turned yellow, and when he approached the pillar of the north he turned completely black. Therefore, the Coyote is also called Child of Dawn, and Child of Skyblue, and Child of Evening Twilight, and Child of Darkness. In this manner, Coyote increased in importance (as one of) the (first) nine peoples of this world.

In the east there was also a basket of white shell, in the south a basket of turquoise, in the west a basket of abalone, and in the north a basket of jet, while in the center lay one of red-white stone. The baskets at the cardinal points covered perfect discs of white shell, turquoise, abalone and jet which, they say, formed the food of these nine people. The basket in the center, however, contained smallpox, whooping cough, nervousness, paleness or pulmonary diseases, and every fatal disease. Indeed, First Man and his companions were evil people who practiced witchcraft, they say. Their wish alone was sufficient to inflict these diseases and to cause death through them, they say. That, however, was not known to the newcomers. Nor (was it) even (known) that one of their own number, the Spider Ant, was of an equally malicious disposition. They therefore suspected no evil intent on the part of the inhabitants of this world.

It so happened that now a pillar of white light descended upon the basket in the east, and a pillar of blue light upon the basket in the south, and a pillar of yellow light upon the basket in the west, and a pillar of black upon the basket in the north. Upon the basket in the center, too, there descended a pillar of black, blue, yellow, white, and of various colors; that is to say, the pillar was black at its base, then in turn, blue, yellow, and white, while its tip was varicolored.

Right here is the beginning of the *haneełnéehee*, Moving-up Rite, which therefore also has the *hayaatéii*—the prayer out of the east, out of the south, out of the west, out of the north, out of the zenith, and out of the nadir. The black portion of this pillar of the center represents dark medicine against secret evils, and it is the beginning of the *haneełnéehee* rite. The blue portion denotes the beginning of *anaají*, the War rites. The yellow portion refers to prayers for other purposes than these, while the white portion shows the origin of *hózhǫ́ǫ́jí hatáál*, the Rite of Blessing, a sort of remedy for the classes of chants represented in black, blue, and yellow, all of which refer to malice or ghost spells. Thus, this is the beginning of the various chants. That portion of the pillar which is varicolored represents the diverse evils that are visited upon present-day humankind, this representing the source of all evils. The *haneełnéehee*, then, is the first of all rites, closely followed by the War Rite, which is (related) to the former (like) a younger brother. Both have a connection with the Rite of Blessing, the songs of which may be used in war and raids, as well as in witchcraft and evildoing.[2] At this point the War Rite leaves the *haneełnéehee* and branches off.

Meanwhile the Spider Ant quickly made friends with the people of this world(-level). He freely associated with them and soon had the confidence of Coyote who explained these secrets to him. "That basket in the center there holds diseases and evils of all kinds," he said to the Spider Ant, who in turn reported this to his companions. With that, Stag Beetle and Red Ant went to First Man, while Black Ant sought Coyote. "What is to be done?" said Stag Beetle to First Man. "What of

---

[2]Reference is made here to a division of chants which is not clearly identified. Briefly, we have in Navajo *diyink'ehgo*, Holyway chants which sanctify and render immune to disease; then *hóchǫ́ǫ́jí*, Ghostway chants, which remove influences of corpses and their ghosts. The third, *hózhǫ́ǫ́jí*, Blessingway chants achieve a complete restoration even from the effects of disease and any remnants of these diseases. It corrects faults incurred by omissions in the performance of any chant, rite, or smaller ceremony.

Editor's Note: Probably means: "...which may be used to counteract (or neutralize) the evil results of war, raids, witchcraft, and evildoing."

our coming here (Is it agreeable, and if so, how will we depart)?"
Likewise Black Ant consulted Coyote. "I know," said First Man,
"I know, my Grandchildren. By the pillar of the east I know, and by
the pillar of the south I know, and by the pillars of the west and north
I know, and by the pillar of the center I know how it will be done," he
said. Then again the chiefs spoke their minds, four times they spoke it,
whereupon First Man and Coyote began to ascend to the upper
regions, and all present (ascended) with them. When they grasped the
pillar in the center it began to raise and to lift them upward. By
entering this pillar, then, it is evident (implied) that they also carried
with them every evil contained therein, inasmuch as (all kinds of)
colors, as mentioned, represented all kinds of evil.

Now while the first world was known as First Speech, the next as
Second Speech, the next as Third Speech, they entered from the
present Fourth Speech (level of the Dark World) into the Red World.

2

The Red Underworld

WORLD-LEVEL OF THE FIFTH SPEECH

The color of the fifth world(-level) was a glossy red and is therefore in the Red Underworld. Here, they say, they found two persons, Sphinx Man and Sphinx Woman. Before leaving the fourth level, First Man had gathered the four pillars of light from the east, south, west, and north, had rolled them into diminutive balls which he carried to the fifth world(-level). The Sphinx, too, had pillars of light at the cardinal points which resembled ridges—a white one in the east, a blue ridge of light in the south, a yellow one in the west, and a dark ridge of light in the north. Nevertheless, First Man placed the white ball in the east, the blue ball in the south, the yellow one in the west, and the dark ball in the north (as a gift to Sphinx). And when the Sphinx blew towards these balls they changed the various colors of the cardinal points, and it seemed as though he and First Man were on very good terms with each other.

Now that was his "smoke." And when he blew towards the east his smoke(-ball) became white and it arose. And when he blew towards the west the ball became yellow and it rose likewise. The two rising columns spread daylight over the world. Thus the people could see. And when he blew towards the south, the ball there became blue and it rose, and when he blew towards the north the ball there turned dark and it rose, both blue and black columns united (above) in spreading darkness over the face of the earth. (It became night).

The Sphinx was yellow in color and a fearless fellow. And seeing the strangers he said: "Why, how did you get here? Whence do you come, my Grandchildren?" "Oh, we are from another world," said the chief of the first level, "but meeting First Man we joined his companions at his place." "Yes, my Granduncle," First Man now said, "we met them there, and came together from the other world. What do you think (of a way of passing on)?" "Oh, I don't know," said the Sphinx in turn. "I am big, but not very wise, and I know not how to get at things." Thus he spoke, they say. But Small Yellow-Ant, Stag Beetle, Black Red-Ant and Red Ant, the chiefs, urged him to tell them. Four times they urged, yet he seemed unmoved. Red Ant prepared a smoke of *azee'* which he offered to the Sphinx. That he readily

(9)

accepted and filled his pipe for a smoke. This he blew eastward, but as it would not follow that direction he inhaled the smoke again. He then blew the smoke southward, but inhaled it again as it made no attempt in that direction. He was equally unsuccessful in the west and north, and then blew the smoke downward. Again he was forced to inhale the smoke as it would not follow that direction. He now blew the smoke upward, and when it followed this direction, all entered the smoke and in it they passed to the sixth world(-level).

WORLD-LEVEL OF THE SIXTH SPEECH

This (realm) also was red in color. In the east there stood a pillar of white, in the south a pillar of blue, in the west a pillar of yellow, and in the north a dark pillar. Into this world First Man and Coyote, with their companions and the nine peoples of the first world, had entered. The people of the fourth world (First Man, etc.), however, were first to enter, and by agreement all future moves and plans were left to them (to decide). First Man and Coyote, therefore, were first to speak (and to act) here. First Man took a cane of white shell and stretched it toward the east, and white arose. He stretched a turquoise cane toward the south where blue arose, a cane of abalone to the west and yellow arose, and a cane of jet toward the north where a dark column arose. The columns of white and yellow in the east and west supplied daylight, those of blue and black in the south and north caused darkness.

In the center of the world he placed a white perfect-shell-disc, but it would not move. He then tried turquoise, abalone, and jet perfect-shell-discs in succession, but they, too, remained immovable. But when he replaced these with a perfect red-white stone disc, it began to move. "This is not good, Children; it portends evil," said First Man. The blue column in the south and the dark column in the north had risen when First Man placed the perfect red-white stone disc in the center. It moved continuously, causing the earth to tremble so that people were frightened and got up. It was night, then, as it were. When they spoke again (on the second day), the earth shook more violently, so that even the blue-black arch above seemed in disorder. That explains an earthquake. When the third speech of leaving was made, the shaking of the earth had become so violent that people were scarcely able to stand. And after the fourth speech the trembling and rocking had increased to such an extent that First Man hurriedly gathered his white shell wand from the east, the turquoise wand from the south, the abalone wand from the west, and the jet wand from the north side. With that the perfect disc of red-white stone in the center began to rise. Seeing this, all stepped on it and were lifted up into the next world. That is the beginning of the Male Branch of the Shooting Chant, which now branches off here.

WORLD-LEVEL OF THE SEVENTH SPEECH

The seventh world was of a red color and was the home of the Cat or Feline People—the Mountain Lions lived here. And (it was the home of) the Wolf, called Big Trotter—also (of) the Wildcat, the Puma, the Badger, the Kit Fox, the Wildcat of the canyons, with Spider Man and Spider Woman. All these peoples lived here. In the east their houses were white and the Wolf lived there. In the west their houses were yellow and the Kit Fox and Badger lived there. In the north the houses were spotted and the Puma and Wildcat lived there. The white houses in the east varied in shape, some being bulky, others (square) like a (modern) house, still others having the shape of a (conical) hogan. The blue houses in the south, the yellow houses in the west, and the spotted houses of the north, too, varied in shape. It appeared, too, that the people were at war with one another, and that they had small regard for fair play. Indeed, the strangers soon experienced that these were tricksters and evildoers bent on killing one another, and (that they were) occupied solely with manufacturing arrows. The dwellers in the east made arrows of white shell—those in the south arrows of turquoise, those in the west arrows of abalone, while those in the north manufactured arrows from jet—with which to destroy their neighbors.

Yet the chiefs of the first world(-level) associated with these people in this manner: Small Yellow-Ant with the enemies in the east, Stag Beetle with the enemies in the south, Black Red-Ant with the enemies in the west, and Red Ant with the enemies in the north. First Man, however, (being a wizard) made medicine (by the *haneełnéehee)* and produced a Wildcat from the east, a Puma from the south, a second Wildcat from the west, and a second Puma from the north. He then built a house very similar in shape to the houses of these people, and placed the two wildcats at the doorway on one side, and the two pumas on the other.

When the Wolf in the east saw this he made an arrow each of white shell, of turquoise, abalone, and jet. He shot the white shell arrow, but the Wildcat at the doorway reached forth and caught it with his left hand. He shot the turquoise arrow, but the Puma on the other side of the doorway reached forth and caught it with his left hand. He shot the abalone arrow, but the (second) Wildcat at the doorway reached forth and caught it with his left hand. He now dispatched the jet arrow, but the (second) Puma reached forth and caught it with his left hand. Thereafter the Wolf ceased shooting, and when all of his people dispatched their entire supply of arrows, they failed to inflict harm, owing to the power of First Man. The latter now turned to the Wildcat at the door saying: "How are they (the arrows)?" He answered: "The arrows in my left palm are still alive." "And yours?" turning to the Puma. "The arrows which we hold are still working," said they. Therefore we know that the *adilgashii*, the shooters or wizards, cannot injure the *haneełnéehee*, inasmuch as its power exceeds that of the wizards.

First Man then took the white shell arrow, and returning the shot, killed four of their number at one shot. He then dispatched in turn the turquoise arrow, the abalone arrow, and the jet arrow, and with each shot slew four of their number. Thus sixteen of their people had been killed. And when the Wolf People realized this they cried aloud: "Grandfather, Brother, Relative, Friend! Do not shoot again! Our power is as nothing compared with yours! Revive these sixteen, and we will give you our songs in return!" "T'is well," said First Man, but as he made no attempt in their direction they again pleaded with him to come to them. "No," he said, "if I shall sing, you will come to me." Thus they were compelled to carry their dead to him. And when he had revived them, the Wolf People donated four songs for each person slain, or a total of four times sixteen, making sixty-four songs. In this manner First Man acquired many songs, and the Wolf People returned to their homes.

In the south, also, the Mountain Lion People made arrows of turquoise, of white shell, of abalone, and jet, which they dispatched at First Man in the order mentioned, without injury to him; for the arrows were caught up by the Wildcats and Pumas (who were) stationed at the doorway. A repetition of questions and answers took place, as on the previous occasion, whereupon First Man again dispatched the arrows, killing four enemies with each discharge. It will be remembered that Stag Beetle had joined the people in the south. He now approached First Man, saying: "This will not do! You ought not to abuse your power in slaying people in this manner. But revive them and we shall pay you with our songs." First Man again refused to hold the ceremony at their homes, but forced them to carry their dead to him. In addition he exacted two times forty-and-four, or eighty-eight songs for his services.

Editor's Note: This story not only explains the purpose of Wolf and Mountain Lion songs in Navajo ceremonialism, it also reflects—in the context of the history of religions—the ascendance of anthropomorphic over theriomorphic deities.

The songs and prayers of the hunt take their origin from the Wolf People of the east and were much in use by old hunters. Another lodge of the hunt originated with the people of the south claiming especial proficiency in capturing deer with their songs. They employ the pith or core of bayonet yucca in killing deer.

Now the Kit Fox and Badger People of the west also made arrows of abalone and white shell, of turquoise and jet, in the color order mentioned, which they discharged at First Man. The result was a sad repetition. The sentinels at the doorway, the Wildcats and Pumas, caught them in their left hands, and reported to First Man who dispatched them at his enemies with the same deadly accuracy. Kit Fox and Badger now turned to Black Red-Ant, who had joined them, saying: "We have exhausted our power. See what you can do for us!" Thus the Black Red-Ant upbraided First Man, and said: "It is not proper that these people shall remain dead. They should live! And if you will revive these sixteen for us, we have one hundered and two songs as compensation, seeing that your power is so much greater than ours!" Thus they brought the corpses, which were revived and the songs (were) paid.

The Wildcat and Puma of the north fared little better when they dispatched their jet, white shell, abalone, and turquoise arrows at First Man. The incidents repeated themselves as before. Red Ant acted as intermediary, and a promise of one hundred and eighty two songs for the revival of the victims was exacted.[3]

After these events, a delegation consisting of Small Yellow-Ant, Stag Beetle, Black Red-Ant and Red Ant visited First Man, the first being their spokesman. "We are conquered," they said to him. "We fancied that our power was greater than yours." "True, true," said the others in approval. "Upon our arrival here we believed our power far in excess of yours, but we have since learned that yours is a greater power, Grandfather,[4] Brother, Uncle, Kinsman! We submit to you! Ordain and direct as you see fit, and we shall always follow."

For this reason, when medicine men accompany a war party, a sandpainting is drawn of two wildcats and two pumas holding a bow and arrows in their left hands, which represent the events which are narrated here.

It appears, however, that this submission was only feigned, for one night Small Yellow-Ant visited Stag Beetle in the south and said: "It is

[3]I have condensed this section—instead of repeating the facts recorded for the east side, namely, catching the live arrows in their left hand, the questions and answers concerning these by the doorguards, shooting the same arrows back at the enemy, etc.

[4]"Granduncle" seems more correct than "Grandfather". I have omitted possessive "my" or "our", which in Navajo is always added to terms of relationship.

too bad! We have lost all our songs, but we must recover them in one
way or another." That message Stag Beetle carried to the Black
Red-Ant in the west, who in turn carried it to Red Ant in the north.
And when they had all agreed to it, Red Ant notified Black Red-Ant in
the west again, who in turn apprised Stag Beetle in the south, and
through him, Small Yellow-Ant in the east. Accordingly, then, the Ant
People of the east once more made arrows of white shell, those of the
south arrows of turquoise, those of the west arrows of abalone, those of
the north arrows of jet. "Ha! I, too, can make arrows of power,"
boasted the Ant chief of the east. "And I, and I, and I," said those at
the other points in response. "Let us but have our bows of power, and
we shall see!"

Now the chief of the east had in his possession a strip of (zigzag)
lightning, and the chief of the south a strip of straight lightning, the
chief of the west a strip of rainbow, and the chief of the north a strip of
reflected sun-red, of which materials each made a bow. Thus they had
four bows—the chief of the east a bow of zigzag lightning, the chief of
the south a bow of straight lightning, the chief of the west a bow made
of rainbow, the chief of the north a bow of reflected sun-red. Each
placed his bow on the ground before him, but the bows would not
move. In the east, the Wolf People now decorated the bow with olivella
shell beads, adding one at each end and one at the center of the bow.
In like manner, the Mountain Lion People in the south, and the Kit
Fox and Badger People in the west, and the Wildcat and Puma in the
north, each placed olivella shell beads at the ends and center of their
bows.[5]

Meanwhile, however, First Man blew upon his own white shell,
and it spread out like a blanket with which he covered himself. This
he repeated with his turquoise, abalone, and jet jewels, covering
himself with these spreads in the order mentioned. Over these he
placed a cover of white flint, another of blue flint, another of yellow
flint, another of dark flint, and finally a cover of varicolored flints,
thus covering himself with nine armors, as it were, for he suspected
some treachery. Presently, too, the chief of the east dispatched his
arrows, then in succession the chief of the south and of the west and of
the north, each discharged four arrows at First Man. But the arrows
merely glanced off his armor and passed on in the opposite direction,
where they took deadly effect. In this manner the archers in the east
were slaying those in the west, and vice versa, and the archers in the
south were killing their friends in the north, and vice versa.

---

[5]While *yootgai* properly means "white bead," I have retained the popular name
"white shell."

And (as an outcome of these events) it is even so today, when witchery is ineffective, the power of a proposed victim of witchcraft increases, such as his power by song and prayer, or the influence of his rites. Instead of losing his power it increases, because the evil influence of witchery is always visited upon the wizard who tried, but failed, to do harm.

Thereupon First Man divested himself of his armor, which he rolled into small balls and laid aside. The outlook was anything but pleasant for his enemies. Meanwhile, Coyote had taken it into his head to investigate a little. Going east, he turned white and inspected the place. "Ha," he reported with a chuckle. "Those people over there are groaning and writhing in pain. Their houses are dotted with white specks, as though they had been struck everywhere." And now that his curiosity was aroused, he turned south, changing blue. He reported that some were dead, others groaning with pain, still others trying to support their companions. In the west he changed his color to a yellow and found the great majority in agony and the houses well shot up. Turning north his color changed to a jet black, and (he) reported from there that the houses were striped in blue and white with specks of yellow and red and all colors, from shots, as it were. "Hm!" said First Man, "what might be the cause? What do you think they have done?" "Oh well," said Coyote, "they probably repeated what they tried before, but instead of injuring us, their arrows turned upon themselves."

He had scarcely finished speaking when they heard voices in the east, then in the south, and west, and north. Presently, too, they saw two old men approaching them—one, Beet Beetle, carrying his pots, the other, Spider Ant, covered with blood for he had been wallowing in the blood of the victims round about. "Grandfather, Grandmother," said Pot Carrier[1] to First Man and First Woman, "we want to leave this place. What is to be done, what do you think?" "We have visited the people round about," said Spider Ant, "and have seen misery everywhere. Have pity on them, and allow us to depart." "I make pots for these people," continued Beet Beetle,[1] "and can not afford to have my craft destroyed completely." "Well," said First Man, "let me see what I can do while you step outside."

With that he made a white smoke and blew it eastward. He then drew it back and swallowed it. The smoke removed evildoing, evil spells and thoughts of the people in the east, all of these evils he swallowed. He then made a blue smoke, blew it southward, and inhaled with it all the witchery, cunning and devilry, of the people there. With a yellow smoke, which he blew westward and inhaled again, he removed any power for evil which those people possessed.

Finally, he made a smoke of mixed colors which he blew northward
and inhaled again, whereby those people lost their power of (bean-)
shooting, man-eating, and similar powers. By thus removing these evil
powers from the peoples of the first world(-level)—Small Yellow-Ant
and associates—this power now entered the nine people of the fourth
level. These were: First Man, First Woman, (the other) First Man and
First Woman, First-Made, Second-Made, First Boy, First Girl, and
First Scolder. In the meantime, Coyote again had made the rounds,
visiting the people in the east and at other points, and reporting that
all seemed well and that no evil could be found among them. With
that, too, the people of the east and south, west and north approached
First Man, saying: "We are conquered. We submit to you. Let your
say be our say. We are satisfied." Thus far, all this happened.

We have now heard of the first to the seventh world(-levels).[6]
First Man now went eastward, and there he laid down a streak of
zigzag lightning which, however, did not move forward. On the side
of this he placed straight lightning which, likewise, did not move
forward. Next to this he placed rainbow, but it held its position. He
next tried reflected sun-red and sunray, but they, too, remained immovable. Finally, he placed sunlight there which moved to the east
just a trifle. He now stepped forward four steps, the distance the
sunlight had moved, but it refused to move farther on. He now carried
the lightnings, rays and lights to the south, repeating the performance,
but with no other result than that the sunlight moved forward four
steps, but no farther. Similarly it happened in the west and in the
north. "Well," he said, "I do not know how we shall leave here, my
Grandchildren!"

He now placed a piece of jet the size of the forejoint of the index
finger on the center of the earth and in an upright position—on this,
in succession, pieces of the same size of turquoise, of abalone and white
shell, and finally of red-white stone, thus making a wand of various
colors. On the east side of the jet wand there were four footprints, and
similarly on the south, west, and north sides of it. The four sides of the
turquoise, of the abalone, the white shell and red-white stone, each
were provided with footprints. On these they stepped and forthwith
were carried into the next world—because First Man had imparted to
these footprints the power to carry them upward. As a matter of
course, First Man never neglected to carry all his powers from one
world to the next.

[6]Each of these worlds are called *saad* (speech), thus signifying Speech or World
one, two, etc.

3

World-Level of Eighth Speech in a "Yellow" Underworld

The world which they had just entered was yellow in color, an unattractive place without vegetation, stone, or tree. One single old man and his wife, and another old fellow were living here. These were Salt Man and Salt Woman, and the Firegod. And this was *saad tseebíí*, the eighth world(-level). They were much surprised at all the strangers and therefore studied them for some time. On this account, even nowadays a stranger excites curiosity. First Man, however, finally greeted him: "*Shicheii*, my Granduncle," and Salt Man returned the welcome: "*Shicheii*, my Granduncle." In like manner First Woman greeted Salt Woman: "*Shichó*, my Grandmother," and she in turn welcomed First Woman with: "*Shichó*, my Grandmother." Firegod, too, was greeted with "Granduncle" by First Man and he, too, exchanged the compliment.

Other people, too, were seen here. There were Yellow Red-Ants, the Yellow and Dark Black-Ants, the Red Red-Ants, and the speedy kind of Large Black-Ants. These, it was found, were identical to the people of the first world who, when they met people like themselves, were friendly to them.

There was also the Big Snake, the Endless Snake, Bullsnake, Arrowsnake, and Flying Snake. Then there was the Snapping Snake, Stubby Rattler,[7] and Watersnake. There were the Yucca People, and the Cactus People, too. All of these people lived here. And when white arose in the east and yellow in the west, and (when) the two met above, it was day, and when blue from the south and black from the north joined overhead it was night. Big Snake carried a perfect-shell-disc[8] and horns on his head.

Then there were also the Black Snake, the Blue, Yellow and White Snakes, the Glittering (pink) Snake, Snake People who were spotted with all colors. All of these were wicked people. They looked at, and studied one another while First Scolder unconcernedly roamed about

---

[7]Some of the snakes mentioned here are probably mythical. Just what exactly is meant by the "Big" and "Endless" Snake is difficult to identify. The stubby rattler is called *tł'iish bichó'ii*, Grandmother of Snakes.

[8]The Navajo *hadaat'e* denotes a shell which is not perforated, either whole or disc-shaped.

to look the place over. "What sort of a fellow is that, boys," they said, "who goes about here with no respect for anything!"

Meanwhile, First Man placed a streak of yellow color in the east, and above this a streak with a mixture of red and yellow. This immediately caused the column of white in the east to remain fixed, so that it did not rise again. These yellow and red streaks were the yellow and red diseases which First Man put there to stop the light. The people soon noticed that the white column did not rise, owing to the yellow and red streaks, and they held council among themselves. "What can this be! We have not seen such a thing as this before." In this manner they held council four times and accused the newcomers of effecting this change. "Do you not think so?" they asked the Salt Man. "I can not say," he said, "I have given it some thought but have not been able to solve it."

And when none could offer a satisfactory explanation, they decided to dispatch couriers eastward to investigate the matter. But when these arrived at the spot where they had fancied the streaks to be, they found themselves as far distant as they had been when they started, for the streaks receded as fast as they approached. They, however, approached again, and again, and again, four times, only to find that the streaks receded with their approach. They returned, therefore, and reported the matter to their people. But curiously enough, the streaks had returned with them to their former position. "What can this mean?" they said among themselves, but none could answer.

Still, after each of their four councils, the voice of one speaking in the south was heard to say: "And what if something be known about this matter?" Four times they heard the voice, after each council they heard it. Finally one spoke saying: "We have now held council four times, and every time this voice is heard. Why not investigate the matter!" This they did, and found an old withered crony called Big Fly. "Was it you that spoke?" they asked him. "No, no!" he said. "I did not utter a word." "But we heard you speak!" "Oh, I didn't mean anything, I know nothing about this matter."

One version maintains that they questioned him four times; another that they questioned him twice. The present version says they questioned him but once.

"Ah!" they continued to press him. "Now we know in truth that you know. Come, come, and tell us!" "Well, then, I do know," said the Big Fly. "First Man is doing this. The lower yellow streak reminds us of the emergence from the lower worlds. The second streak, or the yellow below the red, represents vegetation and pollen, while the red represents smallpox, excessive pains, whooping cough, and every other fatal disease which First Man himself put there. It is not good, however, to speak of this while the streaks are visible." These words of Big Fly set them to thinking again; hence the Wolf spoke to them, and the Wild-cat spoke in two councils.

Yet another addressed them, a person comely in appearance, with blue mouth and splendid voice. He was an Owl *(nik'e'ni)*[9] and an entire stranger to them. Still another addressed them. (He was one) who, while good-looking, possessed a very hoarse voice, and this was the Kit Fox who spoke last. This explains the fact that not all chiefs have good voices; one or the other is possessed of a poor and weak voice.

They next endeavored to have the streaks removed, but could think of nothing valuable to offer First Man. Finally, the Horned Rattler[7] hit upon the perfect shell which he carried on his head. This he offered to First Man, who thereupon removed the streaks. Thus he obtained one of their precious stones. Therefore the Horned Rattler is now bald and spotted with red and black, where formerly he carried this precious stone. First Man then put the streaks under his garments. But the Rattler added: "Henceforth my sacrifice will consist of white shell, and of turquoise, and of abalone shell, and of jet and red-white stone." But these very stones formed the food of First Man, and also of his companions of the fourth world(-level). This food, it will be remembered, was placed there in baskets from which they ate them. They now consumed this food again.

But when it was made known what First Man had done, everyone looked upon him as a wicked person. They discussed this in four councils and agreed that he was steeped in malice. Coyote, however, who roamed everywhere, overheard this statement and reported their views to First Man. And when they upbraided him for his trickery, he admitted all. "It is true, my Grandchildren, I am filled with evil. Yet there is a time to employ it, and another to withhold it."

Not long after these events, First Man placed a piece of turquoise in the south, and a piece of jet opposite in the north, both of them joined overhead (in the shape of an inverted V). Next he set a piece of white shell in the east, and opposite, in the west, a piece of abalone, and these two joined overhead in the same manner. Just a little aside of the pole of white shell which joined the south and north poles, he placed a piece of red-white stone. He then breathed upon them, and behold, a white hogan arose in their stead.

He now added four shelves or chambers of white shell to the eastern pole of white shell, and four turquoise chambers to the south pole of turquoise, and four abalone chambers to the west pole of

---

[9]*Nik'e'ni* usually refers to a species of owl.

abalone shell, and four jet chambers to the northern pole of jet. The northeast pole, made of red-white stone, received no chambers, as this pole merely accompanied the others and rested on the northern pole.

He next placed a small piece of jet in the center of the hogan, and when he breathed on it, the stone expanded, forming a circle which touched the inner base of each pole. In the center of this spread he placed a small piece of turquoise, and when he again breathed on this it spread out over the entire surface of the sheet of jet. In turn he repeated (this procedure) with a piece of abalone shell, which he placed on the center of the sheet of turquoise so that when he breathed on it, it covered the turquoise completely. He finally placed a piece of white shell on the center of the sheet of abalone shell, and when he breathed on it, the white shell expanded in a circle covering the other three sheets as with a spread. In this manner he had made four floors in the hogan, one of jet, the second of turquoise, the third of abalone shell, and the fourth, or uppermost, of white shell.

First Man and his companion then entered and took seats in the rear part of the hogan, under the west pole facing east, and in this order:

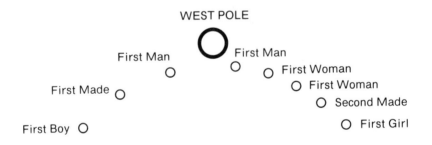

First Scolder remained at the doorway below the east pole, changing positions back and forth between this white shell pole and the lean-to pole of red-white stone.

After these the rest of the people entered, taking their positions in a semicircle along the southern part of the interior, then along the northern interior of the hogan, until it was filled. When First Man saw this, he blew towards the east, south, west, and north so that the interior was enlarged. Others who entered formed a second semicircle in front of those present. Again it proved too small, and a fourth time it had to be enlarged, until the four semicircles were completed and all had entered.

Meanwhile, as said, Coyote had taken a position at the doorway, (below the) east pole, and thus addressed the assembled: "My Grandchildren, what are you doing here, anyway?" And, changing his position to the opposite upright (pole), he murmured to himself:"You never mentioned a word to me about these proceedings." Now he knew full well what was to be done.

When all were seated, First Man arose and assigned places to the various things to be, placing them on the south and north sides in front of the assembled people as follows:

He then beckoned to two in the audience to step forward, and Owl (nik'e'ní) with the Badger responded. Into the mouth of the former he placed a piece of turquoise, and into the mouth of the Badger a piece of white shell, in order to purify these stones. The stones thus purified are called bizá naast'áán, "That which has been placed in its mouth." Both

---

[10]Naadą́ą́' dijoolí, rounded corn, usually implies female corn.

stones were perforated in the center. Just in front of himself, to the north, he had placed a turquoise basket with the finished rim, pointing east, and into this he placed the purified turquoise. Aside of this to the south he had placed a basket of white shell whose finished seam pointed east. And into this basket he placed the white shell which had been purified in the mouth of the Badger.

He now spread out, side by side, four unwounded buckskins with their heads pointing eastward. And taking the purified turquoise from the turquoise basket, he tied this over the heart of the first buckskin and attached the purified white shell from the white shell basket over the heart of the second buckskin. Over the heart of the third buckskin he attached a black flint agate, and over the heart of the fourth buckskin a blue flint agate. Thus he dressed the buckskins, which lay in a line before the baskets, the first one lying to the north. Moreover, the dressing of each buckskin was accompanied by two songs. Similarly, with song, an additional buckskin was cut up into strips in the rear of the hogan.

"This buckskin with the turquoise shall be the male," said First Man. "And this with the white shell shall be the female, and this with the dark flint agate shall be the male, and this with the blue flint agate shall be the female." He then placed the following medicines at his left (the north) side: dark medicine, blue medicine, (watercress, *Masturtium obtusam*), yellow medicine, (evening primrose, *Cenothera grandiflora*), and sparkling medicine, (cadweed, *Gnaphelium sprengelii*). At his right (south) he placed the following: witchery, bean shooting,[11] evil wishing, and insanity.

Between these, in a line from west to east, he placed the following: collected stings, collected footclaws, collected foreclaws, and all varieties of collected irritants. These, with the four buckskins, were for the medicine pouch of the *haneełnéehee*, from which rite all others start. He then prepared the other paraphernalia for this pouch (*jish*).

Four of the strips, which had been cut out of the additional buckskin, were now placed aside of the first buckskin, and four each aside of the second, third, and fourth buckskins. Two of these strips were long enough to reach over the shoulder to the opposite hip, while two were smaller and intended for wristlets. Accordingly, a long one was decorated with footclaws and flints,[12] and was intended for the left

---

[11] By "bean shooting" is meant, to secretly cause foreign particles, such as charcoal, jewels, or bones, to become lodged in one's body, thereby causing indisposition and even death. One method is to mix these with medicinal herbs and to give them to the patient as a potion. The more common belief is that the witch shoots them into his victim's body.

[12] Flint most probably implies an arrow point made of flint. Presently, at any rate, such small arrow points are part of the medicine pouch.

shoulderband, while the second, a small strip, was adorned with fore-claws only, as it was intended for a wristlet on the left hand. The third strip was decorated like the first and intended for a shoulderband over the right shoulder, while the fourth was decorated exactly like the second and intended for a wristlet on the right hand. These were the strips for the first buckskin. The strips for the others were prepared in exactly the same manner. It is not permitted to speak of these subjects in midsummer, owing to the activity of claw-footed animals. This much First Man contributed to the medicine pouch *(jish)*.

They now asked Badger for a contribution to the first buckskin. He presented a dark flint headplume, which was then added to the male buckskin. Next, Gopher was asked, and he contributed a blue flint headplume which was assigned to the female buckskin. And the Badger presented another, a yellow flint headplume, which was added to the third buckskin. And the Gopher presented another, a vari-colored flint headplume, which was added to the fourth (or female) buckskin, so that each was provided with a headplume.

While this work was in progress—they commenced just as the white appeared in the east—First Man sang one hunmdred and two songs from the west to south (inside) the hogan, up to the doorway, and First Woman (sang) one hundred and two songs along the north (interior) of the hogan, up to the doorway (where Coyote continually changed position from one side to the other). This was timed so that the various medicines, which had been placed on the north side, and the witchery, etc., which had been placed on the south side for the completion or dressing of the medicine pouch, were ready about the time that First Man and First Woman finished with their songs. Consequently, these four (dressed) buckskins are in truth the medicine pouches *(jish)* of the *haneełnéehee* (Moving-up Rite), two male and two female pouches. In consequence, also, this is the first medicine lodge, and these are the first medicine pouches. The two hundred and four songs, the medicine (good and evil), the plumes and flints, all belong to the four pouches of the *haneełnéehee*.

And when First Man had spread out another unwounded buckskin, he distributed to each, to First Woman and his other companions of the fourth world, a portion of the dark medicine and of the other medicines mentioned above—also a portion of his witchcraft, of bean shooting, and of evil wishing, and of his power to impart insanity, so that each received a share of this also. He also gave them a portion of *azee' noots'eeh* and *azee' deit'inii* medicines,[13] which he had not shown before.

---

[13] I am unable to identify these plants.

He also gave the Spider Ant a portion of each of these articles just mentioned. But he sprinkled them over himself, and therefore he is red on top and yellow below, and his sting is very sharp and painful. Beet Beetle, too, received his share which he put into his pot, whereas the others, to whom he distributed a share, carried them in shell bundles in their garments. Thus the Bumblebee and the Mud Dauber each received a portion, and therefore their sting causes swelling. And the Horned Rattler, the Track Snake, the Arrowsnake, the Flying Snake, the Pine- or Bullsnake, the Rattler, Stubby, and the (Grandmother) Rattlesnake, each and all received a portion. But as they had no place to put them, they swallowed these articles so that their bite is (now) deadly.

The Yucca and the Cactus also received a portion, but they merely dipped their points and needles into the mixtures, so that now the prick of the yucca and cactus causes swelling. The Yellow Black-Ants, the Large Pine-Ants, the Stag Beetle, the Dark Black-Ants, and the Red Black-Ants were also remembered, so that if the Black Ant, for instance, bites your scrotum, it causes much pain, while the bite of the others also is painful and causes swelling. All these people, therefore, are evil and wizards, because witchcraft was presented to them by First Man.

He also gave portions of them to the other people listed earlier, hence these, too, practice witchcraft. He also distributed portions among the Wind People, such as Black Wind, Blue Wind, Yellow Wind, Striped Wind, Left-handed Wind, and Spotted Wind. Finally, (he distributed portions) to Dark Thunder, to Blue Thunder, to Yellow Thunder, to Striped Thunder, to Left-handed Thunder, and to Spotted Thunder. Wherefore these, too, are evil and witches. First Man was sufficiently provided to supply all.

All of these, being evil, cause sickness and death among the Navajos. Each has his own (prescribed) prayerstick for sacrifice. Some require prayersticks in white, others in blue, yellow, and black. White bead, turquoise, abalone shell, and jet jewels are required, as well as iron ore, harebell pollen, ordinary pollen, and flag pollen for their sacrifices.[14] The Holy Ones inhale this sacrifice and thereby sickness is removed.[15]

According to this version, then, there are thirty-two different ways of injuring us, although there may be more than this. For these there

[14]My notes at this point are fragmentary. The informant did not go into details about the sacrificial offering for each individual divinity.

[15]The Holy Ones are those endowed with witchcraft. To judge from other accounts, the sacrifice takes the very common form of a smoke prepared for the petitioned.

are just as many remedies, consisting of stones and lichens, of plants, their seeds, flowers, leaves and roots, trees with their limbs and bark, many of which may be used as medicine.

Thus the cottonwood with its root, its pulp, its warts, the juice from its cracks, its branches, leaves, core, and its bark, is altogether useful in medicine and ceremony. The same is true of oak, pine, spruce, juniper or cedar, of *nikiihí nákaad*,[16] a tree similar to spruce. (It is) also (true) of the wide spruce and needle (blue) spruce, of the piñon tree, of cedar and its berries, of scrub-oak. True also of the sour berry, service berry, of the red bush and the chokecherry, while the branches and pollen of sumac are also used ceremonially.

The wild cherry, too, is a ceremonial medicine. Likewise, the wild rose, the seeds of a plant called *haich'a*, and the goldenrod and other Bigelovias, and the plant *ch'ilzhóó'*, and *naats'aa'ííł'į*, the greasewood, cliffrose, black and gray greasewoods, the Chenopodium *(tó iichíí')*, the hedge mustard, bulrush, the cattail, and the round-leaved flag, the *tł'éego iilchii'*, a water-plant, and water spruce, watercress, the *táłkááʼbéésh*, and *tó bik'ésti*, the reed *(lók'aa')* vervain, the large and slender thoroughworts, red medine, black stem medicine (gromwell), false mallow, wild sunflower, the large and slender rattle pods, Oxytropis and Leguminae, Eriogxonum racimosum, lightning-struck stone and wood, *kéłdiłii*, Frasera speciosa, a greasewood (Sarcobatus), then corn,[17] squash, beans, watermelons, sugar melons, etc.

All these herbs or parts of them are used in the *haneełnéehee* as medicine or as sacrifices to remove the evils already mentioned. After the medicine pouches had been made and their contents distributed among the people present, First Man enumerated them as remedies for (these) said evils. On that (lower) world, however, these plants were not yet in existence.

Whenever these medicines, just enumerated, prove ineffective on men and women, young and old, a prayer "which prays out from below" *(hach'ee yaatee'ii)* is employed. It is recited by the singer, (together) with the patient, wherein they together travel to the homes of the supernaturals (gods) below the east. The patient repeats each phrase as pronounced by the singer.

After reaching the home of the divinity in the east, and (after) placing their petition there, the prayer makers then return by retracing each step of the journey until the starting point has been reached

---

[16]Some of the trees and medicines mentioned are unidentified. I have given their names in the vernacular.

[17]There are probably a number of sacred names in the list which are used in invocations, thus *ła'ąį́ nitįįh* for squash, and *ła'ałʼéé' nit'įįh* for corn. Because it was impossible to identify a number of plants, these have been omitted.

again. Step by step, the evil is removed and the patient restored to his
former healthy condition. This accounts for the name "to pray it out."
Pollen is then placed on the tongue and head of the patient and otherwise is used freely by the singer.

The same prayer is repeated to the holy ones dwelling in the south,
in the west, and north. The prayer to the nadir (below) must be said
with great care as the evil ones have their homes in that region. The
return part of this section of the prayer to the zenith removes every
vestige of their influence. A short petition is then added to a circle in
the center, another to a second enlarged circle and so on to four circles,
one always larger than the preceding one.[18] This *ch'ee yaatée'ii* is used,
as said, whenever the prescribed medicines prove ineffective.[19]

First Man foretold all these things at that time and enumerated
them as parts of the *haneełnéehee*. Therefore they are used today in
this rite. Its medicine pouch, too, began to be made at this time. For
himself, however, First Man reserved the turquoise and white bead
pouches (the first and second buckskins). The third and fourth buckskins with the black and blue flint agates (male and female pouches)
were made for the Navajos of the present day.

In the pouch of First Man, the left shoulder strap was a zigzag
lightning, the right shoulder strap a straight lightning, the left wristlet
was of rainbow, the right wristlet of reflected sun-red, the headplume
of sunlight. These he retained with the remark that in the other world,
Earth People could not preserve them. Therefore the shoulder straps
and wristlets used by the Navajos today are adorned with animal claws
and with serrated flints, as ordained by First Man at the time. The
haneełnéehee singer therefore must be in possession of the dark flint
agate pouch. Otherwise he cannot conduct the ceremony, nor (can he)
recite the *ch'ee yaatée'ii* prayer.

At the time of the institution of this rite there were no mountains,
trees, stones, no darkness and no light, no sun and no moon.

After the conclusion of the ceremony described above, the people
left the hogan, (now having) in (their) possession all evils which First
Man had given them. The people spoke of this and held council about
leaving the place. Big Trotter (Wolf) spoke, and Mountain Lion spoke,
and Blue Fox spoke, and Weasel spoke. Four (of them) spoke, but

---

[18]Just what is meant by this prayer to the four circles is not quite clear.

Editor's Note: Compare the final chapter, Upward-Moving Way Performed,
where four directional circles of pollen surround the washing basket "on the morning
of the last day." This link is a possibility.

[19]At present the patient may specifically request this prayer.

without reaching a definite plan. And they held council again and again and again, four days, as it were.

First Man now placed his white bead (wand) in position, but there was no light because, meanwhile, First Scolder (Coyote) had tied down the light in the east and west, in the south and north, unknown to the others. It appears that the people had been bantering with him and, because he roamed about and scolded much, they had called him *mą'ii* (Roamer) and *hashké* (He-scolds). "I am not *nanishmá* (roaming), I am not angry *(hashishké),*" he said testily. And in order to regain his prestige, he tied down the light pillars so that all was dark.

Again they held council among themselves over this strange occurrence, and four times they held council in darkness. Meanwhile Coyote lay down and took matters easy, and First Man alone was aware of what Coyote had done. It also happened that after every speech in council they heard somebody remark: "Why do you not ask that fellow lying over there." And the speaker was the Bat. They therefore prepared a sacrifice for Coyote of white bead, turquoise, abalone, and red-white stone.

And when the first was ready, Big Trotter (Wolf) offered it to him saying: *Hayoołkááł tádilwoshii mą'ii łigai yoołgai niyééł áshłaa*— "Dawn who cries in White Coyote, of white bead I have made your sacrifice."

And the Mountain Lion of the west presented his saying: *Nahootsoi yitádlwoshii mą'ii łitso diichiłí niyééł áshłaa*—"In the twilight he who calls, Yellow Coyote, of abalone I have made your sacrifice."

And the Blue Fox of the south presented his saying: *Nahodeełł'ish yitádilwoshii mą'ii dootł'izhí dootł'izhii niyééł áshłaa*—"In the skyblue he who calls, Blue Coyote, of turquoise I have made your sacrifice."

And the Weasel of the north presented his saying: *Ch'ał'eeł yitádilwoshii mą'ii diłhiłii bááshzhinii niyééł áshłaa*—"In the darkness calling, Dark Coyote, of jet I have made your sacrifice."

This evidently pleased him, for he arose and, running east, untied the white pillar, then that of the south, west, and north. And again the white arose in the east and the yellow in the west and it was light again and the speech *(saad)*[20] was, as it were, holy again. Thereupon First Man took down the hogan, rolled it into a small ball, and laid it aside. The people of this world then were wicked and remained so when (they were) ready to enter the next world.

---

[20]The speech here may refer to the world in which they lived as well as to the councils of the Holy Ones.

First Man now planted a piece of jet, of turquoise, abalone, white bead, and red-white stone in the center of the earth, making five in all. Each of these grew to the height of four fingers[21] and (they) were thus enabled to enter the next world.

[21]The width of four fingers equals a trifle over two inches. Here this measure is multiplied five times, each of five jewels being increased.

4

World-Level of "White Yellowish" Color

This world was of a white yellowish color and appeared to be better than the one they had just left.[22] Toward the east there was a white mountain or ridge, to the south a blue, to the west a yellow, and northward a black mountain. Round about the country seemed to be dotted with hills, ravines, and gulches. And they wondered much what it might be. The Coyote, as usual, had investigated the eastern portion and reported that some people lived there. These were surprised at the stranger and seemed unwilling to be friendly, but after he travelled to and fro several times, they finally made friends.

And it developed that the following peoples lived here: Big Trotter (Wolf), Mountain Lion, Blue Fox, Badger, Wildcat, Puma, Meadow Wildcat, Cliff Wildcat, Cat of the Valleys, Elk, (male and female) Deer, male and female Antelope, Virginia Deer, Big Skunk, Spotted Skunk, Big Squirrel, Slender Squirrel, a Rock squirrel, Ground Squirrel, the Mouse, Field Rat, Kangaroo Rat, Small Field Rat, Field Lizard, Field Mouse; all these lived here.

And there were also the Otter, Beaver, Muskrat, *atiin dzołdizí,* and *nahook'é dzołdizí,* the Dark Bear, Blue Bear, Yellow Bear, White Bear, the Silvertip, Yellow-Chin Bear, the Grizzly (?), the Wide-Foot Bear, Black and Gray Pine-Squirrels, the Dark Porcupine, Yellow Porcupine, Blue Porcupine, White Porcupine, the Badger, the Gopher, the Locust, White Locust, the Turkey, Owl *(naak'eeni),* and Owl-with blue-mouth, Owl, the Hawk Owl, *dzidiłdí'ii*-Owl, the Magpie, *bijéiji dootł'izh, na'a'á'ii* (the Spotted One), Large Crane, Small Crane, the Pointed Snake, the Jackrabbit, the Cottontail, the Rat, the Prairie Dog, Dark Weasel, White Weasel, Blue Weasel, Pink Weasel, some with blackish breast, some with white breast, and bluish breast,[23] the Yellow Coyote, they say, and the Yellow Weasel.

And their houses were made of dark moss, of blue moss, of yellow moss, of white moss, and of variegated mosses.

---

[22]This should be the eighth world or the last chamber of the second division among underworlds. The division is not strictly outlined by the informant.

Editor's Note: Father Berard entitled this chapter "Blue World" and added the above footnote. All the same, the first sentence introduces a world of "white yellowish color." Apparently we are still dealing here with a world-level of the Red Underworld. Shades of yellow blend into light and natural reds better than into blue.

[23]I am not familiar with these weasels. My text notes indicate that *ła' bitééł dzidíńthéél* refers to a lark of black, white, and blue breast.

The Gray Lizard lived in a house of dark moss, Blue Lizard in a house of blue moss, Yellow Lizard in a house of yellow moss, White Lizard in a house of white moss.

Squirrel *(tsék'i naazoolí)* lived in a house of variegated moss, and the house of *nihahonoots'eeh*[24] was of red moss; therefore the breast of the Arrowsnake is red. And the house of Flying Snake *(nihonoodǫ́ǫ́z)* was of striped moss, and the house of *tábąąh hastł'ish* was of mouse-colored moss.

And the house of Black Fish *(tałtł'á naaldooí)* was made of dark moss, the house of Male Fish *(tátkáá' naaldooí)* of blue moss, the house of Yellow Fish *(tók'i naaldooí)* of yellow moss, the house of White Fish *(tók'i náálghaałí)* was of white moss.

And the house of Frog *(tábasdáii)* was made of dark moss, the house of White Frog *(tábasdáii)* of white moss, the house of Green Frog *(tó yidoodǫ́sii)* was of blue moss, the house of Tadpole *(naak'élii)* was of white moss.

And the house of Small Water Bugs *(tó yinaabéłii)* was of dark moss. And the house of Water Skipper *(diichiłí yináhidi'nahii)* was of abalone shell. The house of Otter *(tsenásii)* was made of dark mirage, the house of *tsinásii* of blue mirage, that of *ko'násii* of yellow mirage, of *tónásii* of glittering mirage. These are the four sacred names of the Otter.

And the Water Monsters *(téhoołtsódii)*, the dark, blue, yellow, and white lived here. And the Water Horses black, blue, yellow, and white lived here. And Man-eating Fishes too, black, blue, yellow, white and striped in color. All these were wicked people.

And *tó ałná'oosdlį* (Waters-flow-across-each-other) was there. This was the juncture of rivers, one flowing east to west, one north to south. The waters flowing east and west were rapid and furious. Those passing under this from north to south were placid. The water of the river flowing west curved there to the south and was warm; the river flowing southward from north was cold and curved to the west, so that the warm and the cold waters met at the south. And the river flowing

north from south curved to the east and was warm; and the river flowing eastward from west curved northward and was cold, and here also the cold and warm waters met, then whirled from here to the east, to the south, to the west, to the north, so that all the waters met and the people mentioned above lived here surrounded by waters.

---

[24]*Nihahonoots'ee'* is the sacred name of Arrowsnake. Perhaps the preceding *tsék'i na'azoolí* is the ceremonial name of Squirrel.

5

World-Level of
the Eleventh Speech

LIFE BY THE RIVER

And they had emerged at White Speck of Earth *(ni' hahoogai)* and dwelt about here, and this is *saad łats'áada*, the eleventh speech or world.[25]

Now the Cat People argued with the newcomers as to which of them should act as chiefs. "We should be chiefs, too," said those of the lower world. "That shall not be," the others replied. Both therefore wished to be chiefs, but could not agree. Finally they compromised the matter. Big Trotter (Wolf) of this world was one chief, Mountain Lion of this world, also, but Big Trotter of the other (lower) world was the third chief, Mountain Lion of that world the fourth chief. They lived in the east, in the south, in the west, and in the north, in the order mentioned.

The houses in the east were white, those of the south were blue, those in the west were yellow, those of the north dark and of mixed colors. The Wolf chief in the east lived in a white house, Mountain Lion in the south lived in a blue house, Wolf in the west lived in a yellow house, Mountain Lion in the north lived in a dark house.

On the roof of the house of the chief in the east were four chambers from which he spoke to the people. This was similar to a ladder, the lower rung of which was of jet, the second rung of abalone, the third of turquoise, and the uppermost of white shell. And the house[26] of the chief in the south was arranged in the same manner, and in the west, and in the north. The uppermost chamber or rung was made of turquoise in the south, of abalone in the west, and of jet in the north. Passing through the house, they would ascend to the top of these chambers and address the people from the uppermost rung.

At light (dawn) the chief in the east addressed the people. He spoke of the labor to be done that day, of the ditches, of digging and hunting. And when he had finished, the chief in the south was heard. He spoke

[25]The informant seems to be ahead of his story, and probably omits an event, or confuses some events of the ninth, tenth and eleventh worlds.

[26]The sketch accompanying the text reminds one of a Pueblo house from which ladders extend. The address was made from the top rung.

of the newcomers and what was to be done with them, what the people thought of them, and so on. And when he had finished, the voice of the chief in the west was heard to repeat what had been said by him of the east; and he of the north was heard to repeat what had been said in the south. "The speech of the chief in the west is the same as that of the chief in the east," remarked the people. "The two chiefs of the north and south also spoke alike. There is no difference in their thought and speech."

And the people played games there and gambled in the plaza. They played hoop and pole; three different kinds of (seven-card) dice and the bounding stick-game, and *télii* and *tsí'ii* (probably dice games), and *woshii, nézhii,*[27] and they ran footraces out to a certain point and back without stopping, and "football" they played with black, blue, yellow, and white sticks—the white ones in the east, yellow in the west, blue in the south, and black in the north.

This game was played in two different styles. Sixteen sticks would be placed in line in front of one of the villages facing the plaza. These sixteen would represent a club (of four) from each of the four villages, and accordingly the colors would be different; for instance, when they started the game from the eastern village, the lineup would be as follows: black, blue, white, and yellow on the north end. The object would be to kick the sticks to the opposite side, and betting was done on the respective representatives of one village against those of another. Thus they kicked the stick from one village to the opposite village and exchanged in this manner.

The game might be played also by lining up sixteen players in front of each village in the central plaza, the object of the players being to run around their village. The players returning first to the plaza were winners and received the stakes. This course always must be that of the sun, "the way the sun travels," called "sunwise." One turns to his left and completes the course of a circle and never starts a circle or semi-circle to his right.

They spoke a different language there than we do. Thus, *yáshii* meant down *(góyahdi), dáshii* meant up *(wódegi).*

A valley there was called *hasgháál.* Bad lands *(honooji)* were called *honoodáázh.* A meadow or basin was known as *házhmeezh.* A ridge or dune was *honaa'ái.* Dried wood was called *kazitah.* Side of a mountain (was called) *nábinbidí.* Over the mountain, on the other side, was called *áshigói.* For "I am going among friends," they said *shik'éí deeyá nadineeshtł'il,* and for "give me a bag" they used *táts'aa shináá' bee*

---

[27] I suspect very much that *télii, tsíi'ii, wóshi, nézhii* are names of particular dice in seven-dice and bounding stick.

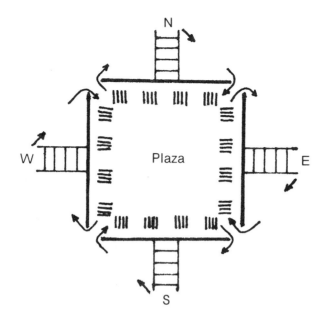

Model of various villages
Chambers on the house tops of the chiefs indicated by ladders
Lines around plaza are possible positions of "clubs"
in the football game
They also outline the course over which the game was played

iishtł'í'. For "spend the night" they used *tł'óół yáale,* and for "I'll return," they said *dayoonił,* and *dáyago* for "I'll wash myself," and *doo yaateel* for "prepare some food," and *t'óó shaajah* for "come and eat." And they also had dogs. When they called to them they said *bi, bi, bi,* instead of *hágo, hágo, hágo* (come here!), and *lę', lę', lę',* instead of the present *akóh* (get out of here).

And the White Dog belonged to the white column of light in the east. The Yellow Dog (belonged) to the west where the yellow column rose, the Blue Dog to the south where the blue column rose, and the Black Dog to the north where the dark column rose.

And the various peoples and tribes of this world were very friendly toward one another and dwelt in perfect harmony there. Each worked at preparing the ground for farming, at making ditches and planting. Big Trotter had white corn, Mountain Lion furnished the yellow corn, Blue Fox the blue corn, and Badger furnished black corn.

And *nádleeh* (the hermaphrodite)[28] was there also, they say. "Have you all you desire?" they asked him. "Yes," he answered, "I do not

[28]The *nádleeh* is a man doing the work usually assigned to women.

Editor's Note: See also Father Berard's later essay in American Tribal Religions, Volume 2.

wish for more. I can make grindstones, and baking stones, and also pots, and earthen bowls, and earthen spoons. I also have gourd seeds, and also own squash seeds, and watermelon seeds, and sugar melon seeds, and seeds of *n'dílkal*, a poisonous gourd, seeds of jimsonweed and of *ilhoschaaí*, and of poisonous milkweed, and poison ivy, and of *shilátso*, another poisonous weed, and of *tsin diwozh*. All these I have in my possession," said *nádleeh*. "You have all you might wish for," they said to him.

Nádleeh now placed twelve millstones in front of the village in the east. The women assisted him. And in front of the village in the south they placed twelve, and in the west they placed twelve, and in the north also. They then placed twelve baking stones in front of the millstones in the east, south, west, and north, and also twelve pots in the houses in the east, south, west, and north.

And Big Trotter spoke in the east on preparing the gardens and fields. Mountain Lion in the south spoke on the hunt of game (animals) and (of) seeds, and Big Trotter of the west repeated what had been said by the chief of the east, and Mountain Lion of the north repeated what had been said in the south. And the people went out to prepare the fields. *Nádleeh*, however, being chief of the culinary department, directed the preparation of the flour and the baking on the stones.

In the east a basket had been placed and turned (upside) down. Blue Fox,[29] and Yellow Fox, and Badger, and Weasel sat there and beat the basket-drum to a song, while the maidens ground the corn. This they did in order that the maidens might keep time while grinding. And four of the same[30] people sang and beat the drums in the south, the west, and north for the grinding maidens there. Time and again the maidens would take a pinch of meal and sprinkle it on the heads of the singers, who would return the compliment. In this manner the food was prepared.

And the others planted white corn, and yellow corn, blue corn, varicolored corn, squashes, watermelons, mushmelons, small gourds, milkweed, and gourds. In this manner the farms were prepared.

They also went hunting the deer, the elk, the antelope for venison. Big Trotter used a black bow and tail-feathered arrow. Mountain Lion had a mahogany bow and an arrow of *gishtsoi (?)*, and they also had *ch'ilhocháí* bows and *tsindiwosh* bows.[31]

---

[29]Blue Fox is a translation of *mạ'ii dootł'izh*. I use Kit Fox and Blue Fox interchangeably. Yellow Fox and Yellow Coyote are identical.

[30]That is, the Blue and Yellow Fox, Badger and Weasel.

[31]These two woods are not identified. The account omits the fabric of the other two bows.

They lived here for what would now be about a year. Then (in the spring) they increased their farms, clearing off a larger tract. They were happy and content, (they) amused themselves with games and dancing and had a good time generally. The harvest, too, was so great that they were forced to build storehouses in the east, in the south, west and north to store their crop of corn and venison.

Another year passed and the chiefs in the spring again spoke of the farm and the chase, each in his turn. Again the fields were increased, the harvest was great, and the storehouses (were) filled.

In the beginning of the next year (in spring), the chiefs in turn spoke of the farm and the chase. The fields were increased and they cleared as much as they might manage. The harvest was enormous so that the storehouses were too small and a large amount of the crop had of necessity to be put into the houses. And the chiefs in the east, south, west, and north each named the storehouses, *t'aht'ó'* (white, blue, yellow, and black according to the color of the direction).[32]

Now First Man, First Woman, (the other) First Man and First Woman, First-Made, Second-Made, First Boy, First Girl, First Scolder, these nine held council. "It will not do to let things go on in this manner," said First Man. "The people are always the same. They have plenty to eat, more than they can use. There ought to be more of them. There should be increase, there should be birth." Thus he spoke four times. "We must make a hogan as before in a supernatural way (in a divine manner)," he said.

He then planted white bead shell in the east, turquoise south, abalone west, and jet in the north, and placed a red-white stone in the center. Now, the hogan built by First Man on a previous occasion was made of poles leaning against each other (a conical hogan). The present hogan was to be *yaa dah askáni*, a round hogan. This is a model of the present hogan, in which the support consists of four uprights on which a flat or slightly sloping roof is built.

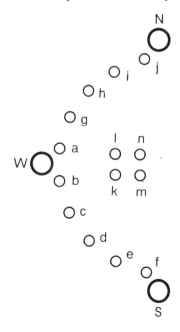

[32]My feeling is that this should be written *da't'oh* and that a corncrib or cornrack is meant. In, or on, these the ears of corn were hung up for preservation.

Editor's Note: According to Irvy Goossen, our linguist, this transliteration seems impossible.

And for the Sun-to-be he put down a piece of turquoise (see "a");
for the Moon (see "b") a piece of white shell. For the future Dawn he
put down a piece of white shell (see "c"); for the future Evening
Twilight (see "d") he placed a piece of abalone; for the Sky-blue-to-be
he placed a turquoise (see "e"); and for Darkness (see "f") he placed
a piece of jet; for *sisnajini* Mountain-to-be (see "g") he placed a piece
of white shell, they say. For Mount-Taylor-to-be (he placed) a piece of
turquoise (see "h") and for San Francisco Mountains-to-be a haliotis
shell (see "i"); and for Perrin's Peak a piece of jet. And placing a piece
of jet (see "k") he said (that) this would be the future Sky; and a piece
of turquoise (see "l") to be the future Earth; and small pieces of stones
of various colors he placed (see "m"); and taking a small heap or ball
of various stones, shell, turquoise, haliotis, and jet, he placed them
at "h."

All these valuables First Man carried with him in miniature, as did
also the other eight. And they also carried the material for the future
Sun and Moon, and so on, and the sacred mountains in this shape. The
better class of people—worthless and evil members were not allowed—
now commenced to file in, taking their seats on the south and north
sides of the interior. They were arranged as on the previous occasion,
farthest to the west First Man and his companions, and the rest of the
people in four rows on each side, with First Scolder prancing at the
door and leaping from one side to the other. They all wondered what
this strange meeting and the display of the various precious stones
might portend.

But First Scolder (Coyote) whispered to his neighbor: "That turquoise over there will be the Sun, perhaps." And, jumping across to the
south side of the door, he whispered: "The white shell there at the end
will be the Moon, perhaps. And the white bead shell next to it will,
perhaps, become Dawn. Next to it is haliotis. That, I presume, will
become Evening Twilight. But that turquoise next to it, why, it just
looks like Skyblue. And that jet next to it, it seems to me, will be Darkness in the future."

And he jumped over to the north side of the door. "Do you see that
white bead shell up there ("g")? he whispered to his neighbor. "It is
just like *sinajini* Mountain. And that turquoise next to it, my Grandchildren, is much like Mount Taylor. And that abalone, this way, looks
very much like the San Francisco Peaks. That is what it will be, no
doubt. And there is a piece of jet; to me it appears like Perrin's Peak.
We will see, however, you never can tell."

And again he jumped over to the south side. "This jet (see "k") is
just like the Sky," he said in a low voice to his next neighbor and
returned to the north side. "Do you notice that turquoise there (see
"l")? It seems very probable that it will become the Earth." And again

he leaped over to the south side. "That stick of mixed stones is a puzzle to me," he whispered. "What do you think will become of it, my Grandchildren? I rather think it will be the genitalia of man." And leaping over to the north side, he whispered to them: "That small pile of jewels of various colors is to be the genitalia of woman."

First Man then rose to speak: "What do you think will become of all the things which you see here, my Grandchildren?" "We do not know, Granduncle," they said. "We have been trying to find out, but cannot imagine what they are intended for." "Of course not," said First Man. "How could you know—with what little sense you have. You know nothing." On hearing this, however, Coyote leaped to the other side of the door and walked along the south side of the circle to where the stones lay, sat down there and crossed his legs.

And pointing to the turquoise (see "a") he said to First Man: "What is that turquoise there for? That will be the Sun, won't it?" "I suppose so," said First Man. "And this white shell here (see "b") looks as though you would make the Moon of it." "Just so," answered First Man. And mentioning c, d, e, f, he told First Man what they were to be, as also the various mountains, g, h, i, j. And First Man answered: "Just so it will be." And when Coyote pointed to the jet and turquoise (see "k" and "l") telling First Man that they were to be Sky and Earth, the latter only stared at him. And pointing at the mixed jewels, he said: "These you put here to be genitals of man and woman. I think you put them there for that purpose. What is your opinion?" Coyote asked First Man. He said nothing, but Coyote resumed his place at the doorway and said to the people: "My Grandchildren, none of you has been able to guess these things. Yet I, who have little sense and am constantly roaming over the country have guessed all of them. Therefore, each and every one of you had better take a hand in this ceremony since it concerns everyone—young and old, men and women. There shall be birth!" he announced.

Now there sat at the south side an old man with crossed legs of whom very few had taken notice. He carried in his hand a *jish* (medicine pouch) made of a fawnskin.

They now began to dress both male and female genitals. All were expected to contribute. Wolf and Wildcat, Kit Fox and Badger, each gave their vomit. And a male organ of red-white stone and a female organ of red-white stone.[33] And for each part, seventeen songs were sung, and thus they were dressed.

---

[33]It is not clear from the text where the organs were placed. From the expression, "they were dressed," it would seem that First Man shaped both organs using, perhaps, the vomit of the animals as a binder for the mixture of jewels. At the time, the interpreter was rather inclined to avoid details in such matters.

And again Coyote approached asking: "What have you made here?" But First Man said to him: "Tis strange. You know everything. You are always running in the dark and everywhere, you ought to know what it is." Coyote, however, looked them over and remarked: "Why, they are not alike. They do not seem to be finished. Hm! They are so different from one another!" And extracting four hairs from his left beard, he placed them with the genitalia of man, and extracting four more from his right beard he placed these with the genitalia of woman. And placing his hands over both he remarked: "This will be my contribution."

First Man then gathered his precious stones and put them aside. He only distributed these organs among the men and women that they might give birth. By showing them the purpose of these parts of the body, he revealed to them something which they had not known or practiced before. And again, he is the source of an evil which before did not prevail.

"We have done well," remarked the Coyote. "Why should the same people always inhabit the world? Let new ones arrive. It is better that young men and women and children continue to come. Indeed, we have done well." And waving his hand sunwise, from east to south to west to north, First Man gathered all of his treasures and the hogan, and, clapping them together four times, made a small ball of them.

And by his power he folded the light columns of the east and west together and raised the column of blue and black in the south and north, respectively, and the people went to sleep. And when the column of white arose in the east, and that of yellow in the west, it was found that the women were pregnant. And the chief of the east and of the south and of the west and of the north spoke of the the farms and the chase as usual. In addition, too, they spoke of the children to be born.

When they had spoken four time (days) in this manner, two children were born who were twins, one with the male and the other with the female organ, a boy and a girl. And the following birth was that of a male child which was again followed by the birth of twins, and then by the birth of a girl. After that no account was kept, for the births increased rapidly.

They again planted and danced and made merry and were content and satisfied and proud of themselves. They ate all and various kinds of food and venison, such as sweetbreads and biscuits and mush, such as the Navajos now relish. And they planted again, and their storehouses were filled with grain and vegetables and venison. And they planted for the seventh time and their storehouses were filled and their dwelling houses, even to the doors.

And they planted for the eighth time and things went well with them. The Wolf chief of the east visited with the chief of the south and of the west and of the north, and they consulted secretly about what was to be done. In the east and west the chiefs usually spoke of the farms and ditches and (of) labor in general, urging the people on, while those in the south and north usually spoke of the chase and provisions. Some of the people, however, gambled at hoop and pole and seven-dice, and basket-dice games.

One day it happened that, after the day's work, Big Trotter returned home accompanied by Mountain Lion of the south. When Big Trotter entered his home, he found that his four children had made a mess of his home. They had been playing in the ashes, dishes were strewn over the floor, which gave every indication that it had not been swept, and so on. His wife was absent. "Where is your mother?" he asked the children. His oldest answered, saying: "We do not know. But after you had left this morning, she too went out and has not returned since." They were unkempt and seemed to be hungry, and this sight filled him with compassion. Presently, however, his wife returned. Her hair and eyes were filled with dirt, and she seemed to have been without food for some time. (She had been playing bounding stick all day long.) Big Trotter, however, said nothing to her. Yet, she did not seem to be overworried and took her time in cleaning up and straightening out things. (Other versions accuse her of adultery; this version does not admit this).

When he noticed the indifference of his wife, he spoke to her, saying: "Why have you left the house? Why should you leave the children without food? Isn't it better to provide for them first and then visit with others? I think there are many things to be done about the house in place of running about and doing nothing. It is entirely wrong to leave the children and to neglect them. You should not do these things," he said to his wife. "Hm!" she answered. "If you know so well what is to be done, why not do it? You have nothing to do but talk. Take hold of things here and work instead of talking to others all the time! And since you have so much sympathy for your children, you might take care of them instead of speeching and walking around all day!"

She then sat down and simply would do nothing. She cried and swore and related all that she had done and what she was suffering in return, just as the women do nowadays. Yet the chief said not another word in reply. He lay on his back with eyes open all night. And when the light arose in the east and west, he did not ascend to speak as was his habit, though the other three spoke as usual.

And the people went on the hunt for game by pit-trapping[34] and by burning brush and encircling the game, or by corralling game. In these various ways they captured much game that day. Now, Big Trotter was sorely offended at what the woman had said to him and remained at home and neither spoke nor ate anything. And when the light arose again he was not heard, though the others spoke as usual. Again the people went on the chase and returned with much game. Yet they discussed the matter among themselves, wondering why the chief should not appear as usual. It was not considered proper to approach his house and investigate.

Finally, they decided to send *nádleeh* (being a person of rank) to inquire. He stood at the door of the chief's house and said to him: "Why is it, my holy Brother, that you do not speak as usual?" The chief, however, made no answer and *nádleeh* returned. And again light arose in the east and the chief was not seen, and after the other three had spoken, the people went on the chase and returned laden with venison. And this was the third time that the chief had not spoken and the people wondered more and more and dispatched *nádleeh* again. He reported that the chief would not speak.

And when the light arose again and the chief would not address them, the people dropped their work and the chase and remained at home. "Has anyone slighted him?" they asked. "Or has anyone disregarded his commands and refused to obey?" But it was found that they held him in universal respect and that he had found no trouble in being obeyed.

Now the chief had not eaten anything these four days and finally sent for *nádleeh*. And when he was seated the chief spoke to him: "What are you (all) doing? What are you speaking about that nobody seems to be at work?" And he answered, saying: "They are worried because you do not address them and go out with them. These four days you have not been seen or heard. What is the reason? Has anyone offended you? Have you been disobeyed? Have any of us women offended you (a *nádleeh* classes himself with the women)." "Yes," he replied, "I have been offended by the answers which I received from the woman. I was told that I am worthless and good for nothing, that I do nothing but talk and ought to stay home to watch the children. My friends, my brothers (addressing him in the plural form as a representative of the others), I am offended at this. I can do nothing and I should not speak! Yet, I fancied that I am of some use; though, what I have done and am doing now, others do not seem to appreciate. I do

---

[34]Several pits were dug at intervals, covered with brush and grass, and then the game was driven towards them. A pit-trapped deer or antelope rarely escaped.

not ask anything of those who abuse me; therefore, I have not eaten anything since. Have you anything to eat, my Brother?" "Yes," said *nádleeh* and soon returned with powdered meal (white bread) and corn mush and handed it to the chief, who partook of a hearty meal giving the remnants to *nádleeh*.

"Now," he said, "you will take these dishes to your house again and return to me." And when *nádleeh* returned, he spoke to him: "My Chief, my Brother and Friend! There are a few things which I should like to ask you. Do you understand the dishes and the work in preparing various foods?" "I think I do," said *nádleeh*. "Have you any millstones?" "Yes, I have." "Any baking stones?" "Yes." "Any pots?" "Yes." "Any earthen dishes?" "Yes." "Any spoons?" "Yes." "Any brooms?" "Yes." "Any louse-killers?" "Yes." "Do all these things belong to you?" "Yes." "And can you do these things without the aid of women? Have you seeds other than those belonging to women?" "Yes." "And have you seeds of white corn, and yellow and male corn, and female corn, and completely kernelled corn?" "Yes," he said. "I have it in my possession." "And," continued the chief, "have you blue corn seed, and striped, and varicolored corn seed, large corn?" "I also have them," said *nádleeh*. "Have you white sugar corn, and blue, yellow, and black?" "I also have them." "Have you some black corn, and plants, and seeds of squash, and gourd seeds?" "I also have these." "Have you watermelon seeds, mushmelon seeds, seeds of the small gourd, and of hard melon, and seeds of milkweed, seeds of sage, and tobacco seeds, and of slender corn, and of sheep tobacco?" "Yes, I have them all." These questions he asked.

"It is well that you have all these things," said the chief. "You will now go to the chief of the south and of the west and of the north. Then you will invite the more sensible people, and men of good speech to my house." And they gathered in council there. And *nádleeh* brought in a large stack of leaves of *nábii* and of *ayáni bilizh halchin* (Buffalo grass?), and of the tall and the slender *dinas*, and of phlox. And they smoked this in pipes of clay, of black, blue, yellow, white, and various colors.

After they had smoked, the *nádleeh* invited them to council and to give their opinion. And Mountain Lion of the south spoke saying: "My Brother and Chief! I am of the opinion that the women are bad since they caused this trouble for you and the people." "Tell us your trouble, Brother," said Big Trotter of the west, "what was said to you?" "Indeed," said Mountain Lion of the north, "we will not be abused by a woman or anybody else. Let us hear your trouble, the beginning and cause of the offense done to you."

"My Brethren, my Children and Friends!" spoke the chief. "I have been offended by four little words. When I returned home four days hence, I found the greatest disorder in the house. The pots were covered with filth and dishes with ashes. The children, too, looked dirty and unkempt. Filth covered their cheeks as if they had never been washed. I remarked this to my wife, yet my remarks were out of compassion for the children, not for her. I upbraided her and said: "This is no way to act. If you wished to play bounding stick, why not care for the children first and then play and be merry, as a sensible woman should do?' But the woman spoke to me and said that I only talk, I do nothing, I had rather stay at home and care for the children instead of talking all the time. 'I can do without your talk,' she told me, 'and I do not need you to be industrious (ambitious?); it doesn't concern me a bit whether the others care for your talks; as far as I am concerned, I can get along without your advice.' Thus she spoke to me and that is the whole trouble. I said no more but lay down and would not eat. And therefore you have not heard my voice as usual. Now you may go home and think over the matter and let me alone to my own thought." They left him and went to sleep, and morning came.

And when the white in the east and the yellow in the west were about to meet above (at noon), the chief again sent for *nádleeh*. "You will now clean the house," he told him. "Then you will call the council together to meet at your house. And the three chiefs shall meet there and I, too, will appear presently." This was done and the people gathered at the house of *nádleeh*, and when the chief arrived there he found the house filled with people. "My Elders, my Friends and Brothers," he said, "I have been told that I am worthless and of little good. I have my own counsel, yet I wish your opinion."

Now there were gathered there all the people of the other worlds, such as the Yellow Ants, Stag Beetle, and so on, Sphinx and First Man and his eight companions, and Salt Man and Salt Woman with the chiefs, and *nádleeh*.

Big Trotter of the east spoke saying: "Men, my counsel is to cross over to the other side of the river." "That we shall do!" said Mountain Lion of the south. And Big Trotter (Wolf) of the west: "The counsel is good. As you have said, we shall do." "Indeed," responded Mountain Lion of the north, "if you are worthless, let us leave and live by ourselves!" "In truth, there is but one voice of the chiefs," said the whole council. "What you have decided shall be done."

And turning to *nádleeh*, the chief said: "Do not fear to speak your mind, but speak frankly whether you will go with us or stay with these women." "What shall I do!" said he. "My Chiefs, my Brethren, my Uncles and Grandchildren, I have no desire to stay here alone," said *nádleeh*, they say. The women, on the other hand, played and laughed, sang and danced to the beat of the drums and made merry. Many did not even know what was going on in the council.

"Four days hence we will move. Prepare and get ready for that day," the chief ordered. They dispersed then and went to sleep. And when the light arose in the east, the chief was heard to address the people as usual. "It was told to me," he said, "that I am a worthless person, that I do not work, that my possessions are not due to my own industry. I must see into this matter. Let, therefore, every one of you move with me in three days to the other shore. Last night I said four nights, now it is only three. All males shall go. All male children shall go. Whatever male children are born until then shall move with us. Whatever may be found in the storehouses, leave it untouched. Take only provisions for a few days with you. Others are more powerful than I, eh? We shall see if she can excel us. Let each and every one, therefore, consider what may be needed to cross," said the chief.

He had scarcely finished when the voice of the chief in the south was heard to say: "It shall be done as you say, my brother. We have heard that people say you are worthless! If they will not listen to your demands, let it be so! We shall see!" He had hardly finished when the chief in the west was heard: "Bear in mind what has been said and consider it well and do it now! Prepare what is needed to cross the river. Let all who wish to follow us take hold and prepare!" "We will not think of our girls and wives any more," said the chief in the north, "but leave them behind! I have yet to see the day when woman is man's superior! That's what I think about it, my Brothers. Let us get ready for the journey across the river," he concluded. Thus spoke the chiefs. They then moved towards the shore.

THE SEPARATION

The shore was variously called. (It was called) Black-streaked Shore (tábąąh jíjín) with reference to the soil and watermarks, also tábąąhjí deetł'iizh, Blue-streaked (Clay) Shore, and tábąąh dzítso, Yellow Bank (on account of foam on the water), and tábąąh dzígai, White Bank (on account of foam on the surface of the water). In the diagram these are indicated at "a."

That section of the (shore) country in which they stood was called nastáán ná'ol, Floating Logs (see "b"). South of this, across, was known as táliwosh ná'ol, the Whirling Foam (see "c"). The opposite shore of this, or the southwest side was known as tsin ná'ol, Floating Sticks (see "d"). Opposite this, on the northwest side, was a pool of water, circling and floating along (the rays represent the waves), which was known as tó ná'ol, Floating Water (see "e").

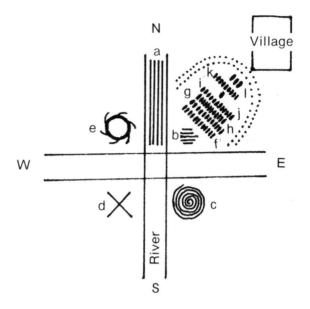

They took positions at the shore. The Wolf, chief of the east, stood at "f" and the people lined up beside him. Mountain Lion, chief of the south, took position at the head of the second row (see "g"), at the opposite end of Wolf. His people lined up beside him. Wolf, chief of the west, stood in the next row at "h" and the people (stood) next to him. And Mountain Lion of the north stood there (see "i") and the people next to him. In order to memorize the positions of the various persons standing there, the medicine man learns them by making marks in the sand with his middle finger.

There were twelve persons in each row, headed by Wolf (see "f"), Mountain Lion (see "g"), Wolf (see "h"), Mountain Lion (see "i"). The people lined up had these names:

Atsiniltł'ish bik'ideesdizí—he who is wound with lightning
Atsiniltł'ish yizeezíní—who stands in the lightning
Hatsoolghał bik'ideesdizí—who is wound with straight lightning
Hatsoolghał yizeezíní—the one standing in straight lightning
Nááts'íilid bik'ideesdizí—who is wound with rainbow
Nááts'íilid yizeezíní—standing in the rainbow
Shá bitł'ááh jilchii bik'ideesdizí—wound with reflected sunred
Shá bitł'ááh jilchii yizeezíní—the one standing in reflected sunred
Shá bitł'óól bik'ideesdizí—wound with sunrays
Shá bitł'óól yizeezíní—the one standing in sunrays
Sháńdíín tsílkéí—sunlight youth.

The other chiefs were accompanied by eleven persons of the same names—except that they occupied different positions, starting from left to right in the first row, then from right to left with the second chief. Those accompanying the third chief took the same positions as in the first row, and those with the fourth chief were lined up like those of the second row. *Nádleeh* took the position immediately behind these four rows of people (see "j"). Behind him are in order, starting on the right hand side (at "k"), First Man, First Woman, (the other) First Man and First Woman, First-Made, Second-Made, First Boy, First Girl, and First Scolder (Coyote). The three last in line (see "l") are: Salt Man, Salt Woman, and the black *hashch'ééh* (Firegod). Around this group of persons the rest of the people stood (indicated by dotted lines), but (they) were not allowed to enter or cross this group. Only men attended this meeting; the women were barred from it.

And the chief (see "f") spoke: "Are we all here now?" And the chiefs at the ends of the ranks (see "g, h, i") responded: "We are all standing." And again he spoke: "What shall be done with the *ná'ol* (see "b, c, d, e")? What do you think? Which one shall we use to cross? And to which side? Surely they are there by some power. How shall we know their use?" (Other versions make no reference to the *ná'ol* at all but let them cross immediately.)

Also, it is tabu to speak of many of the preceding things in summer. The name of Lightning can not be mentioned then for fear of being struck by it. In winter it is possible to mention it without injury, for then they are "locked up," as it were. In summer, too, the Snakes would bite from under the bushes, a Bear may attack you, and a mad Coyote would bite you, and the bad Winds in summer might also inflict injury.

They thus discussed and held council until the blue and black met above (and night came), but they arrived at no definite decision. They were tired and grew sleepy. They therefore turned sunwise toward the village and cooked their meals. After the meal, Wolf spoke: "At dawn you will think over this matter again," he said. Now, until this time there had been no dawn, but since some other power had told him of the dawn, he mentioned it.

When the columns of white and yellow appeared in the east and west, the chiefs in the east, south, west, and north spoke as usual. After eating, all men went out to the place of meeting and filled in the same positions as on the previous day, with the people surrounding them. And when they stood in position and looked at the spots where the *ná'ol* had been, these had disappeared. The water, too, which flowed from north to the center was of a black color. From center to south it

was blue. From east to center it was white, from center to west the
water was yellow. This they saw. "How is this?" said the chief. "All the
things which we beheld before have disappeared. All seems changed."
They accomplished nothing that day, and white and yellow again
were folded together, and it was dark. They then returned sunwise to
the village and after meals they met at the house of *nádleeh*. This,
however, was too small. But the Spider Woman blew to the four
directions and increased the size of the room so that all could enter.

"There has been a change in conditions," they said. "It is not as it
used to be. The waters have become black and blue, white and yellow.
What can this mean?" And they did not sleep that night, but when
darkness disappeared they ate and returned to their positions, each in
his place. And they saw now, that the entire water from north to south
was dark, and from east to west white.

And when the white in the east and the yellow in the west were
disappearing (when it was afternoon), Wolf stepped forward, and
Mountain Lion went to his side; and the second Wolf chief and Mountain Lion (also stepped forward). Then the first named chief spread out
an unwounded male buckskin in front of himself. And the second chief
spread out woven cotton fabric and the third a cotton fabric next to it,
and the fourth a white embroidered fabric next to this.

Now the boy of the first pair of twins, (who was) mentioned earlier
in the story, was called the Boy-who-becomes-the-one-raised-with-
soft-goods, because these soft goods were found in his possession. And
it was he who placed the soft goods. The boy of the second pair of
twins, born third in the order mentioned above, was called He-who-
becomes(-the-one)-raised-with-jewels, and (he) possessed jewels which
he, too, placed on the spreads of buckskin and cotton fabrics. On the
unwounded buckskin, he (the boy) placed a jet. On the woven cotton,
he put a white shell. On the cotton fabric, he placed a turquoise. On
the white embroidered fabric, he placed a haliotis shell.

Next to the jet he put red-white stone and a reddish shell, (thus
placing there) three jewels. Next to the white shell he placed two more
white shells, and this made three jewels. Next to the turquoise, he put
a red-white stone and a reddish shell, which also made it three jewels
for this spread. Next to the haliotis he placed two haliotis shells, so that
each had three jewels.

And next to each of the three jewels, he placed a portion of water
scale. Then he added alkaline clay, taken from the bottom of water,
which was put on both stones and the water scale. To this was added
iron ore, ashes and harebell pollen, ordinary pollen, and water pollen.

The first chief now placed a small piece of white shell, about the
size of a thumbnail, under the three stones which lay on his buckskin.

And the second chief did the same with a piece of haliotis, and the third with white shell, the fourth with haliotis shell. They then walked in file with this offering to the junction of the waters and sat down. And reaching with his hand as far as possible into the waters and holding the jewels there until he had finished a song, he extracted his hand holding only the small dish of white shell in his hand. The three jewels had been offered to the waters. The other chiefs repeated this ceremony in the same manner, each singing a song during the offering of the jewels. They then resumed their original places in the ranks after folding the buckskin and fabrics. In this manner they had made a sacrifice to the water which had shown these ominous signs.

Therefore, even now, when one reaches a stream which causes anxiety, a sacrifice is offered to the water after this fashion. The same songs are employed for this Blessing Rite. The same sacrifice, in the shape of a cigarette, is offered for the reform of a prostitute.

The buckskins and fabrics were again folded and removed. They then returned to their homes in the manner previously stated, and after eating they remarked: "Let us retire and see how our dreams will be." Curiously enough, when at the rise of light the chief ascended for his customary address, he announced: "I dreamt that I had been standing in white corn." "And I was standing in evening twilight," said the second chief. "And I was standing in collected waters,"[35] said the third chief in the west. "And I in child-of-water," said he in the north. Thus they spoke when the people were arising.

And they assembled again at the meeting place and took up their positions there for the fourth time. And when they looked at the rivers they were not as before. They ran smoothly and had no special color. Yet the four ná'ol were not to be seen. "But how shall we cross?" they said. And they held council without result. "It seems to me," said First Man, "that you might use floating logs and floating stick (ná'ol) with good results. I should set floating foam and floating water aside. They do not seem to be of any service anyway. This is my opinion," said First Man.

They now set about to make boats. Along the shores cottonwood, large willow, slender cottonwood, willow, blue willow were plentiful, they say. And they made five of these boats. The Beaver People built the first one of cottonwood. The Otter People, the second of large cottonwood. Muskrat built the third of slender cottonwood, and the

---

[35]Collected waters usually refer to rain or snow waters which collect in pools and cavities. This is sky water as differentiated from "the child of water" found in natural streams and springs.

fourth and fifth boat were built by the three people together of red and blue willow. They built the boats by chewing down the trees.

The first boat was dressed with watercress, the second with watercress *(Nasturtium alpinum)*, the third with water iron ore, the fourth with water-pollen, the fifth with duckweed. These served as a lining to fill cracks. Under the first they threw a rainbow, under the second they threw reflected sunred, under the third (they threw) a stubby rainbow, under the fourth (they threw) sunrays, under the fifth (they threw) sunlight.

On the first one they sprayed black mirage, on the second blue mirage, on the third yellow mirage, on the fourth white mirage, and on the fifth, mirage of various colors. Then translucent stone was put into each boat which made them transparent. And they labored at these boats only at (day-)light four times (four days) and meanwhile discussed the manner of crossing in them.

When the women noticed these preparations they did not worry. "Why should we be troubled that they go?" said they. "Let them! Are they alone our support? Can not we also take care of ourselves? Let them learn!" "We know," replied the men, "that you do not need us. You do not rely on our support, and since you have plainly told us this, we go." And the chief said: "Let it be so! The male children will go with us, and let the girls remain with you." "Well and good," answered the women.

"It is well, my Children, my Grandchildren," said the chief, "let us get ready and go. Gather your pots and millstones and dishes," he said to *nádleeh*, "but have care that you take none belonging to the women." "And you," turning to the men, "get all your property such as you yourselves have made and earned, but leave such as belongs to the women behind." "We are preparing and will do your bidding," they said.

And they collected their clothes, their bows and arrows, needles, sinews, feathers, their awls, knives, and all their own property. "I have plenty of fire," said Firegod. "And I plenty of wood," said Beaver. "And I have plenty of stone," said the Otter. His sacred name is *tsé nási*—Who-sits-at-the-stone. "And I have water (understand water)," said the Otter. "And I have salt," said the Salt Man. "I have water jars and water pots," said the Water Carrier. "Here are the black and blue, white and yellow water pots," he added. "And we all have all of the various kinds of seeds," said the rest.

And they (all the people) put these things into the boats. In the first boat they put white shell, which was to become dawn. In the second, haliotis, for the Evening Twilight. In the third they placed turquoise for Skyblue-to-be. In the fourth they put jet for Darkness-to-be.

Into the fifth boat, however, First Man, First Woman, and their companions placed mixed jewels (white, yellow, blue, black, and so forth), and these were to become fatal diseases of all kinds.

"Hm!" said First Scolder (Coyote), "the boats are made, yet something seems to be missing." "Indeed," they said, "they do not seem to be complete." And turning to the Horned Toad—who was *naayéé' hane'*, wise in transportation—they said: "My Granduncle, can you help us in this matter?" "Oh yes," he said, "just move to the rear a little," and they moved out of sight. Now the boats were placed along the various shores, such as the black-streaked shore, and the other (shores) mentioned above. Facing them he reached into his right inside pocket and brought forth a dark arrowpoint. From the left side pocket he took a blue flint point, and out of his right pocket again a yellow flint point, and with the other hand a white flint point. And placing these on the ground he lapped them up with his rainray (which is his tongue) and put the dark flint on the first boat and in this order (a, b, c, d), and also the blue flint on the second boat, the yellow flint on the third boat, and the white flint on the fourth boat in the same order (a, b, c, d) as shown.

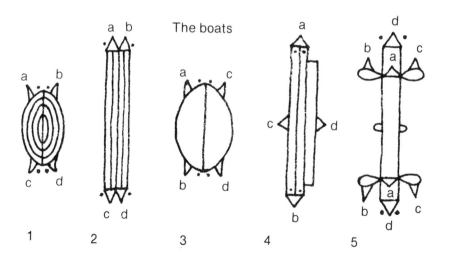

Then he took from his pocket varicolored serrated flint and placed one under the whole bottom of the fifth boat so that the points extended at either end (see "a"). The second (see "b") he placed under the whole length of the left side of the boat, with points extending at both ends. The third (see "c") he placed under the right side of the boat allowing both ends to extend. And the fourth he placed on top of the boat (along) its entire length. With the sound of *kii-ii-yii-ii-í* these four flints united and the boat was finished. He now blew a rainbow under the first boat, and a stubby rainbow above it, and reflected sunred below and sunray over it. And when he blew these, the sound of *zai, zai, zai* was heard. After he had inhaled these four things again, and the boat appeared in full view again, it stood enveloped in dark flint points, much like the back of a horned toad. And he covered the other boats in the same manner (with clouds, rainbow, and so forth) and they were transformed in a similar manner. The second boat (was) covered with blue flint points, the third with yellow, the fourth with white flint points, the fifth with mixed points, all serrated.

And when the people returned and viewed the boats, First Scolder (Coyote) again spoke saying: "They look better, but still something is missing." The Horned Toad now produced a rock crystal and implanted two of them (eyes, as it were) on the front and rear of each boat (indicated by dots on the diagram). "That's better," said Coyote, "but, my Grandchildren, they do not move." "What shall we do?" they said to *naayéé' neezghání* and *tó bá jíshchíní* (Enemy Slayer and Born for Water). *Naayéé' neezghání* then raised his shirt of blue flint, and another, and another, and another (of the same material) and produced a black agate which breathed, and placed it on the first boat. *Tó bá jíshchíní* also raised his blue flint shirt and produced a blue agate which breathed, and placed it on the second boat. And going to the third boat, *naayéé' neezghání* placed a living yellow agate (from under his shirts) into this boat. And *tó bá jíshchíní* placed a white living agate (in the same manner) on the fourth boat.

And walking over to the fifth boat, *naayéé' neezghání* extracted varicolored agate from under his shirts, and *tó bá jíshchíní* produced a club of jet. Placing the two side by side they were welded together and *naayéé' neezghání* placed it on the fifth boat. He now took his dark knife with which he raised the first boat slightly, then breathed on it. *Tó bá jíshchíní* did the same with his blue knife at the second boat. *Naayéé' neezghání* repeated (the same) with his yellow knife, and the two together raised the fifth boat with a varicolored flint knife, and both blew under this one. They then stepped aside and the people rushed over to the boats.

"What now?" they asked. "What about you getting into that one, my Granduncle?" they said to Beaver Man, who immediately leaped into the first boat. And Otter leaped into the second boat. And Frog Man into the third, and Green Frog into the fourth, and the Tadpole into the fifth boat. Instantly the boats rushed into the water, and the five guided them at will and found that they worked readily. The

Americans must have learned this and therefore now make boats similar to these.

Now the first boat was suggested by the color of the four shores mentioned above. Floating logs suggested the second, floating foam suggested the shape of the third boat, floating sticks that of the fourth, and floating water that of the fifth boat. "My Grandchildren," said Firegod, "it seems to me that it is not proper that these things should lie idle here. Rather we should board them."

Now the rock crystals which had been placed fore and aft allowed the boats to travel forward and backward. And these stones (eyes) spread a light over the boats so that one was enabled to distinguish rainbow, stubby rainbow, sunrays, reflected sunred, and sunlight. And the boats lay at the shore. Each man had lunch or food. The *nádleeh* was there with his millstones, and baking stones, and water jugs, his pots, his earthen dishes and spoons.

And for bridges to the boats they used rainbow for the first, stubby rainbow for the second, sunrays for the third, reflected sunred for the fourth, and a bridge of sunlight for the fifth boat. There was a song for each bridge. Each of these bridges was wide, so that the people might enter the boats without delay. Many had boarded the ships when all of a sudden the waters stormed furiously. The waves rose high and rocked the boats to and fro, and Water Monsters were to be seen on all sides.

There were the Water Monsters, and Dark, Blue, Yellow, White, and Pink Fishes, and ball-shaped Water Horses. These were seen on all sides. Many of the people had entered the boats, some were left on the shore. But when they saw these Water Monsters, they held council among themselves what this might mean. The Sphinx, however, remarked: "Leave it to me, my Grandchildren."

He had a hunch on his back and head, and taking the hunch from his head he remarked: "This is the Big Wind." And singing four songs he cast it into the river when presently a very strong wind arose stirring the waves furiously in every direction. And taking the hunch with his left hand from his back, he sang four songs saying: "This is soil." And throwing it upward a violent sandstorm arose of such density as to force the monsters to the bottom of the water. Indeed, these storms were of such violence that one could not hold his head erect. For from the east the White Wind gushed in a whirl, and from the south the Blue Wind, and from the west the Yellow Wind, and from the north the Black Wind, and from above the Striped Wind whirled down.

The people in the boats viewed this scene under comfortable shelter. Those on the shores, however, were forced to the cover of their houses. And the mountain-like waves struck the ships from all sides so that the people in them were frightened and excited. The Sphinx, however, sang five songs and the storm subsided, and the Winds from

the east and west and south and north returned and it was calm. And
the Wind and roar from above was seen to pass upward. And he sang
another song and the boats were seen to float smoothly side by side to
the other shore.

ON THE OPPOSITE SHORE

This shore was smooth and beautiful and they called it the Glittering
Shore. And the waters washed various kinds of precious stone to the
banks: white shell, turquoise, haliotis, and jet. And these occasioned
the various names for these spots, thus, Where-the-white-shell-floats-
out, and Where-the-turquoise-is-washed-out, Where-abalone-and-jet-
are-washed-out. And there flowed out also red shell and water pollen,
and so on, so that the people increased in wealth.

And the Beaver, the Otter, the Frog, the Green Frog and the
Tadpole, the captains of the various ships, returned with the boats.
And for four days they ferried all the men and male children and
newly born males across, together with all their belongings. Meanwhile the women stood at the shore viewing this process with jest and
laughter. And when all the men had left, they laughed and feasted as
before, and the song and drum accompanied their grinding as usual—
because the Blue Fox and Yellow Fox, the Badger and Weasel, these
four "drummers" alone remained, considering the opportunity of
having all the women to themselves (to be) too good (to pass up).
Besides, all the storehouses had been left to the women, the men
having taken only the most necessary provisions. The women therefore
felt secure.

The separatists, however, immediately set about to select a place
for their farms. And this lasted four days. The spot which they selected
they named k'aa'iibah. Their first trouble was with the small children
clamoring for milk. They were able to remedy this difficulty for they
found there in great numbers a plant called "big milkweed," the juice
of which they squeezed into some of the shells found at the shore and
fed the children with it. This kept many of the men occupied. Of
course, the women jeered them from the other shore, inciting them in
the most vulgar fashion. The men, however, paid little heed to them.
In fact, while some of them cared for the children, others went on the
chase and still others cleared a piece of ground for planting. Thus these
four days expired.

Meanwhile, twelve male children were born, a fact of which the
women took advantage. For immediately they went to the shore and,

holding up the children they called across: "Say, we have twelve more males, come over and get them." Immediately the chief gave orders and five boatmen crossed to bring them. The women, however, placed the babes in their cradles on the bank and laughed at the approaching boatmen. They, however, paid little attention to them, neither did they leave their boats. But the Beaver unfurled his rainbow (bridge) and lapped up the children over into his boat. The Otter helped him with his stubby rainbow, and Toad did the same with his sunray, Green Frog with reflected sunred, and Tadpole with sunlight. In this manner they soon had all the children aboard and returned side by side to the men.

In the meantime, *nádleeh* instructed some of the men in the art of grinding the corn and in cookery, for he presided over the preparation of the various fine dishes, such as baked mush, and dumplings, and sweet cake. Others were assigned to making gruel for the children, others to carrying water and wood. In short, he had something to occupy most of the crew assigned to his aid. And at other times the men cleared the field to plant the various seeds of corn and plants mentioned above, which *nádleeh* had taken with him, and cleared a spot which seemed to them large enough.

But after they had lived there about twelve days, the women again appeared at the shore holding twelve male babes which had been born in the meantime. These, too, were carried across by the boatmen in the same manner as on the previous occasion. On this very day, when the children were brought over, they commenced to plant. And *nádleeh* was first to plant.

He went to the center of the field, called Wide Field, where he dug a hole with rainbow, and in the east he made a hole with a planting stick of white shell, and in the south with a planting stick of turquoise, and in the west with a planting stick of haliotis, and in the north with a planting stick of jet. And he planted in these holes white corn—(also) in the center, in the east, south, west, and north. And he sang the corn songs of the Blessing Rite—in which he describes the farm and the corn seed, its stalk, leaves, and all the various parts of the corn plant. The women, too, were planting on their side and they made fun of the men.

While the *nádleeh* was planting, the men stood in a circle around him, observing the manner in which he planted. After he had finished with the five seeds of white corn, the *nádleeh* and his crew of helpers returned to their labor of cooking. The others continued to plant in this manner. Starting at the east corner, where *nádleeh* had planted the corn seed, they planted twelve circles around those planted by *nádleeh*, and they finished in the east again. While one planted, another went ahead in the same circle until it was finished, being careful not to break the circle, and so on until the twelve circles were finished. This is the ceremonial way of planting corn and is observed by many Navajos today. The women on yonder shore did not plant in this manner; in fact, there was little discipline and order there, some giving orders, others snubbing them.

After they had finished planting the corn they also planted black sweet corn, and white, and blue, and yellow, large corn, and black corn, and russet corn, and this was planted in the circle farm. And finishing this, sunwise, they went westward to plant the farm with borders, called the Square Farm.

This was subdivided by borders making twelve squares or blocks which were planted in rows of six to each square and in this order: starting at the southern extremity this square was planted westward,[36] until finished. And starting at the southern extremity of the square, due west, they planted this in the same manner. And turning north, each square was planted in turn until they reached the upper northwestern half. And turning they then finished the lower or eastern squares by planting southward.

And in the southeastern, or first, square they planted male corn. West of this was the second square in which they planted female corn. Turning northward they planted perfect kernelled corn. In the following square blue corn, then black corn in the next square, striped corn in the next, (and other) plants in the next. And turning east to south they planted a sort of squash in the northeast square, in the next square watermelons, in the next mushmelons, in the next small gourds, and in the last square hard melons.

After finishing this field, they returned to the village in the south for their meals, which had been prepared in the meantime. The dishes had been placed in four rows and in such a manner as to allow two rows to face each other while eating. After refreshing themselves, they commenced on the farm called *tábahodisǫǫs*, Striped or Irregular-bank-farm, which was strung out along the eastern side of the square farm. Here they planted the following vegetables: pumpkins, gourd seeds, watermelons, seed of mushmelon, small round gourds, seed of hard melons, seed of milkweed, and sage, and *n'deeshjíín*, and large corn, and *bikázit'á*, and mountain tobacco with whitish flowers, and mountain tobacco with blue flowers, and *dinas* of the tall and slender kind, and phlox, and large beans, speckled beans of various colors, and peas.[37] All of these were planted there. "I thank you, my Grand-

---

[36]This method permitted each plot to be planted sunwise. To avoid a left turn, this sequence was kept up for planting the entire border farm. See diagram, page 100.

[37]Each specimen was planted in a row in front or on the east side of the square farm. The order of rotation for planting is that recorded in the text.

children, my Relatives, for planting all these things," said *nádleeh*. And this was the first planting on the men's side and the first planting on the women's side (after the separation).

Twelve days after the women had sent the second set of children, they again appeared at the shore saying that twelve more had been born. And the Beaver, the Otter, the Toad, the Green Frog, and the Tadpole, their boatmen, went over in the five boats to bring them across in the same manner as on previous occasions. In the following twelve days the men went on the chase and found plenty of venison. And again the women called, announcing the arrival of twelve more babes, which were brought across in the same manner so that on four occasions they had brought twelve males.

The men harvested in due time and the women, too, harvested their crops. And they taunted the men, though, as a matter of fact, the crop which the men had harvested was comparatively larger than that of the women. But the men did not heed them, and since they had taken their games and dice with them, they gambled at seven-card, and hoop and pole, and basket dice, after finishing their work.

At the time when the men had decided to leave the women, it had appeared that seven times twelve children should be born. Some of these had been born on the other side; others, when they took leave, were progressing in the womb accordingly. Others, as has been said, were born in the meantime. By now some of these were of goodly size, others somewhat smaller, some quite small, and the more recent arrivals were mere infants.

One night when the people were asleep, two of them (on the men's side) walked towards the shore where they heard the bark of dogs. They returned and notified the others of this. "You must be mistaken," they said, "go and listen again." They did so and easily distinguished the bark of a poodle-dog.[38] And following this sound past the farm, they located it near the place called Floating Water, but (they) could see no trace of a dog. Yet the sound seemed to come out of the water.

After twelve days had passed, the women again announced that some more children had arrived. When the five boatmen crossed over, they found only four children, which they carried with them. That same night the bark of the poodles was again heard. And the people went on the chase as usual. After twelve days, when the women had announced the birth of other children, the boatmen carried only three male children with them. And again the people went about their work in their customary manner for twelve days. And when two went out along the shore that night, they again heard the bark of the poodle.

[38]*Daasts'ílí* are diminutive dogs, for which I use "poodle."

And when they awoke the following morning, the call of the women was again heard. The five boatmen brought only two children on this occasion. And while some went hunting, others stayed at home, and after twelve more days the bark of the poodles was again distinctly heard for the fourth time and there was no doubt as to where it originated any more.

On the following morning many women were seen at the shore beckoning to the men amid roars of laughter and clamor. "Be quick!" they called, "there are some more male children here." And when the five boats arrived there they found but one child, which again they ferried across. And when the men returned from the chase that day, they had brought some deer, antelope, and elk milk with them with which they nursed this child.

Four days thereafter, the men again spoke of planting. They cleared a larger tract of land this time. But looking across the river they saw that little or nothing was being done among the women. And when the men commenced to plant, their fields were found to be much larger than they had been in the previous year. The round farm, the square field and the strip on its border—each had been increased considerably. And they planted the fields in the very same manner as described above; first the circle, then the square farm, then the border plots. On the other hand, when they looked across the river, they saw only few women planting, one here and there, and instead of cleaning the fields, weeds were seen cropping out everywhere and the farm was considerably diminished in size.

Meanwhile, the men nursed the children as best they could. The junior always received the milk of the deer and antelope, while the others were nursed with milkweed and gruel of cornmeal. Their fields now extended almost to the base of the mountains. For in the east there was a large, almost square rock, from the southern side of which another ledge of rock extended to a point. This point was known as the Rockpoint, the square stone was called the Rock-which-sounds from the fact that when anybody passed it, the sound of *diil diil* was distinctly heard. Next to this Sounding Rock two ridges, broken in the center, extended southward and terminated in what was known as the White Mountain. The two ridges next to this White Mountain were known as the Pair-of-yellow-buttes. The ridges next to the Sounding Rock (were known) as Two-white-buttes or mountains. The break in the center of these ridges permitted the passage around them. Neither of these ridges adjoined the two mountains but stood separate from them. And in the west the formation was similar. Northward stood a massive rock, known as the Rock-to-which-one-spoke. This was turtle-backed and smooth. At the other end (south) was the Blue Mountain. And next to this were the Two-yellow-ridges, while north of this, next to the stone of address, stood the Two-dark-ridges. And the square fields extended to the base of these mountains.

Again, for the third time they increased their farms, while those of the women decreased. And the men hunted and planted for the third time and they were very tired. The four chiefs then held council as to what might be done (to refresh themselves). They then sent for First Man and his eight companions, and the Beaver Man, and the Otter, and sacred Otter Man, and the Big Fly Man. And when they had entered, Big Trotter spoke: "My Elders! We have worked and hunted and grown very tired. We therefore sought you to learn of ways and means to obtain rest and refreshment." "I can advise you," said First Man, "let a sweathouse be made of soft goods and jewels and with song, and let the darkness of the sweathouse be made thereby." "What about you?" they asked the Beaver. "I'll assist with wood," he said. "And you?" they asked Otter Man. "I'll furnish the stones," he answered. "And you?" they asked Big Fly Man. "I'll furnish the fire." "And you?" to the Otter. "I'll furnish water."

And leaving the village, they passed below the Circle Farm and the Rockpoint and around the Sounding Rock to the east side of it. And First Man asked them of what it should be built, and they decided to build it of jewels. They also argued as to where the doorway should be placed. And they decided to face it towards the Rockpoint (west). And while they were building the sweathouse, four songs were sung.

And the Beaver took from his left pocket dark wood, and from the right side blue wood, and again from the left pocket white wood, and from the other pocket yellow wood and placed each at the doorway. And in the song which he sang there and then, he referred to himself and his wood. Sacred Otter Man repeated the same performance with four varicolored stones and sang. And when Big Fly Man was called upon to do his part, he laid down the red fire and the yellow fire. And the Otter placed the black and the blue and the yellow and the white pots there for the water, and the sweathouse was ready.

Now the Beaver Man climbed upon the Sounding Rock and to the tip of Rockpoint and, facing the village, he called out four times: "Come to the sweathouse!" This custom is also observed today even when one person alone enters the sweathouse. He must make this summons. And the people now walked to the sweathouse, divested, and were preparing to enter when they noticed a stranger with them. This was the Owl.

Now when they were about to enter, they noticed that the curtain or cover for the door was missing. "What shall we do?" they said. But when they noticed this stranger with the small horns on his head, they

Editor's Note: The original manuscript reads "horns." But in Navajo our Horned Owl is actually an Earred Owl.

approached him saying: ''Welcome, Old Man! Can you not do something for us?'' ''Indeed, my Grandchildren.'' And reaching with his
right hand into the folds of his garment he brought forth a small white
article. In size this equaled the width of three fingers. With his left
hand he produced a yellow one, with his right a blue one, and with his
left again, a black one. On one side of the sweathouse he placed the
white and yellow, and on the other the blue and black pieces. After
singing over them he raised them, and the white, yellow, blue, and
black unfolded and spread out. And he placed them at the front of the
sweathouse. "The white one," he said, "is a curtain made of dawn, this
yellow one is made of evening twilight, this blue one of sky blue, and
this black one of darkness." Thus there were four curtains, one on top
of the other.

They entered the sweathouse and, since it was small in size, they
enlarged it by blowing toward the four directions. They also sang in
the sweathouse. And while they were singing, a noise was heard
coming from the interior of the Sounding Rock, and it was heard even
after they had ceased with their own songs. They remained in the
sweathouse all day, drinking now and then from the water which was
in the black, blue, yellow, and white pots.

And after they had finished the bath, the Owl rolled up the blankets and replaced them in the folds of his garment. But where the pots
had been standing, water was seen to flow out as if from a spring—the
sacred dark water flowing up, the sacred blue water flowing up, the
sacred yellow water flowing up, and the sacred white water. And after
their return in the evening, they bathed their heads with water from
these four springs which originated there. In those days they had no
soap. After taking their meal, they retired.

In the morning, however, the chiefs spoke of hoeing the ground.
In those days they made use of three different kinds of hoes, (hoes)
made of wood or (of) the shoulder blade of an elk. The first and second
of these hoes were used by taking them in the palm of the right hand
and passing the four fingers through the opening at the end of the hoe.
The thumb of the left hand was passed through the small hole in the
center of the flat board or shoulder blade, and the hoe was then
worked with both hands by scraping the dirt forward with the sharpened end. This was used in a sitting position, the operator clearing the
ground round about within his reach. The third hoe was also made of
wood, curved slightly, and provided with a sharpened edge. A small
stick was fastened at the lower end with an elk thong to insure a firm
grasp. Besides, a thong of elk was attached on the back of the hoe
about the center. Through this loop the index and middle fingers of the
right hand were thrust, while the handle was grasped with the left
hand and operated after the manner of operating a scythe. This was

used in a standing position. And the first was called "both-way hoe," the second "shoulder-bone hoe," and the third "sideway hoe."

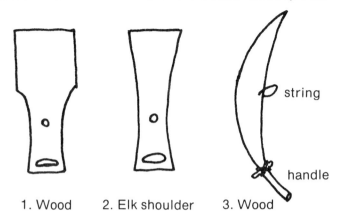

1. Wood   2. Elk shoulder   3. Wood

Within twelve days, all hoeing on the farms had been completed. When the light arose on the following morning they heard singing to the east of their camp. Immediately thereafter many little birds sang most beautifully on the cornfields, where the corn was well in blossom. The small bluebirds, and blue swallow, and yellow speckled birds, and the mockingbirds, and meadowlarks, and large corn beetles, and small corn beetles, all these were heard there. And presently two young men stepped forward from the field and came to the village, and these were Pollen Boy and Corn Beetle Girl. And they approached humming *lo-o-o-o, zaa-hai, zaa-hai, lo-o-o-o.*

And there was a basket of white shell, and of turquoise, of haliotis, and jet, and one a perfect shell basket (—all of) which were half-filled with corn pollen. And the two youths sang a song during which the baskets were seen to be filling with pollen. When filled, the two carried the baskets to the west side of the village where they placed them in a row in this order: the turquoise basket (see "a") at the northern end, the white shell basket (see "b") next, then haliotis (see "c"), and the jet basket (see "d"), while the perfect shell basket (see "e") they placed in front of these. And the Pollen Boy sat down in the turquoise basket, Corn Beetle Girl sat in the white shell basket, Big Corn Beetle sat in the haliotis basket, Small Corn Beetle sat in the jet basket, while White Corn Boy seated himself in the northern half of the perfect shell basket and Yellow Corn Girl in the southern half of this basket. This is part of the Blessing Rite.

With sunlight the Pollen Boy gathered the corn tassel from the cornstalk in the east—of those planted by *nádleeh*. He planted one to the east, south, west, and north of the center of the circle

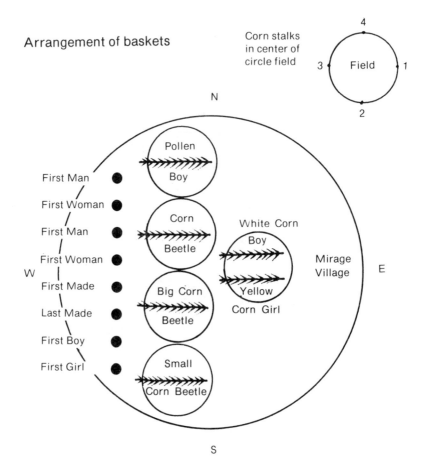

Arrangement of baskets

Corn stalks in center of circle field

farm, as previously mentioned. And Corn Beetle Girl gathered the tassel from the plant in the south by means of sunlight, and Big Corn Beetle that in the west, and Small Corn Beetle that of the north plant. And White Corn Boy and Yellow Corn Girl took (with sunlight) the tassel from the last stalk planted in the center of circle farm, and from the last plant in the square farm, respectively.

These tassels they placed in the respective baskets in which they were sitting. And they covered themselves with a sheet of rock crystal. And First Man and First Woman, (the other) First Man and First Woman, First-Made and Last-Made, First Boy and First Girl, these eight stood behind the baskets. White Corn Boy and Yellow Corn Girl now began their songs, and the other occupants of the baskets and the eight, each in turn, sang a song. In the Blessing Rite, White Corn Boy and Yellow Corn Girl, and the other occupants of the baskets, are mentioned before[39] First Man and his companions.

---

[39]Some informants exclude First Man altogether from the Blessing songs.

The sheets of rock crystal were now removed and placed behind each basket, and the holy youths were found to be covered with pollen. First Man then placed a disc-shaped (unperforated) turquoise shell behind the turquoise basket, a white shell disc at the white shell basket, a haliotis disc at the haliotis basket, and a jet disc at the jet basket, and a perfect shell disc at the perfect shell basket. He and his companions then placed all the various medicines—mentioned as belonging to the *jish* or pouch of *haneełnéehee*—such as dark medicine, yellow, blue, and so forth which, as mentioned above, had been distributed by First Man at the institution of this rite. Some of these were tied in small pouches, others were slender and oblong and of various shapes.

After these had been placed with the discs, the people gathered about and formed four circles around the baskets. The corn tassels were then removed from the baskets and placed to the north side of each, the two tassels of the center basket being placed at the north side. And each of the corn youths stood facing his basket. And First Man then placed the turquoise disc into the hands of Pollen Boy, and the white shell disc into the hands of Corn Beetle Girl, and the haliotis disc into the hands of Big Corn Beetle, and the jet disc into the hands of Small Corn Beetle, and the white perfect shell disc into the hands of White Corn Boy, and the yellow perfect shell disc he placed into the hands of Yellow Corn Girl.

Taking the pollen from the turquoise basket he placed it on the turquoise disc. And of the pollen, on the northern half of the basket, he distributed to the people sitting at the inner circle, beginning at the center and turning to the right. And returning to his basket, he distributed pollen from the southern half of the basket and beginning at the center of the inner circle of people he turned left, giving everyone a pinch of pollen. The pollen of the other baskets was also distributed in the same manner by the holy youths from their various discs to the people sitting in the second, third, and fourth circles.

From the basket in the center, however, the White Corn Boy gathered pollen into his disc of perfect white shell and distributed this to the persons sitting at the end of the four rows. And the Yellow Corn Girl gathered pollen into her disc of perfect yellow shell and distributed this to the same persons. In this manner all were supposed to have received of this pollen. And holding the pollen to their mouths each breathed its breath, as it were, into themselves.

"What now?" said First Man. The person sitting at the southeast end of the inner circle now approached the basket in the center, walking behind it. And moistening the middle finger of the left hand he touched the pollen in the left half of the basket and put the pollen to his tongue; and moistening the middle finger of his right hand with pollen from the right half of the basket he touched the top of his head with this; and taking a pinch of pollen he sprinkled this to the east saying: "*hózhǫ́ǫgo naasháa doo* (may I go in happiness)!" The same ceremony he repeated at the other baskets, and turning sunwise around the baskets he resumed his seat. His next neighbor repeated the same ceremony at each of the baskets, and so on until each and every person in the four circles had blessed himself in this manner.

First Man then instructed them to take the pollen with them and to use it withersoever they might go. Therefore, it is used in all ceremonies and none is conducted without pollen.

First Man then carried the White Corn Boy and the Yellow Corn Girl in the perfect shell basket to the center of the circle farm, and he placed the basket at the east side of the center cornstalk planted by *nádleeh*. Here White Corn Boy walked sunwise around this stalk and the Yellow Corn Girl did likewise, and standing at his (the stalk's) right side, both faced the east and thus they returned to their home. They again became corn. Therefore the Blessing Rite is pure, nothing defiled enters it. And therefore, too, the white corn and the yellow corn are always pure, no other mixes with them. And First Man returned with the empty basket.

And picking up the Pollen Boy, First Man carried him in the turquoise basket to the cornstalk in the east. There the boy left the basket and circled around the group of stalks toward the stalk in the east where he remained, and First Man returned with the basket. And the white shell basket, which contained the Corn Beetle Girl, he carried to the stalk in the west where the girl left it. And encircling the stalk, she settled on the uppermost leaf which grew to the east (see Arrow Two in diagram). All these stalks had twelve leaves, six growing (toward the) east and six (toward the) west. Nowadays corn does not grow to that height, nor has it so many leaves.

First Man again returned with the basket. And taking the haliotis basket which held Big Corn Beetle, he carried it to the stalk in the north where, after leaving the basket, it circled round the stalk and settled on the uppermost leaf (at Arrow Three). And First Man returned with this basket. And carrying Small Corn Beetle in the basket of jet, he placed it on the east side of the stalk in the south, where it left the basket, and after circling around the stalk it settled on the lower leaf (at Arrow Four). And when First Man returned with the basket, he said: "Tonight we will listen." And they all sat up that night to listen. And when the column of light was about to rise in the east, they heard the rustle of the corn, *zai, zai, zai* and the *loc, lo-o-o-o, loc* of Corn Beetle Girl; and the *lo, lo, lo* of Big Corn Beetle, which seemed to shake everything in the field; and the *lol, lol, lol* of Small Corn Beetle.

First Man had brought all these things—Corn Beetles, White Corn Boy, etc.—with him. And the corn grew by means of cloud figures—

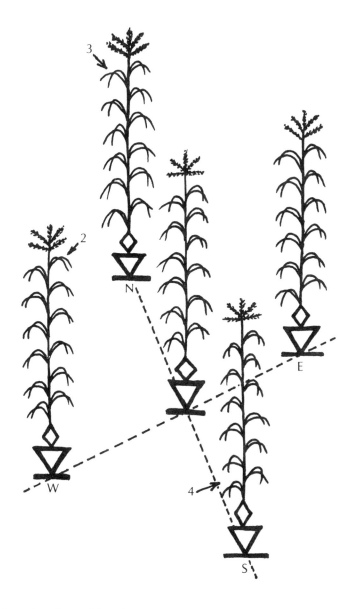

(which are) indicated by the triangles at the base of the stalks. These cloud figures, of which there were four to each stalk, caused them to grow. And the corn at the very center was large corn, in the east parent corn,[40] in the south white corn, in the west yellow, and in the north russet (?). And the names of the corn planted in the first two squares (of the square farm) was male corn and (round) female corn. And

[40]The text gives *naadą́ą́' tsoh* for tall corn, and *nadą́ą́' chó* which I am rendering "parent corn", taking my clue from other accounts obtained later.

between the six rows of these, beans of all kinds were planted. The other plants are mentioned above in the description of the square farm.

Now, when the light met above from the east and west, it did not seem to improve the growth of the corn; though, the squash plant and others seemed to thrive at midday. On the other hand, when darkness arose in the south and north, the corn seemed to progress better. Therefore it is called, sacredly, *ła'atł'éé nt'įįh*, "that which does well at night," while sacredly the squash *(naayízí)* is called *ła'ąjį nt'įįh*, "that which thrives at day." And *naadą́ą́' yiichíí'*, "the awn of corn is red" is (a term) used to express the advanced stage in the growth of the corn. And *naayízí bitáitsoi* (is used to express that) there are yellow-flowers-between on the squash plant.

And therefore it is said of these two, of corn and the squash: "Once begun, it never dies." In other words, there will always be corn and squash and they will always be raised. And whenever it happens that corn will root nowhere, evil is near at hand. There would be no crops, nor increase in families. Of course, this day is far distant, and it has always been a fact that corn is raised.

The men now harvested their crops, and it was noticed that the women, too, were preparing for the harvest. The latter, however, had little else than weeds, while the harvest of the men in melons, corn, vegetables and jerked venison was great enough to fill their houses. And while some of them were harvesting, others enjoyed themselves at various games; still others were on the hunt in the various manners they knew. Some hunted according to the Wildcat Rite, others according to the Ceremonial of Wolf; others according to the Big Snake Rite, all of which contained numerous songs of the chase.

Some returned after a time equal to 9 days, others in 13 days. Some hunted for 15 days, others for 17, and 19, and 21 days. Others returned in 23, and 25, and 27, and 29 days. Another group returned in 21 days, and 23, and 25, and 27, and 29, and 31 days. Thus all had returned. Some brought dried meat, others fresh meat, some carried hides with the hair for rugs, others hides with the hair removed and prepared (tanned). Others returned with seeds of all kinds. In fact, they were well supplied.

In those days there were no horses or burros or asses, but people had to carry their loads on their backs. Therefore they were tired and they went to the sweathouse which was made at the same place and by the same persons. And they sweated for four consecutive days and washed themselves, as previously, in the sacred waters there. On this occasion, however, they washed their heads only on the first day and their bodies on the second, repeated the procedure on their head on the third day and bathing their bodies on the last day.

And again (a fourth time) they planted, and increased their farms in size. They planted first the circle farm as previously described, the the square farm, and after a meal, the border farm. They then added four cultivated tracts to the circle farm, one at each corner, and finished with an addition to the southern end of the square farm. This additional farm was known as *dá'ák'eh njookélii*, the "additional field (?)."

At the village First Man now put down a (piece) of turquoise and a piece of white shell which he had taken from his mouth, and blowing on them they grew in size. Out of the two white buttes (in the east) blue water flowed, and out of the two blue buttes white water flowed. In passing these buttes the sound of *k'ol, k'ol* was heard in both streams.

On the growing *(dinisééh)* turquoise, the first born boy of the twins took his seat, and the other boy (of the second pair of twins) seated himself on the growing white shell. Turquoise and white shell baskets were also placed there. The water carriers now brought some water from the sacred springs in a blue and white water bucket. First Man then poured some of the water from the blue pot at the east, and south, and west, and north of the turquoise basket, then (he) emptied the rest into the basket. And from the white pot he again poured water at the east, south, west, and north of the white shell basket before pouring the remainder into it. "Who shall do this?" he then asked. "What is your opinion?" Presently First Boy stepped forward to the first (turquoise) basket and washed the head and body of the first twin boy. First Girl stepped to the white shell basket and washed head and body of the second boy. Both were sitting on the growing stones.

Meanwhile, First Man placed the following in order: shoes of turquoise, a turquoise shoe seam and shoestrings, turquoise leggings and garters, a turquoise loincloth and garments, a living turquoise agate and two blue perfect shells, then turquoise armbands and turquoise wristlets, and turquoise arm fringes and a turquoise collar band, two turquoise eye pendants and two turquoise ear bands, two discs of rock crystal, one large disc of which was not perforated (for the head), and four slender turquoise headplumes. And he also put down the same garments of white shell, white shell shoes, and so on.

First Boy then dressed the first twin boy in the garments of turquoise, taking the shoes first and the strings, and the the leggings, and the garters, and the loincloth, and so forth. And First Girl dressed the second twin boy in a similar manner with the garments of white shell. All these various precious stones had been the property of First Man.

(Here follows a) figure of the *doo bideedláád*—Non-sunlight-struck-ones—as they appeared after being dressed by First Boy and

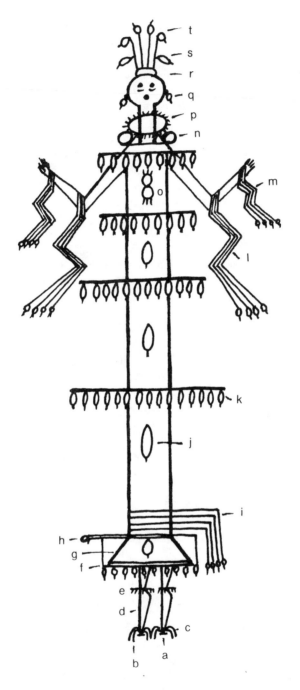

Figure of a Non-sunlight-struck-one

First Girl. One was dressed in turquoise clothes, as here represented, the other in clothes of white shell. The letters indicate: (a) shoes of turquoise and white shell respectively (b) thread or mixed border seams of the shoe, (c) shoestring, (d) leggings, (e) garters, (f) loincloth with turquoise fringes at bottom, (g) the buttocks, (h) "where you take hold of," namely, the grip of the loincloth, (i) the belt with turquoise fringe, (j) discs of turquoise not perforated in the center, (k) turquoise garment supposed to cover the entire frame of the body, (l) turquoise armbands, four strands to each arm, (m) turquoise wristlets, (n) turquoise "epaulettes," (o) living agate by which he breathed, (p) turquoise collar, (q) earrings, (r) turquoise perfect shell head, (s) rock crystals which guide him by their light, (t) turquoise feathers topped by turquoise. The mouth, too, is represented by turquoise, the eyes, under which turquoise is curved, (are represented) by rock crystal. This is the reference to "the turquoise under the eye."

And stepping from the two growing stones on which they had been dressed, they walked to the north and into the chambers on the south side of the village, which were constructed so as to confine them to the house and these chambers. And therefore they were called *doo bideedláád*—Light-does-not-shine-upon-them. Nor were they seen by others.

And they walked side by side into the chambers, the first of which was of jet, the second of turquoise, the third of haliotis, the fourth of

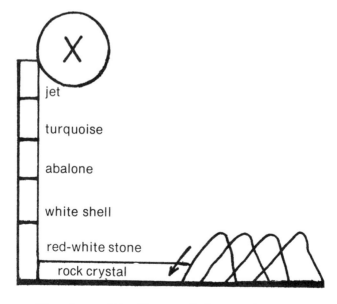

Chambers of the Non-sunlight-struck-ones

white shell, the fifth of red-white stone and the sixth of rock crystal, terminated at White-water-pool (see arrow). And here, too, there were four chambers in which they lived. They returned in the same manner to the village (see "X").[41]

Meanwhile the harvest of corn was reaped, this being the fourth time for the men and for the women also. But, while the men had steadily increased their farms, the women had planted in such a careless manner so as to have their farms fuzzy with weeds. And on the morning following the harvest, the men saw the women staggering along in poor and ragged condition. And they heard them calling by name to their various husbands. They would then raise their skirts, point to their buttocks saying: "Here is your buttocks."

And the Blue Fox, and the Yellow Coyote, and the Badger, and the white and yellow Weasel, who had remained with the women, had committed adultery so frequently that their voices were impaired. Therefore, it is noticed that these animals have no voices and grunt only a bark similar to *waa, waa*. So also men injure themselves by excess in sexual intercourse and lose their voices.

The women also sought to gratify their passion among themselves by running a stick through a perforated disc, each inserting the stick in *vulvam alterius*; then, too, by making imitation *genitalium vivi* of smooth oblong stones and bunch cactuses. In this manner they passed their time.

And the chiefs sent the men on the chase in the usual manner. And it was found that the men, too, were strong in their passions and that they also committed deeds to gratify themselves. There was one among the hunters named *bił hoogai* who had strayed from his party in quest of a doe, which he overtook. And being alone, *coitum habuit cum cerva adhuc viva. Dził ná'ol*, the floating mountain, was not far distant. And walking towards this small mountain, he was struck by Lightning and was killed. And falling, his head lay to the east.

When the others assembled for camp they found that he alone was missing. "The one who is called *bił hoogai* is not "here," somebody remarked. "I wonder where he might be." And they sent two messengers to the east and south, west and north, in search of him. They, however, returned saying: "We have called in every direction, yet he has not answered." And their sleep was disturbed that night. Now there were four brothers: *bił hoogai* who had been struck by Lightning, and *bił jídeetł'ishí shaiyoo'áál*, and Young Man, and *shándíín bił shoogishí*, his younger brothers. The oldest brother, thus, had been struck by Lightning.

---

[41] The account mentions that these things are made, perhaps in a sandpainting, "for protection" against prostitution. A smoke is prepared in a pipe. This is a personal remark of the narrator.

But when the light in the east and west arose they again sent two couriers in all directions in search for the lost brother, and they returned at dark saying: "He can not be found, he is not to be heard." And they discussed the matter that night. "What has become of him? Whither has he gone? He is neither in the east, south, west, nor north. Has he gone upwards? Perhaps downward?" And they went to sleep.

With the rise of the light in the east and west, the couriers again left for every direction in search of the dead one. Again they did not find him. "It is useless. He has disappeared," they said. And scarcely one slept that night. To such a degree were they concerned for the lost one. Still, with the rise of the light, twelve couriers went in search in the east, and twelve in the south, and twelve in the west, and twelve in the north. This day, too, was spent in vain and the parties returned at dark. "Again we have searched in vain," they said. Now the man struck by Lightning had been covered with blue moss and white moss and yellow moss and moss of a copper-gray hue. Therefore, he could not be seen and they had passed without taking notice of him.

"Here we are hunting and wasting our time," said the hunters that night, "while our people at home are working and probably worrying over our long stay. Let us return to report and see what is to be done." Now they had hunted everywhere, but since the body was covered with various mosses they had several times passed over it without observing it. And returning home to their farms they discussed the matter the whole night.

Big Trotter then arose, saying: "My Elders, one of ours is missing. Let us hold a council." And the council convened, and there was the Big Trotter, Mountain Lion, the chiefs of the east and south, west and north, and Blackgod *naayéé' neezghání* and *tó bá jíshchíní* and the Dark Gila Monster, and the Spotted One, the Yellow One, and the White Gila Monster, the Heron, the Curlew, the Bittern and Roundbill Crane, and the Dark Duck, and the Blue, the Yellow, and White Ducks, and the Badger. All these people convened and decided to go out in search for the missing one.

"Has anybody some eyewater, my Elders?" was asked. And the Heron answered: "I guess there is some." "We must do something for this man!" they said. Gila Monster then consulted the directions with his hand to learn where he might be found. And he consulted toward the east, the south, the west, the north, upward, and downward. "I have consulted everywhere," he said. "In the north there is nothing, neither in the west nor east, neither upward nor downward. My hand rested, however, in the south, near *dziil ná'ol* (also *dził ná'ol*)— Floating Mountain. There all is not right. I think we must go there." And the Spotted Gila Monster also consulted his hand with the result that it rested near *dziil ná'ol*. And since nothing definite could be learned in this manner, the Magpie and the Heron sat down to consult, the latter behind the former. And they were stargazers. They, too, reported that there was a streak of white pointing at the same mountain. And turning their faces in another direction they again consulted, reporting: "The light rests on the mountain, not on this side of it nor on that, but on it."

Then the Wolf Chief, the Mountain Lion, and the Badger gave their eardrums to *naayéé' neezgháni* and *tó bá jíshchíni*, and they went out to listen. "Somebody is breathing over there in *dziil ná'ol*," they reported. "Listen again," they were told, "but turn this way (north) and listen." They again reported, saying: "We have heard breathing there. I heard him twice on the same spot," said *naayéé' neezgháni*. "And I, also," said *tó bá jíshchíni.*

That night they did not retire to sleep, but when the first signs of the approach of light showed, they approached Blackgod saying: "My Granduncle, what do you think? Can you assist us in this matter?" "To be sure I can," he said, "I have been waiting all this while to be asked." He then undressed quickly and, making four steps forward, stood on rainbow and moved quickly toward *dzil ná'ol*. The Big Fly, being inquisitive, accompanied and hovered above him in order to bring the first report of the proceedings. Blackgod approached the mountain from the east side and arrived over the center of the mountain as daylight was approaching.

In the center, on the top of this mountain, there was a small pool of water which was covered with moss (scum). This he removed and blew upon the water which spread and revealed a chamber. And blowing thus four times, three chambers were unearthed which led into a large opening. Glancing into this hole, Blackgod noticed an old, dried-up fellow there whose skin was slick (as ice) and smooth. He entered and sat down. And the old crony's name was Smooth Thunder. Blackgod sat against the wall imitating the position of the old sulky fellow, who crossed one foot over his knee and rested his hands back of his head, looking upwards. This house was made of dark water.

"Where is my grandson, Old Man?" Blackgod inquired. "Whoever saw him? I know nothing of your grandson," the other said shortly. "What does that mean anyway? I asked you where my grandson is." "I told you I haven't seen your grandson," replied the other angrily. "How can I tell you when I haven't seen him." "Where is my grandson, I said. Of course you know where he is," Blackgod added testily. "I do not know where your grandson is, I said. Clear our of here. You stink!" said the old man. "Hoho! Did I speak of going? Where is my grandson, I said!" Blackgod replied. "I didn't tell you he is here, did I?" said the other. "Get out, I told you."

Now this Thunder Man had a house of dark water, of blue water, of yellow water, and of white water. And the two fussed in this manner. But Blackgod now drew his knees towards himself and put his feet in position for the firedrill. And placing the stone flint (or lower board) between the palms of his feet, and the *dilyízí* (punk or whirling stick) in one of the holes, he whirled it quickly between his two hands and smoke soon arose. Whirling it again, a cloud of smoke filled the room. At the third whirl fire arose, and at the fourth turn the crackling *dlad dlad dlad* of a bristling fire filled the room, which soon ignited the house. The fire spread with a great roar as if blown by a strong wind. This frightened the old man and he begged Blackgod to extinguish it. He, however, paid no attention to his pleading.

"I'll give you your grandson," the old man pleaded again. "Let me return him to you and I'll give you four songs in addition." Blackgod, however, gathered the stick and drill and put them aside. Now, the dark, the blue, the yellow, and white water chambers were all ablaze. And the old man pleaded with Blackgod saying: "I'll return your grandson and give you four songs in addition." "Alright," said Blackgod, "that is just what I expected you to say."

He then took a small white shell dish and a dark water pot, and a blue, a yellow, and a white water pot from his garment, and poured from them four kinds of water into the white shell dish. To this water he added watercress and another kind of watercress called *tółkáábéésh* and two other plants called *ní'dichíl* and *doo dithįį'*. For an aspergil he used a branch of duckweed which was about two spans long—stem, leaves, and all. This he placed first in an upright position into the white shell dish. Then, dipping into the preparation which it contained, he sprinkled this to the east, south, west, north, and four times in a circle. And the fire was extinguished.

Now, the slick Thunder hid the dead one in the northern part of his house. There he removed the wraps of Scum previously mentioned from the man who had had intercourse with a doe, one after the other until out of the fourth one the corpse fell. But Blackgod said to the old man: "Why, he is dead. Fix him up properly!" "No," answered the other, "I will not. Now that I have returned your grandson to you, you may do with him as you please." "Ha!" said Blackgod, "what do you mean? Still, as you like!"

And putting abalone fire[42] into his mouth, he blew his breath to the east, south, west, and north, setting the house on fire again. And gathering the various pots with the extinguishing preparation, he

---

[42]The expression *kǫ' diichíłi* is not clear at this writing. *Diichíł* may have reference to abalone as a magic, or more probably the stem -*chíł* is related to "crackling, flashing"—like lightning.

brought them to his mouth as if to drink. The old crony now agreed, and Blackgod blew to the four cardinal points and extinguished the fire. And when they were both reseated, Thunder Man sang the four songs, calling on the Scum which he had removed and on Lightning. And the corpse began to move a little. And these songs became the property of the Blackgod. And while before, when operating the fire-drill, he had never sung, he ever after sang these four firedrill songs because he had won them from Smooth Thunder. The latter was also forced to give four songs in addition for the second fire which Blackgod had made and extinguished. And these, too, became property of the (Blackgod's) *haneełnéehee* ceremonial.

Blackgod then ordered the patient to rise and asked him how he felt. "I can't complain," he replied as he stretched himself as one just awakening from sleep. He then left the four chambers followed by Blackgod. And when Big Fly, who had watched the proceedings, saw that they were about to start, he hurried home with the report: "They are coming, they are coming!" He had scarcely finished when Blackgod and his patient arrived. Blackgod had placed the patient on Stubby Rainbow and, stepping quickly behind him and blowing upon it, they thus had been rapidly conveyed to the camp (village). *Naayéé' neezghání* now prepared a mixture of "thunderfoot liniment"[43] in water which he gave to the patient to drink. Then he washed the man's body thoroughly. Thus this happened.

And when the light rose in the east and west, Wolf and Mountain Lion, and the other chiefs spoke in the east and south, west and north, of having a sing (ceremonial). And the people spoke to *naayéé' neezghání:* "Sing the *haneełnéehee.*" "All right," he said. "We will do that!"

And it happened that some of the younger men were standing at the shore to observe the doings of the women. And they saw some of them standing along the shore on the other side as if expecting to hear the news. And one of the men proposed to satisfy them and called across: "There will be a *hatáál* (a sing ceremonial) here, come over and see it." "Is that true?" the women asked. "Yes." This was asked four times. "And can we come over to see it?" they again asked. "Surely, come on!" This was also said four times. And turning his head, (the one who spoke) laughed aloud and shook (waved) his hand towards them as if to say, "Come if you can, but help yourselves across." This also showed that the women desired to change matters and to return.

---

[43]The various rites usually require *kétłoh,* "foot liniment," so called from the fact that it is first applied to the feet, then to other prominent parts of the patient's body.

And from the house these twelve started: the Wolf, Mountain Lion, and Wolf and Mountain Lion (the four chiefs), next He-who-moves-with-the-white, -with-the-blue-, -with-the-yellow, -with-the-black, these four, then He-who-walks-upon-the-earth, and He-who-speeds-upon-the-earth, and He-who-travels-by-sunray, and He-who-travels-by-sunlight.[44] These twelve stood in line in front of the village (to the east) counting their order from one to twelve, (that is,) from north to south. And each had a sun plume tied to his head. And they walked abreast along the side of the jewelled chambers mentioned above, then through the pass between the white buttes, and (between) the blue buttes, and spent all of what was like a day in selecting a spot for the sing-ceremonial.

And they designated a place called *ni'naaldóóh* as the place of the ceremony. And they returned to the village in the same manner and slept. On the following day, accompanied by the rest of the people, they went in the same manner to *ni'naaldóóh*. And Dark Mirage took position in the east, Blue Mirage stood in the south, Yellow Mirage in the west, and Sparkling Mirage in the north. From his position Dark Mirage (Man) blew on a small piece of dark mirage which took the shape of a small hogan. The one in the south similarly blew upon blue mirage, which threw a sheet of blue mirage over the dark one. This was repeated in the west and north making, as it were, four sheets of mirage, one above the other.

Then the dark, blue, yellow, and sparkling Mirage People entered the hogan. Here the Dark Mirage Person blew toward the east, the

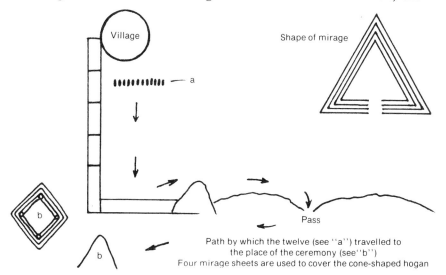

Village

Shape of mirage

a

b

Pass

Path by which the twelve (see "a") travelled to the place of the ceremony (see "b")
Four mirage sheets are used to cover the cone-shaped hogan

b

---

[44]Apparently sacred names of supernaturals are given here.

blue one toward the south, the yellow one toward the west, and sparkling one to the north causing the hogan to spread to enormous dimensions. In this manner the hogan was made and they returned home."In four days we will bring the pouch inside," they said. And four days later many moved towards the hogan with provisions and camped there. A buckskin was now placed on the west floor, inside, with its head facing north. Reflected Sunred, in person, now entered the hogan. He viewed the preparations made and travelled on a trail of reflected sunred to the house of *naayéé' neezghání*. And he carried a white shell in his hand as an offering to the singer.

The *jish* or medicine pouch of *naayéé' neezghání* was made of white shell. The cord with which it was tied (see " b") is of sunray. Braided beads (see"c") were used in sewing it. White shell (see "d"), jet (see "e"), and haliotis rattle (see "f") were inside the pouch, topped with feathers of Black-streaked Rain, feathers of streaks of Big Rain and feathers of streaks of Glistening Rain.

This pouch hung above *naayéé' neezghání* when Reflected Sunred entered. "My Granduncle," he addressed him, "I have come for you." With that he placed the white shell on his left toe, and passing it upward on his left side he brought it around over his forehead, down his right side and rested it on his right toe. And looking at it, *naayéé' neezghání* turned it over. Holding it then close to his mouth, he drew in its breath four times. "There is my *jish*," he said, pointing to it.

Reflected Sunred then carried the *jish* to the hogan, followed by *naayéé' neezghání*. He entered and walking along the north inside the hogan he placed the *jish* on the buckskin. And passing to the south side in the hogan he sat down. *Naayéé' neezghání* also walked along the north side and sat down facing the *jish*. Wolf then addressed him saying: "My Granduncle, we wish you to make put-in-the-mouth medicine, howsoever this may be done." And *naayéé' neezghání* answered: "Yes, (howsoever) it can be done." "Do you need anything?" asked Wolf, "tell us what is needed."

"I need five baskets," he said, "a turquoise, white shell, abalone, jet, and red-white stone basket. The one of turquoise shall hold the *jish*, the one of abalone shall be for the emetics, the one of white shell for washing, but the baskets of jet and red-white stone shall be turned (upside-)down for drums."

His orders were followed and the baskets placed before him. He now took four black arrowpoints out of his *jish*. One of them he placed in the east (crevice of the hogan), one in the south, west, and north, respectively. He then wrapped the patient sunwise into zigzag lightning, that is, from left to right. And taking his knife, he and *tó bá jíshchíní* cut up the lightning in which the patient had been wrapped.

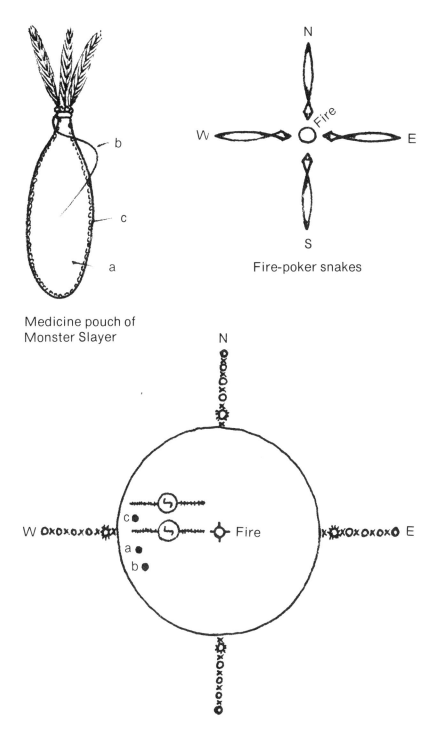

b

c

a

Medicine pouch of
Monster Slayer

Fire-poker snakes

N

S

W

E

N

W

E

c

a

b

Fire

Position of hoops on four consecutive days

He next placed a buckskin on the ground upon which he put one zigzag lightning, and another, and another, and another, and another. All told, five. With the first lightning he made a slipknot, which he held between the soles of the patient's feet and unslipped it. The knot made with the second lightning he unslipped in the palm of his hand, the third on his breast, the fourth between his shoulders, and the fifth on his head. On his head was also tied the white shell which Reflected Sunred had presented to him. Therefore *naayéé' neezgháni* is always represented with white on his head. He then recited the prayer "for protection," after which the ceremony was finished. And they retired.

On the following day various things were brought into the hogan, after which four beautiful young men entered. The first was dark, the next blue, the following yellow, and the last youth was white. "What are you doing, my Grandchildren?" they said. "You have not notified us of this." "No," the others answered, "we haven't said a word to you, still you have come." "Indeed, we have come to assist you." And walking around the fire sunwise, the first lay down in the east with his head to the fire, the next, blue, lay to the south, yellow to the west and white to the north, all with their heads to the fire. And these were the Jet Big Snake youth, the Turquoise Big Snake youth, the Abalone Big Snake youth and the White-Shell Big Snake youth who represented the pokers for the fire. Therefore we speak of the talking poker. Many are not aware of this, and if asked the origin of these pokers they can not tell. Yet this is its origin. These, then, are the Big Snake People. They then made the fire with materials brought into the hogan, and conducted the fire ceremony.

Meanwhile, *naayéé' neezgháni* (see "a") and *tó bá jíshchíní* (see "b") were seated south of the buckskin spread; the patient (see "c") a little to the north of it. The hoops *(tsibąąs)* were now prepared and outside, in front of the hogan, a short run was levelled off. The hoops were five in number, one of sumac, one of oak, one of wild cherry, one of chokecherry, and one of wild rose. (In the drawing, the latter is indicated by its prickly edge.) These were now planted on edge, outside, at the east side of the hogan. Between each of the hoops a zigzag lightning was placed (in the drawing, represented by an "X" between the hoops).

The patient now left his position, followed by *naayéé' neezgháni* and *tó bá jíshchíní*. As soon as the patient had stooped into the first hoop, *naayéé' neezgháni* unslipped the knots at the four corners. He then passed through the second, third, fourth, and fifth hoop; *naayéé' neezgháni* untying them as he (the patient) stood within. And after resuming their places in the hogan, *naayéé' neezgháni* said a prayer to the holy ones in the east, after which the hoop materials were strewn with pollen and carried to a secluded spot which people as a rule do not frequent.

On the following day the same ceremony was repeated in the south with fresh hoops made of the same materials as described above. On the following day the same was done in the west, and on the next day on the north side of the hogan. The spaces between the pokers are filled in with yucca knots which are unravelled. After each fire ceremony the pokers were laid aside for use on the following morning. At present this ceremony is only a five-day sequence. After the ceremony of the hoops had been concluded on the north side, the pokers were carried to the north and placed in the branches of a tree.

On the fifth night the jet and red-white stone baskets (see "d") were turned (upside-)down. In the turquoise basket were two sticks, one of jet, the other of turquoise. Each stick was provided with twelve notches. The red-white stone basket also had two notched sticks with twelve notches, one of white shell, the other of haliotis. These (notched sticks) were held in a slightly slanting position on the baskets and scratched or scraped over their surface with a small stick which produced a rasping noise. (The upside-down baskets function as resonance chambers.) Four men worked then at the baskets which had been placed in front of the buckskin, slightly to the north. These notched sticks also belonged to the medicine pouch. Meanwhile a sandpainting representing *naayéé' neezghání* was made in the hogan. After a short ceremony with drum and song, it was destroyed and the sand carried out. A similar sandpainting was reproduced on the three following days.

On the morning of the sixth day, Wolf and Mountain Lion were sent as messengers to make the invitations for the closing night. Going around the Rockpoint and along the base of the two white ridges, they came to the village and sprinkled meal on the singers there. And they found there a singer of the Hail Chant, and a singer of the Owl Chant,

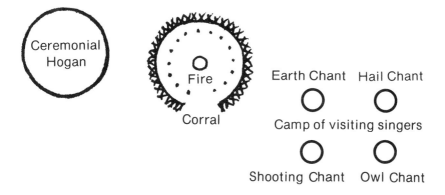

upon whom Wolf sprinkled the meal. A little farther on, Mountain
Lion sprinkled meal on a singer of the Earth Chant and on a singer of
the Male Branch of the Shooting Chant. They then returned to the
hogan. Two days afterward these four singers moved around Rockpoint in the *álíl* (magic paraphernalia) and camped near the ceremonial hogan.

The sandpainting of the fifth night was explained by the informant
as follows: The borders represent the future *sisnajini* Mountain in the
east, in the south the future Mount Taylor, in the west the future San
Francisco Peaks, in the north the future San Juan Mountains or Perrin's
Peak. Each is decorated with four live feathers or sun plumes. The
central figure, with head toward the east, is *naayéé' neezghání* or, as
his sacred name reads, *béésh díłhił bee hooghan, béésh díłhił bił
hadook'éhíí naayéé' neezghání*—In-the-home-of-dark-flint-with-dark-
flint-who-cuts Monster Slayer. He is the founder and first singer
of the *haneełnéehee* ceremonial. Zigzag lightning is shown at the
bottom of his feet, pointed with dark arrowpoints. These arrowpoints
were also attached to his ankles and knee joints, as also to his wrists,
and (they) protrude from his shoulders. Arms and legs are encircled
by lightning. His loincloth is also of dark flint, and three tassels of
rainray are attached at its lower extremities. He is also girthed with
four lightnings shown at the bottom of his trunk, this trunk being
covered with a garment of flint. These arrowpoints are indicated by
the diagonal lines in the small rectangles. It will be noticed that the
diagonal lines indicate four points of flint, points upward and downward, respectively.[45] His front and back are also adorned by pointed
dark flints which are indicated by the points on the sides of his frame.
In his left hand he holds five lightnings, topped with dark flint. In his
right (hand) he holds the flint club which is wrapped in and fringed
with zigzag lightning. Three dark flints are seen (protruding from) the
top of this club. On his head, too, three dark flints are fastened from
which lightnings flash, topped with dark flint. On his head he carried
the feather of life at the butt of which the white shell is sewn. The two
cords, just above this, are *atł'óólzół (?)*. Over his heart the black agate
is placed, by which he breathes. Four lightnings, topped with dark
flint, run through his body which indicates his means of travel, by

Editor's Note: While the description mentions "four points of flint," the drawing
features five pointing up and down at each side. Preference should perhaps be given
to the primary data in the drawing. On the other hand, the number four usually
signifies completeness. Correcting the story to "five" certainly would not sound right.

[45]The figures on the following three days are those of *tó bá jíshchíní* in red,
of *tsowee nádleehí* in yellow, and *łeeyah neeyání* in white. The text, however, offers no
description of these.

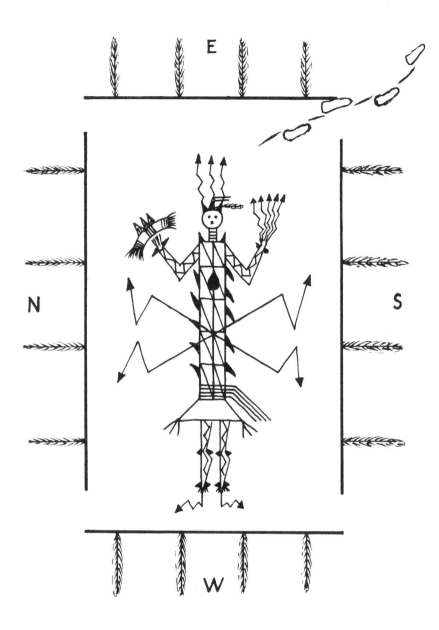

Monster Slayer

zigzag lightning. Arms and legs are decorated with lightning. The lines in the east show the figures of footprints made of cornmeal. The entire figure is in black.

That evening, before the *bijį* or closing night, singing was heard at the camp of the Hail Chanter, and Rain Boy and Rain Girl were seen dancing to the songs. The sound of *zi-zi-zíl* was frequent. At the Owl Chant camp they also practiced, and here Wolf and Mountain Lion were the dancers. At the Earth Chant camp, Sunray Boy and Sunlight Girl danced while Holy Boy and Holy Girl danced at the Shooting Chant camp. In the Hail Chant they used a white shell whistle, at Owl Chant a red-white stone whistle, at Earth Chant a whistle made of a Hummingbird's shin, and the Shooting Chant (used) one of haliotis.

The following (the ninth) night was the closing night. The corral was made, just a little north of the hogan, of spruce, dark spruce, and blue spruce, all branches laid with butts toward the inner side of the circle (see figure p. 77). And they commenced building it just shortly before the yellow in the west had disappeared. In the center of the corral was a large stack of wood. The two drums and the *jish* (medicine pouch) were now taken from the hogan and transferred to the west side in the corral. Fires were built inside the corral and the people filed in to attend the performances. Some remained outside at the camps of the performers, and soon whistles of all kinds were to be heard. The stack (of wood) in the center was set ablaze which illuminated the whole area. And the people gathered in great numbers while the four visiting singers made their camps to the northeast of the corral.

Two first dancers left the hogan. Passing along the north side of it, they entered the corral, encircled the fire four times, and paused in front of the baskets. Each held an arrow in his hand and, facing east, they swung these in front of themselves crying *úhu, úhu*. And facing west they shoved the arrows down their throats as far as the tips of the feathers. And extracting them again, they held them in back of their heads. And passing in this manner along the north side of the fire, they left the corral and returned to the hogan where they removed their trimmings.

Then four other *atsálee* entered, each with an arrow in his hand, and, after repeating the same performance, they retired in the same manner as the others. Then eight entered the corral, each with an arrow in his hand. These also encircled the fire four times, pausing at the baskets and pushing the arrows down their throats in the manner previously described. They left the corral on a short trot and extracted the arrows outside, returning to the lodge to undress.

Meanwhile, many people stood near the Hail, Owl, Earth, and Shooting Chant camps looking on in curiosity. Those of the Hail Chant now entered the corral, encircled the fire four times, then paused before the baskets. Here the performers, namely, Rain Boy and Rain Girl danced. They then returned to their camp. This they repeated eight times.

The Owl Chant now (was next in line) and these performers also danced, namely, Wolf and Mountain Lion, and they also entered the corral eight times. After these followed Sunray Boy and Sunlight Girl of the Earth Chant, and they also danced eight times. After these, Holy Boy and Holy Girl performed eight times for the Shooting Chant.

By this time the white appeared in the east. Now four *atsálee* entered, each carrying a branch of spruce in his hand. They encircled the fire four times and paused at the baskets (drummers) where they drove these spruce branches down their throats, leaving only the tips extending. And holding them in this position they left the corral on a short skip and hop, dragging their feet as they went, then (they) extracted the branches as they were outside the corral. This closed the nine-day ceremony. The brushwork was now opened in the south, west, and north, and through these openings the people left for home. *Naayéé' neezgháni* announced: "The ceremony is finished," and taking his *jish* he left for home, followed by all the people.

Now when the women had heard the singing and dancing on the evening preceding the closing night, and on the last night, they knew scarcely what to do. Twelve women even attempted to cross but were carried downstream by the waves and drowned. And this was the beginning of the drowning over there. And the Blue Fox, the Yellow Coyote, the Badger, and the Weasel, who beat the drums for the women, became hoarse from frequent adultery and could sing no more.

Four days after the ceremony the men began to till their farms again. They did not increase the size of the farms but devoted all their energies to burning and hoeing the weeds. Then they planted on the Circle Farm, on the Square, Border and Extension farms, while on the side of the women nothing had been done. Indeed, their desire for men grew so strong as to induce some again to venture across the river. But these (also) were drowned in the attempt.

The men, on the other hand, were wont to run on the race track to test their winds. This race track was laid out between the Border and Square farms and extended along the whole west front of the latter. They also raced around the Circle farm and played hoop and pole along the Extension farm, while seven-dice and basket dice were played against the house. The favorite game of the *nádleeh* was bounding-stick. To the beat of turquoise and white shell drums (up-side-down baskets), the men also danced in the enclosed chambers with the *doo bideedláadii* (the Non-sunlight-struck-ones). Thus they enjoyed themselves after they had planted and harvested.

In the spring the chiefs urged them to hunt again. And it happened that one of the hunters became separated from the others and slew an antelope. And being late he made a fire and placed the liver of the antelope near the fire. And brooding, his passions were aroused and fixed on the liver of the antelope as a means of gratifying his passions. But looking up he saw two persons sitting just above him, and these were the Holyway Owls. "Why are you contemplating that liver so seriously," said one of them to him. "Do you wish to cohabit with it?" the other said. "Yes, he did wish to do so."

The party consisted of something like thirty-two hunters. Their camp was close to an open space at Dark Mountain, where they gathered for the evening. And when they assembled they found that all were present. But a stranger, too, happened to be in camp one night. This fellow was well-dressed and fine-featured. His neck was long, his shoulders showed a little gray, and he seemed to take pride in contemplating himself. "There is a stranger, a stranger!" they whispered to themselves in the camp. He also was provided with a small broom which he carried in his garment. He seemed very inquisitive, for he walked about the camp studying everything most carefully. This was the Turkey Youth. He was treated courteously by all. Some opened their lunch bags and offered him food. But he refused and would not speak to them. And when they retired that night, the hunters whispered: "Let us watch him and see what he eats." They also were anxious to know who he was, yet refrained from asking. The stranger, however, did not sleep but wandered about the camp as if in search of something lost. He would sometimes close his eyes a little and open them suddenly to see whether or not he was observed.

When the light rose in the east, he seemed to be more talkative for he was observed to say, as if in soliloquy: "Why bother me, shii' di'nidíín, there is light in me!" And his gait, too, seemed to be loftier. "The-man-with-the-light-in-him" somebody dubbed him, and he, the stranger, seemed to be more at home, for he was continually bowing in all directions to everybody. "I wonder," said the speaker, "why he bows to us." But the stranger merely repeated daa shidoolííł, shii'dinídíín, "why bother me, there is light in me." "Has anybody noticed whence he came?" they asked. But the stranger said nothing more than his daa shidoolííł, shii'di'nídíín, "don't bother me, there is light in me."

And when it had become pretty light, they sat down to eat and also invited the stranger. But he paid no attention to them. Presently, however, he shook himself and made four steps in the direction toward the east. They laughed at him, thinking him very haughty, for he made four large and slow strides. He suddenly, however, dropped four white grains of corn and quickly picked them up with his mouth and returned to the camp. And shaking himself again he approached with four rapid strides to the south where again he dropped four grains of yellow corn, which he ate there and returned to the camp. Everybody now observed his actions. And he again shook himself and going west ate the blue grains which he dropped there, and similarly in the north he ate grayish corn.

In this manner he ate his food for breakfast. Now his body was made of these various corns, therefore he ate them. On his head he wore red mirage stone, his tail was made up of eighteen feathers. His wings were his arms—in distinction from his legs.

On this morning the hunters all returned home and the stranger with them. All were good runners, and the stranger, too, was found to be quick and fleet of foot. And since the Roadrunner was of about the same build and features as the stranger, they made friends quickly. They strode side by side and were equally fleet and active. Yet, when the stranger approached the village, he did not seem disposed to enter until the Roadrunner persuaded him to do so. But when he asked him his name, the stranger spoke rapidly: "Why bother me, there is light in me!" so that he was difficult to understand.

Now the White Big Fly whispered to Roadrunner: "His name is Body of White Corn, Body of Yellow, Blue, and Gray Corn, Body of Vegetation, and he lives at Black-mountain-open-space."

And the Roadrunner addressed him immediately: "White-Corn Body, my Older Brother, and Yellow-Corn Body, my Older Brother (repeating the other names)." After this they were the best of friends and were seen together all the time. And the Roadrunner told the Quail of his discovery and he, too, addressed the Turkey: "White-Corn Body, my Older Brother, etc." And he was taken into their friendship. The Quail then instructed the Magpie, who, in turn, addressed the Turkey: "White-Corn Body, my Older Brother, etc." And thus another friend was added. In this manner these three had learned the Turkey's name. All of these were fleet and had good eyesight and remained friends.

In that world these four were holy ones. Now (in ceremonies) their plumage is only an imitation of the plumage and birds of that world. The eyewater of these birds, therefore, forms part of the present day *jish*. And this is the eyewater for consulting or gazing at the stars. The eyewater and plumage of these birds form part of the *haneełnéehee jish* today.

The four Gila Monsters consulted by feeling when *bił hoogai* was lost. And Dark-gila-monster-rough-man, and Spotted-gila-monster-rough-man, and Dark-gila-monster-rough-man and Spotted-gila-monster-rough-man, these four were the ones that consulted by touch. And the earwax of the Wolf, the Mountain Lion, and Badger were

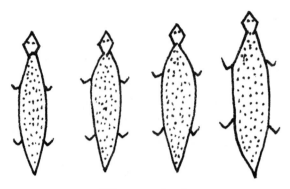

Gila monsters

used by *naayéé' neezghání* in the ceremony for listening. After the close
of the ceremony the *jish* was carried back to the camp again.

It was four days after the ceremony that First Man placed a stick of
white shell in the east, of turquoise in the south, of abalone in the west
and of jet in the north, on the outer side of the mountains and farms.
He then asked for four fine youths who walked out to the white shell
in the east and stood there. Likewise four others stood on the turquoise
in the south, four on the haliotis in the west, and four on the jet in the
north. And blowing toward the east, the four youths turned white,
toward the south they turned blue, in the west yellow, in the north
black. *Sii-ú*, it sounded, and the winds had come into being. In the
east the White Wind, in the south Blue Wind, in the west Yellow
Wind, and in the north Dark Wind.

And folding the four in the east, First Man put them in his garment
and thus they became *diyin* (holy). And he also folded the winds in the
south, west, and north together and put them in his garment. By this
time a slight breeze could be felt. And again he placed four young men
in the east, south, west, and north, and blowing eastward he made the
Striped Winds. Blowing to the south he produced Twisted Wind, to
the west the Striped Wind, to the north Twisted Wind, as in the south.
Therefore these two Winds, as also those in the east and west, are
similar to each other. And they all are things to be feared.

About this time spring again had appeared. The men planted, as
before, without enlarging their farms, while on the opposite shore
nobody could be seen. In fact, the provisions in the four storehouses
were rapidly diminishing. After planting, the men hoed the ground
and, later in the season, harvested their crops, storing them in four
storehouses as they had done at their old homestead. Thus they had
now planted seven times since leaving the women.

And when there was nothing else to be done, the chiefs discussed
the matter of making the *jish* for the Shooting Chant (none had been
provided for this chant). "Wonder how shall it be done?" they discussed for four days. "Boys, let us speak to that quick-tempered fellow

over there," said someone. This fellow came around now and then and always carried a small pouch made of a dirty buckskin which contained a gourd rattle. And this fellow was called Thunder Child, whose sacred name was Coyote-from-the-folded-dawn. "Yes, how will the *jish* be made? We must get it some way, my Grandchildren," he said. "I think we can."

And turning, the Coyote ran to the east singing a song (and turned white). And while he ran to the south, he sang and turned blue, and returning from the south he turned west, singing as he turned yellow. And returning from there he faced north singing "I am a black one" as he went. Thus he sang four songs and this is the beginning of the Male Branch of Shooting Chant (which is not widely known).

He returned also from the north. And when he had finished his songs, a breeze blew from all sides. From the opposite shore it carried the scent of coyote urine so that many became sick in the stomach. And when they looked in the direction from where this smell came, it seemed to them that the women were getting very thin, while the men were looking better every day.

And looking to the east one day they saw an animal, a dog, trotting along, which was of a pretty and white color like snow or white clay. And this was a dog of white shell. Coming into the camp it entered the house of *níłtsą́k'eh hídiłí ashkii* who, picking up an arrow, struck the dog across the back. The dog, however, turned and looked and him four times and in this way bewitched him, then left.

The man presently took sick and fell off to a mere skeleton. And his friends seeing this asked him the cause of his sickness. He, however, did not know. And they desired to have an Earth(way) Chant. (This is said to be a different version from the one previously mentioned.) And they discussed the matter four times without coming to a decision. Finally the Big Fly whispered to them: "First Man and his companions know. Go and get them." "Ah!" they said, "now we know what to do." And they set about to build the hogan at the Sounding Rock. It was made of willows and plastered with dirt and was therefore called the Hogan-walled-up-with-dirt.

Editor's Note: The context in which ceremonial knowledge and paraphernalia are acquired is noteworthy. It, too, reflects conflicts precipitated by a culture change from hunting to planting. As in Hopi society, where the fields are owned by matrilineal clans, and where the men found a significant role in ceremonials mediating the weather and other forces of growth, so also the Navajo hunter ceremonialist buttresses his male ego by developing his ceremonial importance. Ceremonial status must substitute, in part, for the economical status the men are losing with the women's ascendance in agriculture. The men, traditionally hunters, have no claim to planting. This is why they needed that twilight figure of the *nádleeh* to start their planting.

Yoołgai nádleełii (Who-changes-into-white-bead)[46] went after the singer. And approaching First-Made, he placed before him reflected sunred, dark, blue, yellow, and white in color. In size these were as large as the two upper joints of the index finger and four, all told, which he placed before the singer inviting him to conduct the ceremony. He then returned, accompanied by Last-Made (First-Made was the singer) who carried but one basket in his *jish*.

On reaching the hogan, he issued orders to get willows and to lay the twigs with the growing tips toward the hogan. They immediately set to encircling the hogan with four layers of willow twigs, one layer above the other (with butt ends pointing away from the hogan), until the whole was covered in this manner.

·Mud-plastered hogan covered with four layers of willows

He now asked for a basket for the emesis.[47] His pouch was of mirage, his rattle was called *béésh diits'a'*, Flint-sounds, and was small in size. His other *jish* or paraphernalia were round. A cord was attached to the whole *jish* to be carried on the back. Therefore, if dogs cast an evil spell on one, this seems to be something round in one's stomach. Such a round pain, which made him sick, the patient had in his stomach.

He was seated to the left of the singer in the rear (west) part of the hogan. There the singer produced various small paraphernalia from his *jish*, including thirty-two capsules (shells) of acorn which he laid in the southern part of the hogan. Into each of these capsules he poured water to which he added mixed jewels. Then he sang. This is the Earth Chant, also called Dog Chant. The whistle was made of a Humming-

[46]It is possible that by "the one who time and again becomes white bead shell" Coyote is meant again.

[47]My notes read *dilkǫsh* (*dilkos*) *tsah*, coughing (?) basket. I have translated "basket for the emesis." The text in the following does not mention specifically that an emetic was taken at this ceremony, except at the fire ceremony.

bird's shin bone. He sang thirty-two songs in the course of which the patient drank the preparation contained in the thirty-two capsules. He then blew his whistle, encircling the patient as he sang. This finished the ceremony and they went to sleep.

On the following day they held the fire ceremony at which they vomited. The singer then ordered them to remove the uppermost circle of willows covering the hogan and to bring them inside. He then prepared the medicines as on the previous day, and the patient took the thirty-two acorn capsules filled with medicine. After this there was rest. On the following morning the fire ceremony was again held and the second layer of willows was carried inside and the thirty-two medicines were given to the patient. And on the following morning after the fire ceremony, the third layer of willows was carried inside. In the evening the thirty-two capsules of medicine were again prepared and given to the patient. Thus it was given to him four times.

On the following morning there was another fire ceremony and the last layer of willows was carried in. Now these layers of willows were carried to the north every day, with the butt ends facing south, and were left there. And the evening of this day was the closing night which finished the ceremony. And this whole ceremony had been conducted inside the hogan. And the patient became well again, they say.

And when spring came—they had no years, no summer or winter there as such—they planted again, while yonder shore nothing was done, and only now and then some stray person was to be seen. This was the eighth time that they had planted. And again some of the women tried to cross the river, but (they) were carried down by the current. And when the time arrived for hoeing, they (the men) decided that some should stay at home while the others went out to hunt. And counting these in, they counted thirty-two hunters.

They went toward the east to hunt far from their homes, but returning in the evening they found that one of their number was missing. "Where is he? Has anyone seen him?" "Yes," someone answered, "I saw him last at covered water." This was a small lake covered with a thick scum so that the water was not to be seen unless one threw a stone into it. Therefore it was called "the covered water." They had passed this lake and gone east along the base of a mountain called *dził iłt'og (ditł'oii?*—Hairy Mountain, Blanding, Utah), on farther until they reached a spot called *ni' doo ni'óóh,* where they camped.

It was learned, in time, that the straggler had been picked up in some magical way. Therefore he had disappeared so suddenly. In passing *dził iłt'og* he was picked up magically and enveloped in a ball of hail, about the size of a fist, which closed in on him and hid him inside of the mountain *dził iłt'og.* And since he did not appear again,

the hunters retraced their steps walking abreast until they reached
their homes and reported that he was missing. Four times the people
all went out to search for him. And the missing one's name was *halgai
naagháii*, One-who-travels-in-valleys (?).

"What shall we do?" they said after their futile search. And again
they decided to have a ceremony, and moving to the southwest corner
they selected a spot for the hogan. Presently, however, Big Fly called
saying: "I know, I know!" Yet, in spite of their pleading, he would not
give the desired information but ran out. "Make a smoke for him!"
someone whispered. And turning to the Owl, they said: "Can you do
anything for us?" And taking out his pipe, which was half blue and
half white with the lower part a perfect shell, he filled it with mountain tobacco and lit it with a sunray.

When Big Fly entered again he presented it to him, which evidently pleased him very much. "Now, that's the proper way to do," he
said. "I know where he is, but we'll watch this smoke and see where it
goes." And taking two puffs from the pipe he blew them eastward
where the smoke rose and hovered over *dził iłt'og*. "My Grandchildren," they said to the four Winds: "Come assist us to get your
grandchild." At once the Winds started off for that direction. But *dził
iłt'og* was a hard and smooth mountain, and after trying every possible
way to penetrate it, the Winds returned, saying: "It is impossible."
Then the two Striped Winds and Twisted Winds hurried over to the
mountain, but they also returned, saying: "It cannot be cut!" Big Wind
then whirled a powerful wind around the mountain but succeeded
only in stirring the dust at the base of it. "It's useless," he reported.
"Ha!" exclaimed Blackgod, "why can't you do something?" He was
angry and he, too, went to the mountain. Thus, four had been there
before him to try.

He stepped on a rainbow and leaped to the top of the mountain
by seams of it. And taking his firedrill, he whirled it four times, causing
the sound of *dlád, dlád, dlád, dlád*, and the mountaintop was ablaze.
He then lay on his back, facing east, crossed his legs and supported his
head in his hands and waited. Presently a person came out of the
mountain and addressed him in an excited manner: "Extinguish it,
extinguish it, Granduncle! I'll return your grandchild to you." But he
paid no attention to him so that he was forced to plead four times and
offer him four songs in exchange.

Blackgod then sprinkled water from his white water jug four times
on the fire and extinguished it. The person living in this mountain
happened to be the Dark Hail Man. He now produced two dark canes
of rain, and sticking these in the ground in the east, south, west, and
north, he threw them back over the mountain, beginning in the north.

A room or dwelling was thus revealed which had been covered by this blanket-cover. Hail Man and Blackgod now entered the room, in one corner of which lay a ball of hail which the Hail Man moved with his cane toward the center of the room. Blackgod then realized that he had hidden the man in this ball. Hail Man now placed his *jish* on the center of the ball which burst immediately into four quarters. From the interior of this, a tiny ball rolled out which was the person whom Blackgod sought. Hail Man then sang the four songs which he lost to Blackgod who turned them over to the *haneełnéehee*, in (the context of) which they are used (nowadays) as firedrill songs.

The person still lay there without moving. "Bring him to life again," said Blackgod. Hail Man then touched the patient with his cane from the east, south, west, and north and sang twelve songs which became (part of the) property of the *haneełnéehee*. And when these twelve songs were finished, the patient was revived. Therefore, if these twelve songs are sung and medicines (are) administered against witchcraft, the patient becomes well and the witch dies.

"How are you, my Grandchild?" Blackgod greeted him. And after they had left, Hail Man closed the lid of his home and nothing unusual could be seen about the mountain. "There comes the old man with his grandchild," whispered the people when Blackgod arrived. He, however, said nothing but lay down and was angry and tired. "I am tired. You can't do a thing," they heard him say. "Can nobody assist here?" said the others. "What about you, Spider Ant?" At once he called upon the Pot Carrier (Beetle), "Give me one of your pots," he said to him. And pouring water into one of them, Spider Ant mixed this with thunderfoot liniment and five-finger (gamot) which he gave the man to drink, then bathed him with it. Thus this was done.

Again they spoke of having a sing. And taking three with them they went in search of a medicine man. And finding the Rain Boy they offered him collected (rain) waters to conduct the ceremony. And they built the hogan just on the outskirts of the square farm, at the southwest corner. It happened, however, that at the same time, just below Rockpoint, another ceremony, the Bead Chant, was in progress. The Owl Ceremony was performed by Rain Boy over One-who-travels-in-valleys while *doo yínik'įįh* was the singer over *k'íínik'įįh*, the patient.

In front of the two (ceremonial) hogans a fire trench was dug. After heating this the patient was placed with his head towards the hogan and feet to the east. After this they retired. On the following morning another fire trench was dug on the south side of the hogan, on the next day on the west side, and on the fourth morning on the north side. Thus far there was no difference in the ceremonies at the two places. That same night the basket was turned (upside-)down (for drumming) at both places.

The women on the other shore presented a most pitiful sight to behold. Seeing them, one of the men called to them: "Five more nights there are until the corral is built. Today the meal sprinklers[48] are leaving. Better come over!" With this he turned and walked away. They (the women) said nothing.

For the Bead Chant, the Wolf and Mountain Lion were chosen as meal sprinklers. For the Owl Chant, too, the Wolf and Mountain Lion had been chosen. In dress they showed no difference. Their bows only differed, those of the Bead Chant messengers were dark bows while the bows of Owl Chant were bows of mahogany. At the Bead Chant they knew nothing of the Owl Ceremony, and at the latter place they were just as ignorant of the Bead Chant in progress.

For the Bead Chant the Wolf travelled along the base of the mountains to the south side of the Circle Farm, then upwards (west) along the north side of the western extension of the Circle Farm where he met the other messenger who, coming along the border of the Extension Farm to the Square Farm, had intended to take the same route over which the first messenger had just passed. The distance would be about seventy-five miles. But travelling was done supernaturally, on sunrays.

Therefore, both met at "the white shelf of rock" and sat down. "Where do you come from?" the Bead courier asked. "We are having Owlway up above. But where are you from?" "We are having the Bead Chant just below Rockpoint," he replied. "Well, I was just about to go there to invite the people to the Owl Chant." "And I am on my way to invite them to the Bead Chant. Let me see! How can this be arranged? Put your sing off for a few days and come over to our sing. After that, you can take it up again and we'll come." "Oh no," said the other, "we have the fifth day now and can not interrupt. Put yours off!" "We also have the fifth day," said the Beadway (courier). "How is this?"

In this manner they argued. "Well," said the Beadway (courier), "you were coming my way at any rate, and I was going to your place. We need go no farther. I'll sprinkle meal on your head, and you on mine, and we will return." This they did. "But how will they know that we have met and delivered our messages being dressed alike?" asked he of the Owlway. "We can exchange bows," said the other, which they did. "They will now believe us when we tell them that we have met. Some of your dancers should come to ours, however, and

---

[48]The corral is the well-known bough circle which is built for performances on the last night of the ceremonial. On the morning after the fifth night of the ceremonial, meal sprinklers are sent out to invite prominent singers to attend the closing night with their special performances. This implies that the chants mentioned here were nine-night ceremonials.

1. *Daitsoi* eagles at both sides. 2. Lightning attached to his and eagles' feet. 3. Black eagles. 4. String of light. 5. Black hawk. 6. Lightning. 7. Redtail hawk. 8. String of light. 9. White eagle. 10. Lightning. 11. *Atsa dagitgai*. 12. String of light. 13. Four strands of beads. 14. Earrings. 15. Beads. 16. The earring *jish*. 17. Headfeathers. 18. Black arrowsnake. 19. Blue arrowsnake. 20. Wing feathers. 21. Provisions carried by eagles. 22. His neck.

Sandpainting connected with Beadway and Blessingway The figure represents the originator of Beadway, *Do yinik'iih* you will attend to that." "But what about your dancers, will they visit with us?" "Leave that to me," said he of Beadway, "I'll see that they come." And they parted.

Upon their return each told what they had learned, that there is a dance at Rockpoint and that the Owlway will be performed. "See the bows which we have exchanged. He gave me his dark one while I gave him mine of mahogany." And the other courier spoke the same and the people at both places understood. "We agreed," said he of the Owlway, after they had asked him, "that we should each send some of our singers and specialties to the other place. He asked me to postpone our dance, to which I would not agree; neither would he agree to postpone theirs. Finally we compromised by an exchange of the singers (that is, some dancers) on the same night. Therefore, both will take place in the same night."

This happened on the fourth last day of the dance. And the Mountain Lion announced this to the people of the village. And on this and the three following days they made sandpaintings. And they made the Wildcat sandpainting. This consisted of eight figures, two of Wolf, and aside from these two of Mountain Lion, and one of Gray (Wildcat), and one of Spotted (Puma), and two of Badgers. This same painting was made in both hogans.

On the following day, the sandpainting of the eagles was made. This is the same sandpainting as described in the Bead Chant. The same sandpaintings were also made at both places on the two following days.

On the day preceding bidjí, the closing night of the ceremonial, the special álííl and first atsalee dancers arrived from both places. The corrals were made north of the hogans and the same performances as were held on a previous occasion took place here. After the close of the ceremonies, the corrals were opened at all points and the people returned to their homes. And the closing (of the ceremony) was held on the same night at both places.

Twelve days after these events they began to plant again, which is the ninth time. On the other shore, however, all corn and provisions had disappeared, and the women had dwindled down to living skeletons. They proceeded even to search the ash piles for bones in the hope of finding a greasy spot sufficient or meager enough for soup. They were ragged and ghastly. Their adulteries with the four "drummers" were frequent, not to mention their efforts at conception by means of wrapped cactus and other methods already mentioned, in consequence of which many took sick and died.

In the fall the men harvested. There were now very few of the women left and these were continuously appearing at the shore crying for mercy. This gave Wolf occasion to say: "This can not go on much longer. Some change must be made. There is no increase, and for the men to remain much longer alone, I do not consider proper." Meanwhile the cries of the women were most pitiful. "My Granduncle, Brothers, Husbands, take pity on us, we can stand it no longer," they pleaded.

And again Wolf spoke: "Consider, my Grandchildren, what is to be done. We are farming, hunting, and harvesting; we, who are males. Shall this ever continue so? We should consider this well and then decide accordingly." "That's true," added Mountain Lion, "you should sift this matter thoroughly. Your stomachs are filled with such thoughts anyway, and since the question is left to you, you should speak freely." "My mind is made up on this point," said Wolf of the west, "and I think it is high time to become reconciled again. Look to the future and frame your minds accordingly and do not hesitate to state just what you think. The chiefs have spoken, therefore you should decide quickly." "Just so it has appeared to me," added he of the north, Mountain Lion. "The time for reconciliation is at hand. Whatever their failings may have been in the past, we should hold out no longer, my Brethren!"

Wolf now sent for *nádleeh* saying to him: "You will now go to your brother, Mountain Lion, and tell him not to leave tomorrow. Moreover, he will order the people to remain at home and to go nowhere tomorrow. This I tell him." *Nádleeh* then informed Mountain Lion of the chief's wishes. That night Mountain Lion was heard to speak: "All you that are workers will stay at home tomorrow, and none shall leave the village."

And when light rose that following morning, Wolf was heard: "My Children, Friends, my Elders," he said, "you will presently eat and then we shall see what is to be done. After your meal you will gather here and we shall discuss this matter all day, and if need be, all night. But I think we shall have arrived at a decision by that time." And after the meal they gathered in the square of the village. The more prominent people in the center, the others wherever they wished in a circle around them, except *nádleeh* and the cooks. Wolf and Mountain Lion sat in the west (starting from north and in the order named), and the more prominent men occupied four rows each in the east, south, west, and north side of the plaza.

And when they were all seated, Wolf arose to speak. And turning to the other chiefs at his right he addressed the assembly: "What do you think of what I said to you about this matter? Our council concerns that small band across the river. Therefore I have asked you here. My brothers here and I have spoken to you concerning this. Over there they are filthy and unclean, ragged and poor. Some have been drowned, others committed adulteries, still others have abused themselves to such a degree as to injure themselves and die. I am not begging! Yet, I think their punishment has been severe enough. I have even no sympathy for my wife, yet they should not remain over there alone." He then resumed his seat.

Mountain Lion then rose to say: "T'is well as you have said. Your thought and mind has ever been spoken first and never was found wanting. Do as you have spoken." "We shall do as you think, and this, too, is the will of the people," said Wolf. Mountain Lion, the fourth chief, also assented: "I am also of your opinion and think the people will agree."

Now First Man sat on the north side while the Salt Man occupied a seat on the south side. Though it was not permissible to cross diagonally to the other side, owing to ceremonial prescription, First Scolder (Coyote), less respectful than the rest, continually crossed from one side to the other—instead of passing sunwise in the rear as prescribed.

And after the chiefs had spoken, Sphinx Man turned to Wolf saying: "Your idea is very good and should be followed. And being a good idea it is well to say it once, and again, and again, and again (referring to the chiefs), and should not be changed. Therefore we will do as you bid us." And the rest of them chimed in, speaking hurriedly and together as if a lot of frogs had gathered: "What the chiefs say is fine. Let us do that. If we do not make up, there will be no more of us. Come on, let's get them, (and so forth)."

And by this time the white and yellow had met above (it was noon). *Nádleeh* then entered saying: "My Children, Friends and Brethren! Eat now and then you can talk again." "Ah, but we must have a ceremony over them before they can come among us again," some continued. "We can not live with such foul stench." "Yes, that's true. They must be clean, otherwise they may stay where they are." And there was whooping and yelling and confusion among them, just as we see today at councils.

The cooks had set thirty-two dishes in each of four rows on the east, south, west, and north sides and they all sat down to eat. And they partook of bread griddled on stones, of biscuits baked in ashes, of dumplings, of gruel, of griddle cakes and sweet cake, and of roast meats of all kinds. In those days they had no coffee, eggs, sugar, bacon, and so on. On the other shore they went hungry.

And One-who-moves-with-the-sunray spoke saying: "In truth what you have said should be done; we must also look to the future." And One-who-moves-with-rainbow, and Traveller-on-earth, and Traveller-on-mountains[49] joined him in his opinion. This was taken up

---

[49]These are probably sacred names of unidentified supernaturals.

unanimously by the crowd: "What you have said, brothers, must be done. That's the best method. That's right. Bring them over. Yes, but it will not do to bring them among us without doing anything (without performing a ceremony) over them." In this manner the council continued until the yellow in the west and the white in the east were disappearing (it was sunset).

Wolf then rose to speak: "You are agreed then, my Brothers, that this should be done. Your mind is as one. And since it is thus, we must consider ways and means to bring them across. You will therefore remain at home until it is done. It is not necessary for you to work at present. You are well supplied with food and the work to be done is of no hurry. It is your mind which I am following, not my own. I have placed this matter before you and you all have agreed with me. They have been punished sufficiently, some died from their own sins, others from starvation. The fault is not our own. Still we should make every effort to land them across."

Nádleeh, however, approached the chiefs saying: "My Brothers, there remains yet some work to be done. It does not look proper to allow our crops to go to waste after we have spent so much labor on planting. Do you not think it were better to attend to this first and then look after the other part (the women)?" They decided then to harvest first. After this had been completed, Mountain Lion, the chief of the north, stood at the shore looking across. There he saw some of them walking and crawling along, others seemed to be idle and whiling away their time. "What are you doing over there anyway?" he asked them. "Is there nothing to be done over there? Sometime ago you claimed that you were the whole thing for life, but apparently you stand in need of many things."

"That is true," one of them made answer, "we did think that, but it turned out differently." "But I thought," he continued, "you were dancing and singing and having a merry time. How is it that you are lying about idle?" She answered: "We are starving for a living. We want food, and drink, and clothing. But we leave it to you to have pity on us." "Is the chief's wife still alive?" he asked. "There she is," she answered, pointing to her. "She can just about drag herself along." "And what about the second chief's wife?" "She is in the house just about able to breathe." "And the third?" "Do you see that one over there dropping from weakness? That is her." "And what about my own?" "Here she is. I am holding her to prevent her from plunging into the river. I have refused to let her go."

"And what do you intend to do about yourselves?" he continued. "That lies with you. My Granduncles, my Chiefs, my Fathers-in-law, my Uncles and Brothers, see, we beg you, come and bring us where you are." "And is this your will?" "Yes." "Sure?" "Yes." "Really?"

"Yes." "Really?" "Yes." "Well and good," he said. "Gather all your foods, your wares, your clothes and jewels. In the meantime, I'll see what the others say." Then he turned. He was well aware that they had nothing whatever.

THE REUNION

And when the light rose they went to the boats, and the same chief asked again: "Are you ready?" "Yes," they answered. "Then come on!" And when they appeared some were supporting others, while the weak ones were being carried by the few that were still left. They had no provisions, (and neither) clothes nor wealth. They were filthy, ragged and haggard sights, and the smell coming from them reminded strongly of coyote urine and other disagreeable odors. "Where are the boatmen? Go over and bring them," the chief ordered.

And the Beaver, the Otter, the Toad, the Green Frog, the Tadpole—the boatmen—rowed over as usual. The scent was becoming so strong, however, that the men moved to the rear of a ridge to avoid it, while the boatmen were so sickened by the smell that to avoid it they stuffed their nostrils. The women were scarcely clad and more like walking skeletons than humans. Some were too weak to walk or support others. Owing to the smell, however, the oarsmen insisted that they help each other into the boats, which they did.

And when they arrived at the shore, the men sought the opposite direction of the wind in order to avoid the odor. And when some of the women, recognizing their husbands, extended a greeting hand, they refused to accept saying: "No, you'll stay there until you look better. We can not shake hands with such things." Mountain Lion of the north, however, ordered: "Do not let them into the village until they are purified. Make a corral for them on the north side where they can remain. They shall not touch your dishes and wares in their present condition."

And they ordered the women to enter the corral. "But what will we do for a covering for them?" they said when it was about sunset. "What about it, Owl?" "Well," he answered, "I think I can do it." And going to the corral he made a fire there called dinásikį' (?). He also had four covers in his possesion—one of dawn, one of sky blue, one of evening twilight, and one of darkness. "I'll not give them dawn; sky-blue is too good for them; evening twilight we shall also reserve for some other time. But, darkness ought to be good enough for them." So this he threw over them and left. The men also sent food to the women. And since they were very hungry, many of them ate too much. The remnants of the meal were thrown away.

That night few of the women slept, since such as had eaten too much groaned for pain and kept the others awake. And when the light appeared, orders were given to make a sweathouse for the women and to heat the stones "so that they might sweat it out." Four large sweathouses were built for the women. The stones were heated and then placed inside. And for a curtain they used "grass woven fore and aft," and also "grass simply tied together." These they left at the sweathouse.

For a floor mat the Squirrel put down bark. The Big Squirrel with the red back placed spruce, the Toad placed sage, and Ground Squirrel placed yarrow. Taking some of the two latter plants and two kinds of watercress, they crushed these four plants and put them into four pots near the sweathouse, instructing the women to bathe themselves with this. There was also a hot spring near the sweathouses in which they told the women to bathe after the sweating. Then the men returned to the village.

The sweathouses had been built at the base of a yellow adobe bank, from the rear of which this hot spring flowed and emptied into a small pool to which tracks led. It was therefore called Figures-at-the water-place. Their food was carried to the sweathouse by the men, who left it at the pool telling the women not to eat very much; they might eat a little and then re-enter the sweathouses.

And when the white and yellow had disappeared, giving way to the blue and dark in the south and north, they ordered the women back to the corral again after they had bathed themselves. In the meantime they had picked up the old clothes of the women with long sticks and carried them far from the camp. And lighting them with the tsénáásíkǫ' (fire), they turned their faces to avoid the scent. In lieu of the old clothes they brought what was called "rough garments" which they placed near the camp of the women. These garments, then, the women donned after their sweating, and (they) entered the corral in this dress. "They do not smell as strongly as yesterday," the waiters reported after their return.

On the following day the Squirrel and his group left the material for the floor spreads and the four pots with medicine near the sweathouse as on the previous day. Again the women sweated all day. The "rough clothes" were burnt as before and (melted?) garments (were) substituted. "They do not smell very much now," said the waiters who brought the food to the women. After each sweating the floor mats were carried out. "What do you think, Old Man?" they said to Watersnake. At once he brought branches of willow which he put into the sweathouse for matting.

And again the women sweated all day and bathed themselves in the hot spring. And the men burnt the (melted) garments and substituted dark garments for them. "They look a great deal better now and begin to laugh," reported the waiters that night. "And what do you think?" they asked of the Kangaroo Mouse. He used white earth (?) for matting in the sweathouse. And again they burned the dark garments.

Meanwhile the Toad and Green Frog had been in the hills, gathering sweet-smelling herbs which they crushed and placed at the sweathouse. Buckskin clothes were now placed there. And that night the waiters reported that there was little, if any smell and, though peculiar, "it is not harmful."

That day two old women visited the camp. The color of the one was grayish, that of the other gray with a yellow breast. They were a peculiarly looking couple with very wide mouths. "Whence do you come, my Grandmother," the men asked them. "Oh, from somewhere," they said. "And where are you going?" "Over there (to the women). We shall do our part now. Tell Pot Carrier (Beetle) and *nádleeh* to come."

And when these appeared, the two women greeted them: "How are you, my Granduncle? (speaking to Pot Carrier) Have you any dishes?" "Yes," he answered and placed a dark and blue dish before them. "Have you any?" they asked *nádleeh*. "Yes, here they are," placing a white and yellow dish next to the other two. And it was found that they were alike in shape. "Do your part now, my Grandmother," the people said to the old women. "That we will. Yet, we are not very strong. Will somebody carry these dishes for us?" And the Pot Carrier made a bundle of the dishes and carried them to the women's camp. "Tis well," said the old women who were none other than the Marsh-Wren Woman and Snowbird Woman.

Wolf now spoke: "There are two persons over there; tell them to come to me." Not seeing anyone, the people wondered to whom he was sending them. But Big Fly came to the rescue, saying: "I know who he means," and brought The-boy-with-the-scent-of-wares and The-boy-with-smell-of-jewels. "I wish you to assist us a little," said Wolf, "therefor I sent for you." And the first carried a small bundle of *ajáájí halchin* (?), the other of *alá be'él'į* (?).

Meanwhile Pot Carrier had filled the dishes with water. The Marsh Wren Woman now placed collected dews into each—(into) the black, blue, white, and yellow dishes—while the other old woman sat (to the) side of the women near the corral. And the small bundles of the two boys were also given to the women who added *ajáájí* and *alá be'él'į* to each dish and then kneaded the whole with their hands. "Now get in," they said to the women, "and get washed, my Grandchildren." And they first bathed their heads and then the entire bodies of the women. And in this manner that happened.

The inspector, Turkey, also came around to see what was going on. He had nothing more to say than *shíídidíín*, "light is in me." But, running to the east he shook himself and dropped four white grains of corn and repeated this in the south, west, and north—dropping four yellow kernels in the south, four blue ones in the west, and four gray kernels in the north. "Get those four grains from all the points," the Snowbird Woman told the women, who did so. "Now grind them to meal and sprinkle it over you." They did this and therefore some women are white, others black, and yellow, and of all colors. "Now let them go around in the village," the old women said. But the men objected, saying: "No, let them occupy the houses on the north side of the village, but they shall go no farther." Again they decided to go on the chase. Large and small of every age left for a general roundup. Some hunted by corralling, others by crawling up to the game, others by burning, and so forth—some according to 'the rites of the Wolf, others according to that of Mountain Lion, some observed the Big Snake Rite, and so on. And it happened that one night all dreamt of Whirling Winds coming up. Even the Winds dreamt this. And they saw in the east, where the light usually appeared, a streak of sparkling white instead. And in the south a blue streak, in the west a streak of sparkling yellow, and in the north one of sparkling black. This was their dream. And when the light arose they related their dreams, which none understood. And for this reason they were not in good spirits and returned home with what venison they had been able to collect.

Their bundles were immediately taken in charge by the women, who carried them to the homes of their respective husbands. They looked much healthier now and each made herself useful about the home by putting things in order and cleaning up, sorting the meat, and so forth. And when their husbands entered, they extended their hands in welcome: "How are you, my Husband? You were right. We are not in a position to provide for ourselves but must rely on you." And they shook hands and (those who) had mothers and sisters and nieces greeted them heartily. They noticed no foul odor any more. Others, however, accused them of their crimes and breach of faith and would not be reconciled. This explains (how) in our own day some husbands readily forgive while others accuse their wives of their faults and became jealous. That is because it happened (began) happening) there.

And when the white and yellow appeared, Wolf, as usual, arose to speak: "Arise and get your meals, we have something in view." And calling *nádleeh* he said: "Go to the people and tell them that some have had bad dreams, seeing signs in the east, south, west, and north which

must be discussed. Therefor we will meet." *Nádleeh* did as he was told.
And they discussed the matter all day, saying that they would yet learn
what this might forebode.

They planted for the tenth time and were ably assisted by the
women as they are used to do today. Some dropped the kernels into the
holes, others prepared the meals. In those days the planting stick was
of a different shape than that of today. A straight round stick was
hewn down to a convenient thickness. And this was done in a manner
to leave two notches on either side, just above the point. The stick was
placed on the ground and pressed down with the foot, after the manner of using a spade. It was then twisted and extracted after which the
grain was dropped into the hole.

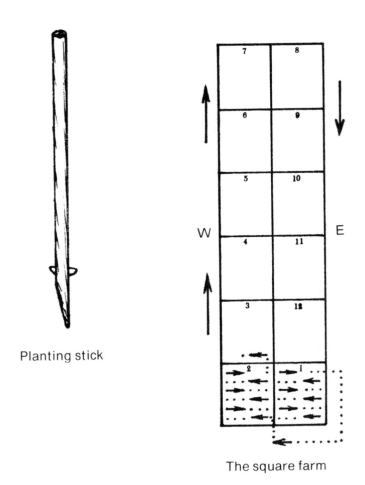

Planting stick

The square farm

Everyone was busy planting. They planted on the Circle, the Square, the Border, and the Extension Farms, and even (included additional) small vacant spots. Therefore, the Navajos plant on a nice little plot of ground wherever they may find it. And when the yellow and white met above (at noon), they returned to the village for their meals. There the dishes had been placed on the west and north sides of the plaza in four rows. These rows ran south and north on the west side, while on the north they ran east and west.

While the people had been at work in the fields, First Man had secretly dropped mixed stings into the food before they had been distributed on the plaza. This he did because some of the people were practicing witchery, bean shooting, adultery, and so forth. "Eat!" they told the people when they arrived. But after they had eaten, all the witches, bean shooters, adulterers, and crooks felt a terrible itch over their whole body. They began to scratch themselves vigorously, while the others did not suffer any pain at all. And when the white and yellow disappeared they still continued to scratch themselves, nor did they find relief that night.

But when the white reappeared they were covered with marks from their fingernails and with blood and swelling. About noon they were so completely bloated and covered with blood that they could move no more but lay down and groaned. Big Snake was one of the latter and he went to *naayéé' neezghání*, offering him twelve songs in return for his cure. He came and made the medicine which he put into a bead basket.

It was gall which he added to the water. *Doo yiniki* had brought the gall, and eyewater of the eagles with him from above. And at the Bead Chant, below Rockpoint, he had given some of it to *naayéé' neezghání*. Therefore he was in possession of it now. This he kept in his club which he closed with the three dark flints. In his right hand *naayéé' neezghání* is pictured carrying the club on which the three flint points are shown.

This medicine was called *anábin*, an antidote, and was the only gall there at the time while today different substances are used. *Naayéé' neezghání* was used to taking this from the club whenever it was to be administered and to carry it over his breast in a small pouch. From this pouch he then dropped some of the medicine into the water while he sang a song. Then, if today one is bewitched and approaching death from it, this mixture is administered.

The Big Snake was ordered to drink some of it and to rub his body with it, after which he recovered and scratched himself no more. The Rattlesnake, too, paid two songs and was cured in the same manner. The Sphinx also was in a sorry plight, itching and swollen. "If you can

cure me," he said to *naayéé' neezghání*, "I'll give you four songs in
return." And after *naayéé' neezghání* had given him to drink of his
medicine and rubbed his body with it, he was well again.

Then there was Spider Ant, with his black breast and red stripes
covering his back, who had little life left in him. And he, too, begged
naayéé' neezghání. "There is little life left in me," he said, "and I have
nothing to offer you, but if I recover I'll return the favor some time or
other." Therefore, singers are at times called upon to perform the rites
without compensation, which is done owing to this occurrence—
because *naayéé' neezghání* gave him (medicine) to drink and (to) apply
and Spider Ant recovered.

He had, therefore, ministered to four patients who, in turn,
mingled with the others. (The sick), by rubbing their bodies against
those (who had been treated), were cured of their pain. In this manner
all were cured. And while witchery, and so-called paleness, had been
practiced publicly, it was from that time on confined to strict secrecy
by those knowing these arts.

It happened, too, that a brother and sister *copulam habaerunt*,
after which they plunged into the fire which consumed them. If,
therefore, close relatives commit incest, they take (they contact) a spell
and plunge into the fire, they say. Others, becoming completely
deranged, approach the fire too closely and burn their clothes. For
there it was the Moth who committed this crime and they always get
too near the fire. Some people became deranged and epileptic. This
Moth, they say, works its way below the skin on the forehead, pricking
so that the person scratches himself and becomes crazy to such an
extent as to froth at the mouth and roll himself on the ground, and
finally to land in the fire. Therefore, there are crazy people among the
Navajos. The moths, therefore, are evil people. *Quosdam quoque
veneficos rem cum matribus suis habuisse dicunt ot quidem impune.*
And this also happened there.

And they were about to plant again. Meanwhile, children were
born to them, boys and girls. The boys were said to be unruly while the
girls were well behaved. And shortly after they had planted (corn)
again, the weeds also appeared and were choking the corn. It was
noticed, too, that four were spitting blood which surprised the people
very much. "How is this?" they asked. "How has this happened?" And
they had discussed this four days when Dark Big Fly, Blue Big Fly,
Yellow and White Big Fly visited them.

"Whence do you come, my Grandchildren?" Wolf asked them.
"We came from close by," they said. "How far from here?" "The place
is quite near and called Meadow-at-the-water," they said. "And what
is your mission?" "We are just calling."

And Wolf placed food before them. But Wind Child (Little Wind) whispered to him: "That is too good for them; rather, make a black, blue, yellow, and white cigarette for them. That should be good enough." And having no tobacco, he sent for the Frog Man, saying: "My Granduncle, I need some of your tobacco for my guests here, I have none." "This is fine," said the Frog, evidently much pleased at being called. "Guests should be treated in this manner. I'll gladly furnish the tobacco." And the guests consented.

Frog Man then filled his jet pipe with dark-flowered tobacco, and his blue pipe he filled with blue-flowered tobacco, and the haliotis pipe with yellow-flowered, and the white shell pipe with white-flowered tobacco. And the pipe stems were of light sunrays. And from here the (Anglo-)Americans must have gotten the idea of pipe stems.

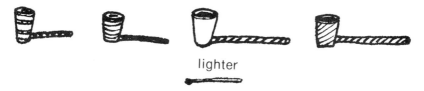

lighter

Pipes—jet, blue, haliotis, white shell

He then lit the pipes with rock crystal, and after he took one or two puffs at them, smoke was seen coming from his mouth, his arms, sides, and legs, enveloping him in smoke. He then handed the jet pipe to Black Big Fly, the turquoise pipe to the Blue Big Fly, the haliotis pipe to the Yellow Big Fly, the white shell pipe to the White Big Fly, each of whom smoked until the pipes were empty.

"We have had our smoke now," they said to Frog Man. "Indeed," he replied, "but you, too, must now tell us something in return." "We can say but little," they remarked, "but those who cause spitting of blood are the young men from Meadow-at-water. More we can not say. Consider ye this again, my Granduncle." And they left them again.

And after consulting, the two, Frog Man and Wolf, selected a piece of jet, (pieces) of turquoise, of abalone, and white shell, none of which were perforated, then sent for White-shell-youth-who-stands-in-sunlight. And placing the precious stones in his hand, they dispatched him to Meadow-at-the-water, whence the four Big Flies had come. He boarded a rainbow and on his ears he had Child-of-wind to guide him. If he went too far to the right the (Little) Winds whispered, "Turn to the left." And again they warned him when he turned too far to the left. In this manner he reached Meadow-at-water.

Here he found a small body of blue water covered with varicolored moss. And going to the east end of the pond, he blew over it four times after which it opened before him, allowing him to enter. He found there a dark place which was a jet house. Over the door in the east he saw a dark object, in the south he noticed a blue one of similar shape, in the west another of yellow color, while that in the north was white. These were the big stars. In the center of this place stood a column of rock crystal which illuminated every corner of the room. He saw four persons, fine looking youths, there. One of these was black, the others blue, yellow, and white.

The black one was seated at the north end, the others next to him along the west part of the room. Each was seated on a small round stool of various colors. The black one occupied a dark stool; the blue, yellow, and white one (all occupied stools) of their respective colors. On his head the black youth was decorated with a blue extension (which featured) a sparkling black tip. The blue youth was decorated with a black extension (which had) a sparkling blue tip. The yellow (one was decorated) with a white extension and a yellow tip, the white (on) with a yellow extension and a white tip. Their names were Loco-weed (?) Youth, Poison-Ivy (?) Youth, Poison Marsh-Plant (?) Youth, and Jimsonweed Youth.

Among themselves they were very friendly and they looked with friendly mien upon the stranger. They were very beautiful and the stranger, too, presented a fine appearance. His body was straight, his limbs well matched. "Where do you come from, my Granduncle?" the youths asked him. "Oh, I come from over there. I heard that you live here, therefore I came, my Grandchildren." "Yes, we live here," they said.

At once the stranger took the jet from his garments, approached the Dark Youth and passed it from the left foot around his mouth and down the right side to the big toe, where he left it. And with turquoise, and abalone, and white shell, he repeated the same ceremony on the Blue, Yellow, and White Youths, respectively. And looking at the jet, the Dark Youth said in a low voice: "T'is you, Dark Big Fly, who is responsible for this. You are the only one who knows of my sacrifice." But the (Big) Fly spoke up saying: "I have been here all along. Don't blame me." Similarly the others, each in turn, blamed their respectively colored Big Fly, but each in turn denied knowledge of anything unusual.

And picking up the offerings, the youths each inhaled his breath. "The people over there are sick, but not fatally. What can happen to

Editor's Note: Each apparently blamed their opposite plant person—i.e., White (east) blamed Yellow (west), and Blue (south) blamed Black (north), and vice versa.

them? We shall come in four days," they said. Therefore singers today give the same reply to messengers. "And we will bring our own medicines with us," they added. Therefore today some singers carry their own *jish* themselves, while others have it done by another.

And the courier returned to the village. But the people soon grew impatient at waiting so long. But when on the fourth day the white and the yellow joined above (at noon) the medicine men arrived as they had promised. And coming from the east they entered the house of Wolf sunwise, the black one in the lead followed by the blue, yellow, and white ones. The patients were named Whose-body-is-dark-medicine, Whose-body-is-blue-medicine, Whose-body-is-yellow-medicine, and Whose-body-is-white-medicine. All four suffered from spitting blood.

And when the youths had been seated, the first (the black one) spoke: "We do not know very much, yet we will try if anything can be done." And the others repeated this. Now they were fine looking young men of splendid physique. They were well proportioned, of well rounded limbs and harmonious outlines. In short, they were pleasant to behold. Everybody admired them. A fine looking person is therefore always admired, and everybody takes interest in him.

And seeing the patients, they asked whether they were conscious. "We do not know, but they seem to be alive yet," the others answered. The Black, Blue, Yellow, and White Youths then produced their pipes, each of his respective color. And the jet pipe (of the dark one) had a turquoise bottom, while the pipe of the Blue Youth had a jet bottom. And the bottom of the haliotis pipe was of white shell, while the white shell pipe was fitted with a bottom of haliotis.

And the tamper of the first youth was of jet, that of the second was of turquoise, that of the third of haliotis, and that of the fourth of white shell. These tampers were used to stuff the pipes. Each lit his pipe with sunlight, the tip of which was fitted with rock crystal.

And the first handed his (black) pipe to the patient called Whose-body-is-black-medicine, and the second to the Blue-medicine-body, and the third to Yellow-medicine-body, the fourth to the White-medicine-body, each urging his patient on to smoke. The pipes were filled with dark-flower tobacco, with blue-, yellow-, and white-flower tobacco. Nowadays a different kind of tobacco is used. Each in turn accompanied the filling of his pipe with a song. But when the patients drew in the smoke, they fell over and were motionless.

The singers, however, produced some ashes—dark, blue, yellow, and white—and breathed over them in their hands. And touching the feet, legs, thighs, breasts, shoulders, backs, and heads of the patients, they revived them. "What is the matter with you?" they asked the patients. "You should smoke. Try it again."

They succeeded in taking one good draw but fell over in attempting another. Again they applied the ashes and pressed them, reviving them as before. "Why do you fall over when you smoke? Get up and try again." And taking the pipes they took three whiffs which made them unconscious again. After they had been revived, they again accepted the pipes but, while holding their own, the pipes trembled visibly in their hands and they clutched the stems in their mouths. Again the ashes were applied and their limbs straightened out.

The pipes were now refilled and the smoke blown on the patients four times, after which they had no difficulty with smoking. And again the pipes were filled and the Black Youth breathed over the people who sat in a circle of four rows. He then handed the pipe to the person sitting at the end of the outer circle who passed it along the line. The blue pipe was handed in the same manner to the person at the end of the second row, who passed it along. The same was done with the other two pipes for the third and fourth rows of people so that everyone smoked.

First Man now removed the white in the east and the yellow in the west so that it became dark before the usual time. "What is up?" said Frog Man. "It is dark, it is evening." "This is too bad," said the medicine men. "Over there the people will do just what we have done now," said the youths. "I'll remember that," Frog Man replied. "I think I shall be living there too."

When darkness set in, the youths refilled their pipes, passing them around as before. The smoke, however, made the people crazy—with the exception of Mountain Sheep, the Elk, and the Skunk. (These) persons did not lose their minds. And the Black, Blue, Yellow, and White Youths breathed ashes on the people and they came to (themselves) again, after which they pressed their limbs. Now, since it did not affect the three persons mentioned, the horn of the Mountain Sheep and of Elk, and the tail of Skunk are now used for a smoke when people become unconscious. Then they retired. The singers, however, placed pokers between themselves and the people and slept apart from them. And they returned with the return of the white and the yellow. The patients were well again and nothing ailed them.

And for the twelfth time the people went out to plant. The children, who had been born in the meantime, were quite large. And while they were at work, a stranger appeared who seemed to be possessed of very little sense, for he ran everywhere, even to places and into directions and in a manner which clearly showed his disregard for everything sacred. This was *chahałheeł ałk'inaadeeł*, another Coyote.

Being a quarrelsome, impudent sort of a chap who disregarded everything (that was) sacred to them, they were much vexed at his temper and hated him. "Let us feather an arrow for use on him," they said. And having selected a place for this ceremony, they crossed two rainbows and stood them upright. And breathing on them (the two rainbows) became a hogan. "Let somebody go to the place Where-dark-rock-was-made and notify the people there," they ordered.

At once the Little Wind left for that place. Kingbird and Chicka-dee lived there. And these two youths soon arrived, for they were fleet of foot and with their large black eyes they quickly took in their immediate vicinity. The Black Squirrel was now sent out to gather the pokers and returned with one of pine and one of spruce, each (being) about the length of an arm. The Coyote paid little attention to what was going on, neither did anyone inform him. Therefore people (such as witches) do not tell others what they intend to do.

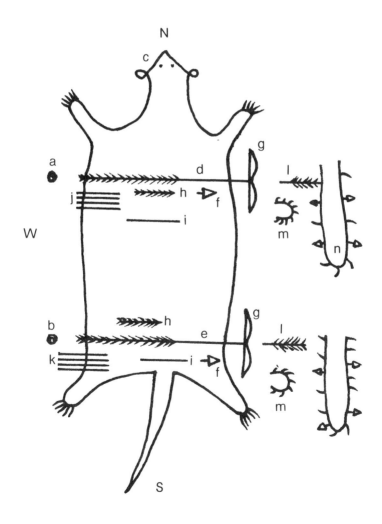

The two sticks, one of pine (see "d"), the other of spruce (see "e"), were then placed, by Kingbird (see "a") and Chickadee (see "b") who were to feather the arrows, on a spread of an otterskin (see "c") with claws and all. Then the arrowpoints (see "f"), and the bows (see "g"), and the living plumes to fasten to the arrow (see "h"), and the unwounded buckskin (see "i"), thongs to fasten the point to the shaft, and the yucca (see "j"), slim yucca (see "k") to wind around the end of the point and shaft, (these) were all placed in the positions indicated. And the feathers (see "l") for tying to the loins, and the fingerclaws (see "m") for the wristlets, and the shoulderbands (see "n") with claws and arrowpoints of the *haneełnéehee* (paraphernalia) completed the requisites.

These had scarcely been placed in order when the Coyote came without an invitation. "What are they doing?" he whispered to The-youth-without-a-mind, who sat next to the door. "I do not know," he answered. And jumping across to the other side he whispered to I-don't-go-up-young-man: "What are those old fellows doing over there, anyway?" "I don't know," he also answered. Now they had told him not to go across the path but around in the usual (sunwise) manner. Yet, he paid no attention to that. In spite of their injunction, he crossed to the other side and, shading his eyes, said: "I wonder what they are doing there. I do not see well." Again he passed to the other side, whispering to his neighbor: "Tell me, what are they doing there anyway?" But the other, getting angry, said to him: "If you wish to know, why not go over and look for yourself. I do not know." And the Coyote indeed leaped over to the place.

Now *naayéé' neezghání* was directing the ceremony and the Coyote impudently asked him: "What are you old fellows trying to make here?" "Oh," said *naayéé' neezghání*, "I don't know, we are just laying these things out." And he repeated the question four times without getting any satisfaction. "Hm!" he said, "that is hardly worthwhile. Why not put your time at something more sensible? Why not make things in the proper way? That otterskin there is about the only thing worth anything at all. What are those sticks for anyway? And those flints, what do they amount to anyway? I see some wristlets and shoulder bands there too. Did you ever see anything as common? I guess you picked them up somewhere. Well, look at those two (birds) over there. What are you doing with those ugly fellows? Puh!" And seeing the black, blue, yellow, and white clays, he said: "Damn that stuff. I ran all over the clay and have yet to see clay that is holy. Is that what you call 'holy clay'? I suppose you are dressing (feathering) that arrow. How will that pierce the flesh? Blast it all, that will do no harm."

And when they made no reply, he continued: "What is the use of idling away your time with such trifles. Better lie down and sleep.

That's too tame to hurt anybody." And turning up his lip, he said:
"Come on, try that on me." And going east he looked back at them
saying, "wá, try that on me, try that on me, wá, wá, try it, try. Death
must be pretty near at hand if that thing will injure anybody."
    "We'll see," they said. "You had better not talk that way." But he
mocked at them still more. "That struck my leg," he whined. "I am
struck in the side. Oh, my heart! That arrow pierced it," he said to
naayéé' neezghání. "Did you ever hear it said that a piece of pine
should injure anybody? Pshaw!" He was about to leave when they
warned him, saying: "Nobody is allowed to leave." And after he had
held his peace he started suddenly, saying: "I must urinate," and
walked out. And when he returned, he resumed his place, saying:
"Don't see why I should not go out. Am I sick? And why should I wait
just because of that nonsense."
    They now dressed the arrows accompanying the ceremony with
a song. The Coyote, however, was ever impudent and jeeringly said,
"I wish you would finish soon." And extending his feet, he said to
them: "These (my feet) they (these arrows) can not overtake." Kingbird and Chickadee attended to the feathering of the arrows. The first
(attended) to that of the pine (arrow), the other to the spruce arrow.
The flint points were wrapped with yucca thongs, together with live
feathers around the arrowshaft. The tips of the points were then
dipped into rock slide[50] and lightning rock (sacred soils).
    Meanwhile, the Coyote was restless, moving from one side to the
other. The Kingbird and Chickadee then touched the palms of their
feet with the arrows, right and left, then their shins, the legs, the
breast and back, and the forehead and top of their heads. They then
fastened the shoulderbands and wristlets on their shoulders and wrists,
and the buckskin thongs on their heads. And picking up the arrows
they held them in their right hands, the bows in their left, and attached groove to string. The Coyote, however, was unmoved and
faced the north. He said incredulously: "Wááh, that must be very
holy!"
    Naayéé' neezghání now sang and the arrows began to move in
their hands. After finishing the song, the archers blew over the arrows
four times when they left the strings, the pine followed closely by the
spruce arrow in the direction of the Coyote. When he saw them come
he made his escape through the door. But the sound tsii'í of the arrows
was heard close on his heels. He ran to Bluewater Pool into which he
plunged; still, the arrows followed him. He circled at the bottom of the
water; yet, the arrows were ever at his rear. And leaving the water, he
ran to Red-flag-patch (?), the pine and spruce arrows a close second.

[50]I am only suggesting a translation for these two stones.

He ran to Blue-water and to Water-sprout (?), and to Striped-rock-ledge (?), and (to) the hogan in the dusk of Black-rock, yet the arrows were after him.

Turning he went to *tsé elyá* (?) in which there were dark, blue, yellow, white, striped, and spotted chambers through which he madly rushed, ever pursued by the arrows. He hid from bush to bush, tried for the moss and other holy places until the flesh was worn from his feet and raw. Still, the arrows urged him on and on, though he was panting and tired and thin. In the north there was a place called Hole-in-the-rock, so called from a diamond-shaped small aperture in the rock. Into this he finally thought to escape. But the hole being small, he was not able to squeeze through so that his whole rear half stuck out of it. He tried in vain and screamed pitifully, his scream of *wá, wá* filling the air. But the arrows struck his anus, the spruce arrow piercing just above the pine. Out of this rock a spruce may yet be seen growing, (together) with a pine (branch) as one (tree). Therefore, the *haneełnéehee* uses these arrows to dispel evil, shooting them over the hogan. This is the origin of this practice. And thus this happened.

FLOOD AND ASCENT

And it happened when the blue and dark were rising (in the evening) that the cry of a child was heard. "What can this be?" said they. And hearing it again they located it in the neighborhood of Floating Water. But when they reported what they had heard and where they had heard the cry, the others laughed at them saying: "Go on, that isn't true. How could a child be over there? You must be mistaken." But after they had harvested their corn, again the cry of a child was heard.

The Heron went over to investigate, but when he reported that a child was to be heard crying there, they discredited him. Now Bittern went over and returned with the report that "there is a child." On that evening another stranger, Yellow Coyote from the west, appeared in camp. And when it had become quite dark and the child was heard, Curlew and two others walked over, saw the Floating Water and returned with the report that they had heard the child cry. Now the Coyote had followed them without being observed, and he saw that they were watching the floating pool. On the following evening, after returning from their work, again they heard the crying and sent the Snipe with three others to look. Again they were followed by the Yellow Coyote. They reported that there could be no doubt but that a child was crying over there. And they believed it but wondered what it might be. On the following day they tilled their farms. Then Wolf, the chief, spoke: "My Elders, what does this mean that a child is crying over there? What do you think of it? An occurrence as strange as this should be discussed." And they held council.

To reassure themselves, some walked over to the Floating Water but returned to the chief's house with the old report. "Well, what do you make of it? Whose child can it be? How can we learn?" they said. And they held council all night while the Yellow Coyote sat among among them listening.

On the next day they went out to work again, but in the evening the child was heard again. And after discussing the matter in vain for some time, they retired. They attended to their work the following day. And when they again heard the cry of the child, they did not retire but held council. After finishing their work on the following day, they were very tired and desired sleep. They therefore retired early.

But on the following morning, one called *náhoogaik'eełáałi*, announced: "I had a dream, and I dreamt that somebody was born; yet, who or what it was that she gave birth to I can not remember." "Can't you really remember? Try! Tell us your dream," said everybody, much interested. "Well," he said, "it was the Holy Girl that gave birth. This I dreamt." Now this virgin was wont to go to the shores and the people had noticed she was approaching delivery, though it was known that she had no husband. And indeed she had given birth at the shore to something in the shape of a ball, of black color, but without legs or arms. "But what it is, we do not know," said they who had seen it. And in the meantime the child on the Floating Water did not cease to cry.

Finally, Wolf again spoke saying: "This is bad. At first we hear the bark of a dog, then this continuous crying of a child, and this mysterious birth, and finally this dream. And worst of all is this virgin giving birth without a husband, and to what? A ball, a shapeless black mass, without legs or arms. What is it? This is a bad omen. Let us discuss it, my Elders, all of you," said Wolf. Despite all discussion, however, they were not able to solve the mystery.

On the following morning the ball had increased in size and taken a glossy color. The girl who here gave birth later on became the Bear Maiden. For four days they discussed the matter, recalling to mind what had happened below and what they had been doing, but found no solution. After the third night the ball had again increased, and on the fourth morning it was still greater in size.

Now the girl herself dreamt one night. "'You only imagine that you have given birth to that thing; in reality you did not,' somebody said to me," she related. "Who the speaker was, I do not know, but he told me to think the matter (to be) over. And he continued: 'It is the child of

Folded Dawn (?). It's the child of Folded Evening Twilight,' he said. 'It is a gourd,' he told me," she said she dreamt. And thus that happened.

Meanwhile, the ball had grown in size and began to move. They conversed of nothing else but the ball, even taking turns in watching its progress at night and day for twelve days. The ball then burst open of its own accord and two humans were there. Eagles and bird, thus, have eggs to bring forth their young. The gourd, thus, is also used for sacrificial purposes.

All the while the cry of the mysterious child was heard. After four days the gourd children were quite large (rough-surfaced). Both were males. In discussing the matter Wolf remarked: "Such as this, that people should see and dream of things in this manner, has not happened before. It does not look well. It must be evil." And when he slept, he too dreamt; and being frightened he awoke. "I dreamt," he said the next morning. "I was told to think over the matter which now does not appear as bad as it first did. I am relieved ever after this dream and am not worried over late occurrences, and I think you, too, will take my view; therefore I have mentioned that I am not ill at ease anymore." Thus this happened.

Now the two boys, who in the meantime had grown quite large, seemed to be sulky for they would not answer when addressed. Nobody then paid special attention to them. However they, as a rule, slept at the village. It happened then that some, who had spent a wakeful night, noticed that they left at early dawn for a walk. And when light had fully appeared, it was observed that they were missing. And when inquiry was made, it was learned that nobody knew their whereabouts and they sent out in search for them. And the messengers reported, saying that they had found four footprints in the east and four in the west which had then disappeared and could not be retraced despite all their diligence. They had therefore not found them.

Meanwhile, the (Yellow) Coyote was yet among them. Eight days after the episode with the boys it was observed that the tracks of the Coyote led to and from the shore. And that night they again heard the cry of the baby and knew not what to make of it. Neither could they understand how the boys had disappeared so suddenly. At dawn the Coyote was again seen at the shore. He had learned what was the secret of the Floating Water and had stolen sunlight from the Light People.

With this he enveloped the child, drew it to the shore and hid it in his garment. The child lay in a cradle of rainbow, the footpiece of which was of reflected sunred, the lace strings of zigzag lightning, the hood of stubby rainbow, and the carrying straps of sunrays. After the Coyote had captured the cradle, he replaced the stolen sunlight. When the light then appeared in the east, they all noticed an indistinct glare in the east, and south, west, and north.

And calling couriers, Wolf sent two in each direction to investigate the matter. They returned at noon saying that they had found a rolling water (in each direction). "Are you certain of this?" asked the chief. "Yes," they replied, "we examined it carefully." Meanwhile the Coyote went aside to look at his find and taking it from his garments he noticed that it changed to a black, blue, yellow, white, and pink color which he thought was very pretty. He replaced it in his garments and returned to the village.

Towards evening he again left and taking the child from his garment, he inhaled its breath four times and touched it gently on the mouth four times (so that it should not cry). He then replaced it and returned. And this is the beginning of theft. And when the people slept they heard the cry of the babe no more and they remarked this.

At light (daytime) the streaks at the four points had increased in size and again the couriers were dispatched with instructions to approach them and learn what they were. "What is it?" asked the chief when the couriers returned from the east. "It is water of about this depth (two feet). It does not flow rapidly, nor rush wildly, but barely moves." And the other couriers returned with the same report.

It was about noon when somebody remarked: "What is that?" And they saw the missing boy returning from the east. And turning they noticed the other returning from the west. The boy in the east carried a large reed of twelve joints in his hand. The other in the west carried a similar one. And while the people could distinguish the water that day, they made light of it and were not disturbed in their sleep.

And when at daylight they again saw the streaks much closer, they dispatched the couriers. The Coyote was very unconcerned. "What is it over there?" the chief asked the couriers upon their return. "It is water and about above the knee," they said. We tried to wade in it but immediately it became furious, rising and falling back, so that we quickly receded." And when the others had like reports, they became alarmed. Wolf alone of the chiefs would speak. "What is this?" he said. "Why should these waters rise and come upon us, my Grandchildren? Somebody must have stolen that child, otherwise we should hear its cry. But do we hear it? No. Therefore someone has carried off the child of Water Monster, therefore these waters are upon us. Is this your opinion also?"

Now they had not known fear, but the rising and furious waters really disturbed them. "It is not through any fault of ours that this has happened," said First Man. "I suppose we must face it." "I suppose there is no way out of it," said First Woman. And Salt Man also agreed saying: "It is true, we must face it." Meanwhile the waters continued slowly to move in on them and it was utterly impossible for Wolf to hold council that night, owing to the general confusion. And since First Man had tied down the lights it was completely dark.

And the people turned to First Man and his companions for aid. "I'll try," said First Man, "but I really do not know what can be done." And taking dark, blue, yellow, and white mirage, he made mountains of each and placed them one on top of the other. And presently the light appeared again. But about noon the roar and thunder of the waters were heard and they saw the waves rolling toward them and receding with greater fury than before. And confusion reigned supreme.

"My Grandchildren," said First Man, "It is time to save yourselves. Get on the mountains which I made." They lost no time in climbing them. And looking behind, after they had reached the summit of the Dark Mountain, they remarked: "The water has covered our farms completely." But the rising waters left them no time for respite so that they were forced to ascend the Blue Mountain also. From the summit of this peak they were able to view their old hunting grounds and their entire fields which were completely covered with water.

"This is certainly fierce," they said. And when some were slow in climbing they called on the Turkey: "My Granduncle, can't you help us out?" And putting his tail (which now is white at the tip) into the water, it seemed to retard its progress so that they were able to ascend. Yet, when the Turkey followed them, the waters immediately began to rise again. And when but little was to be seen of the Blue Mountain and they had crowded at the base of the Yellow one, they again called on him to hold the waters until they might ascend. Again by the power of his tail—which became white from the foam of this flood—he checked the rise of the waters, which rose as soon as he followed them upwards. And when the others had begun to climb the White Mountain, and (when) little more was to be seen of the Yellow one, he followed in their track, holding the waters in check until they were all up when he followed. But when only the tip of the White Mountain was to be seen and the Turkey had to check the waters continually by the force of his power, they said in alarm: "What now? The waters are coming upon us." And turning to the Gourd children they asked them: "Do you know of anything?" The youth of the east then produced his reed and, touching the ground in the four directions, he planted it in the ground in the east. He then blew on it four times so that the reed expanded, making a large opening into which they all entered. On the interior of this they stuck rock crystal which diffused sufficient light to guide them. The Turkey entered last, constantly checking the water. And the reeds grew in proportion as the people ascended from joint to joint. And always the Turkey waited until one joint had been climbed before taking his tail out of the water, which continued to rise forth-with.

But when they had entered the last joint, he complained saying: "I am tired. This water is frightening me." And this word was passed upward. But they called back saying: "Coax him to stay there." But Big Fly had better counsel: "Give him a smoke," he said. "That's all he wants." And immediately the Frog Man filled his pipe and gave it to him, saying: "Here, my Granduncle, smoke." "All right," said the Turkey, "I'll smoke. In the meantime you may devise some means of getting out of this." And again he checked the water with his tail, now and then closing his eye a little, completely enjoying his smoke.

The other youth now planted his reed immediately above the other after he had first motioned to the cardinal points. He then blew four times over it as his brother had done previously.

In this manner the smoke became a sacrifice for the Turkey. And since the youth of the west pointed his reed to the cardinal points before he tied it to the other, the singers of today also raise to the cardinal points whatever is to be tied on the head or other parts of the body of a patient. And blowing to the four directions, the joints of the reed were large enough for all to enter. And as soon as the water reached one of the joints, the Turkey would check the water with his tail. And the joints would increase as they proceeded. In this way they had nothing to rely upon but the reed and the Turkey.

They had passed probably four joints when they stopped to hold council. "What can have brought this upon us? Why is this water following us anyway?" And they began to be suspicious of each other, closely observing every move of others. And noticing the indifference of the Yellow Coyote, they pounced on him, saying: "It's very strange that you should appear so very unconcerned about everything. Own up, did you do anything out of the way, perhaps?"

He, however, made no reply. He merely remarked: "I haven't done anything. Had I done anything wrong, you certainly should have taken notice of it, since it is difficult to conceal anything from you. Why should I speak in council? I am not wise as others are. Let the wiser people speak their minds." And they were unable to discover the fraud, since the Coyote played the innocent so well. But when they had made another four joints of the reed, they again stopped to hold council. "It is well known," they remarked to the Coyote, "that your people are always up to some mischief, and we are convinced that you have brought this on us." "Don't speak in this manner of me, my Grandchildren," he said. "You wrong me. Look at me. Haven't I always been among you and followed you all this way? You are mistaken if you lay the blame on me." Here at the eighth joint the reed began to sway to and fro as if blown by a strong wind. The Turkey, too, became stubborn again so that prospects were anything but bright. They soothed the latter, however, by offering him a sacrifice of mirage, red stone, and abalone. In this manner the red-white stone became the heart of the Turkey, the abalone his moving power. Therefore the Turkey has no hair on his legs. He inhaled the breath of them and resumed his place in the water.

And in a favorable moment, when the Coyote was out of listening distance, the others held council to watchfulness. "He says he is innocent," they said, "but he must be up to some trick. This certainly could not have happened by accident. Let us watch him then." They started again and reached the last joint, for they knew of nothing else to be done.

The reed now reached a hard and glossy roof above, at which they stood gazing helplessly for the waters followed them and they knew not what was to be done. "What about this?" they remarked to the Locust, "do you know anything?" "All right," he said, "probably I can do something. But watch that Coyote in the meantime." And they cornered the Coyote saying to him: "Why do you always run among the people? You had better stay here on one spot. We know that you have done this, but just how it happened we will find out." Those of the others, who had canes of jet, turquoise, and so on, poked these against the solid roof but could not make an impression.

They then asked *naayéé' neezgháni* and Horned Toad to try. *Naayéé' neezgháni*, however, cut four zigzag lines with his knife into the roof, which he crossed by four straight ones. Horned Toad then pierced it from the east, south, west, north, and center, and it became soft. *Naayéé' neezgháni* then produced four small bundles, from which he selected a piece of bluish material of the size of a thumbnail, which began to sing. And henceforth people began to have fingernails. And during this song the roof became very soft. Wolf then began to dig but was tired very soon. Mountain Lion continued digging until his claws had almost disappeared. "My," he said when he retired. People therefore now, too, exclaim "Wa, oh my!" when they become tired.

And while Wolf and Mountain Lion and the Bear were taking turns in digging, the Locust was preparing to investigate. In his possession were the small White, Blue, Yellow, and Dark Winds. And in order that the Coyote should not notice what was going on, some kept him busy and held him at bay in one corner saying: "You must not run around now, just stay where you are."

The Locust in the meantime left his shell while his White Wind entered the body of the Coyote, of which the latter was unaware. Indeed, he fancied that the Locust stood in person where he saw his shell. And after surveying the whole body of the Coyote, the Locust returned to his shell. His Yellow Wind now left his body, and the

Locust again searched every joint and muscle of the Coyote but returned the report that he had found nothing. The Blue Wind was then dispatched. But after searching the skin of the coyote he also returned saying there was nothing to be seen. The Coyote now was getting nervous and wished to walk around. They told him, however, to be quiet. "There is nothing there," the Blue Wind reported. "I searched him from toe to head and saw nothing, except under his arm. Here, there is a small ball which he has hidden in his garments. I worked my way around it and saw that it throbs a little."

The little Black Wind was now dispatched from the body (shell) of the Locust and tried to enter the Coyote below the chin. Finding that this was impossible, he passed through his ear and under the skin, working his way to the heart of the Coyote. Near the ribs he found something. He inspected it closely and found that is was about the size of a finger joint—because the Coyote had the power to diminish his find to that size. And after he had satisfied himself that it pulsated, he returned, passing (left to right) under the skin of the Coyote over his eye and made his exit from the corner of the eye, back to where his body was standing. Therefore, you will notice that when you close your mouth and hold your nose and blow, you drive the air (wind) through the corners of your eyes, because the Little Wind passed out there.

The Coyote was now getting so restless that he made use of all kinds of ruses to escape, saying that he was tired from sitting, getting stiff and cramped. A guilty person, therefore, makes use of any pretext to get away as soon as you begin to speak of his crime. With some it is business, or that they don't feel well and they are suddenly very anxious to get away.

And the Dark Wind reported, saying: "From the upper rib, where the third rib is, there is a small ball which moves and breathes." The Coyote and the Turkey were getting more restless every moment, the latter especially, since he was anxious to know what was being done above. He asked then to let him know. The Wolves and the Bear, however, continued digging at the roof. "How are they progressing up there, anyway?" the Turkey asked. "Pretty slowly, and it is very tiresome. But it seems we are striking softer and muddy ground." "Mud, did you say? Well, then there is hope."

The Turkey soon reported that the waters were rushing furiously, and raising his tail out of the water he splashed the foam over his entire body; therefore the Turkey is spotted white. The Locust in the meantime had donned his shell body and addressing the others he said: "My Grandchildren, I know there is some evil in that fellow. You had better search and see what it is." And to the Coyote he said: "It appears, Old Boy, that something is not quite right with you. Moreover, there is a standing rule with us that everybody, young and old, should be searched, which applies to you as well."

"Oh," the Coyote replied, "there is no reason why I should be searched. There is nothing wrong with me. I am not afraid." "Search him then," the Locust ordered: "All right," said the Coyote angrily, "search me. There is nothing wrong to be found on me. Why should you search me?" "Oh," said the others who had grabbed him, "we will search you whether it is you or not. We know well enough that you are dishonest." And they searched near his heart where they knew he had hidden the ball.

They found it (to be) of hard sunlight and palpitating perceptibly. But all the while the Coyote swore that he had nothing. Therefore, thieves today always protest their innocence when they are convicted of theft. "Hello there, Old Man, thought you had not stolen anything. How is this?" they said to the Coyote. He, however, laughed and smiled, thinking he had played a good joke and that they looked upon it as such. "Oh yes," he said with a smile, "I picked that up at the Crossing Streams. Why, that's the child that you heard crying. I guess that is the reason why all this happened," he said laughingly. But they were in no disposition to join his laugh, in fact they were at a loss to call him any vile name. "You double-faced loafer, you," someone exploded. He, however, laughed the more.

First Man now produced a perfect abalone shell and a perfect reddish abalone into each of which he placed five jewels of various colors. The Coyote then blew four times over these and the child fell from the ball. And since he had inhaled the cry of the child, he now breathed four times upon it and again the child was heard to cry. And picking up the first named shell, First Man carried it with the jewels, and First-Made picked up the other shell with the jewels, and both carried them to the water. They then dipped them into the water, held them under the water a moment, and released them. First Man next placed the child upon the waters and immediately these ceased to rise. Therefore, whenever you dig into the ground you will always find water, because they (the waters) remained at that level.

When this happened the people were much relieved. And turning to Badger, they asked him to assist them. At once he dug his way into the mud but soon returned covered with mud of all colors, black, gray, yellow, and blue. He still carries the marks of this adventure. "I can do no more," he announced.

They next approached the White Locust, who answered: "We'll see, my Grandchildren." And boring through the hard ground he made his way up until he had reached the other side, just as he does today. And looking out he saw that the place was covered with water and rolling waves. And in order to get a better view of the country he built a small wall near the opening upon which he crept. Yet he saw nothing but water over the whole face of the country, in the east, south, west, and north.

He then sent his Little Wind back to tell the people that there was much water up there. "We thought so," they said. But while the Locust sat up above viewing the country, an old person, called White Nostrils, approached him. In his hand he held a reversing stone axe[51] which he swung four times at the Locust, who never winced. He now produced two arrows, one tail-feathered, the other yellow-feathered. The one he thrust into his (own) mouth and extracted it at his anus, reversing the motion with the other arrow. And rubbing them across his mouth, first the one then the other, he cast them before the Locust saying: "If you can repeat that, the land is yours."

The Locust, however, thrust one of the arrows through his right side, the other through his left side, and passing them over his mouth as the other had done, he threw them at his feet saying: "It's pretty easy to thrust an arrow through two openings as you have done, but repeat what I have done." "Oh no," said White Nostrils, "you have more power than I, my Elder Brother." And returning to the water in the east, he swam off.

He had scarcely left when from the south another white streak appeared on the water. This White(-Septum)-nosed-one (was) reversing (his) stone axe four times at the Locust. And swinging his axe, he said to him: "What right have you to live here and inhabit this world?" But he did not wince. He, too, repeated the same performance with the arrows while the Locust retaliated with his own feat. "You have the power," he said and returned to the south. Presently another White Nostril appeared from the west making four thrusts at the Locust with his axe without succeeding in making him wince. And he, too, was excelled by the feat of the Locust with the arrows. And he returned to the west saying: "I can not do it, my Older Brother, you are superior to me." And presently another White-nosed-one appeared from the north, swinging his axe most threateningly. And he, too, was put to shame by the feat of the Locust and returned.

In this manner the Locust won the country for the people by excelling these four monsters in power. But the Locust had prepared for this by bringing his vital organs to the tip of his nose. It was easy then to take the thrusts of the arrows. Furthermore, his eyes were covered with mica (stone shale) so that he might see without incurring bodily injury.

At that time there were no ducks, no animals, no creeping nor walking things on the earth, for they were to be brought there from

---

[51]One who wielded this axe and was ignorant of it would receive the blow himself.

below. Neither were there any trees, grasses, nor plants. These, too, were brought up. In fact, there was only water covering the earth.

In this manner then, the Locust could not be hurt. And because he thrust the arrows in his sides, he (now) makes a noise below his wings. And because of the mica which protected his eyes, you never see a locust close his eyes but you always find his shell on the tree. And when the Wind rages he seems to be most happy and at home, and many of them come out of the ground because they had the Winds there. And the Locust comes out of the ground and returns to it on this account.

And after this had happened the Locust left the Black Wind with his (shell) body and returned to his comrades below. His name is Youth-who-turns-about-on-the-earth   and   Youth-to-whom-Black-Wind-reports. "It is an unpleasant place up there and a country covered with water," he reported to them. The other Winds—white, blue, etc.—had always reported to them what had been happening to the Locust. "We have a hard proposition, my Grandchildren," he said, "and I think we had better discuss the matter." Now there was one called *náask'idi* (Hunch-eye) and another, Mountain Sheep, among them. And when the Locust had spoken, they approached these two saying: "What about it? Can you assist us?" "Oh yes," they said, "we can, my Grandchildren."

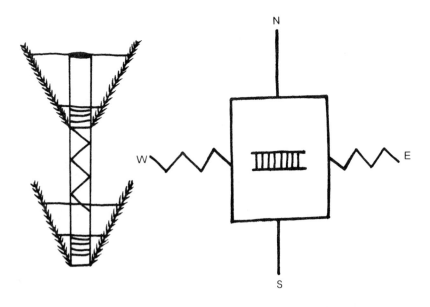

Huncheye's cane   Sandpainting

Hunch-eye was in possession of a cane which was covered with a lightning of four zigzags (see "a"), and its borders or sides were covered with four straight lightnings. These border lightnings represent the flashing lightning of summer nights. The four lower and central rings in the drawing represent lightning with which the cane is wound.

The Mountain Sheep also produced two crooked and two straight lightnings from his horns—represented in the sandpainting as "c" and "d" at four points. Therefore the lightning never injures the horn of a Mountain Sheep. And they both ascended through the hole which the Locust had made. Hunch-eye held the cane in his left hand and rainbow in his right; the Mountain Sheep a feather in his left hand and rainray in his right. And they ascended on ladders (see "e") which the Locust had made on the side of the walls. And coming out in the east, Hunch-eye held his cane slantingly in that direction, and blowing upon it, a streak of lightning shot beyond the waters from it. And the Mountain Sheep repeated this in the south with his rainray, but straight lightnings shot from it. And they again shot their lightnings to the west and north; Hunch-eye (shot) the zigzag lightning toward the west; the Mountain Sheep (shot) the straight one to the north so that the waters might recede.

Presently a great noise was heard on all sides, for the waters separated and rolled to the four directions. And there were seen the Water Monster, the Monster Fishes, Water Horses, the White Nostrils, Children of the Water Monster and White Septums, Children of the Water Horses. These, together with the rushing waters, made such a tremendous noise that the two became frightened and quickly made their escape to their brethren below.

"It's frightful up there," they said, and after they had told what they had done, the people turned to Spider Man and Woman for help. The Spider Man then blew a dark web to the mouth of the opening and followed this with a yellow one, while the Spider Woman furnished a blue and white one so that there were four webs covering the opening. And these hung over it as four curtains, a black, yellow, blue, and white one so that no water might pass through it. And this prevented the water from rushing upon the people below, for even today you do not observe water passing through a spider's web.

The noise and rush of the water above lasted something like four days—after which it ceased. The Spider Man and Spider Woman then inhaled their webs again and the light shone through the opening. And again they sent the Locust up to investigate. "There is quite a change up there, but it is very muddy," he said. "Here and there you can see lakes and pools of water, and in the distance some objects which are the young of the Water Monsters, Water Horses, and Monster Fishes which they left behind on their way to the ocean. Therefore, today these are in the ocean.

After Locust had reported what he had seen, they summoned the Black, the Blue, Yellow, White, and Speckled Big Winds and sent them up. And they ate wind and went up. And they unloosed their winds in all directions for four days and returned. "My, but we are tired," they said, "we have done enough. The surface does not look well yet." And they summoned the Twisted Winds, the Dark, the Blue, the Yellow, the White and Glossy, these five Winds they dispatched to harden the ground sufficiently to support the people. And after they had labored four days, they returned, saying they were tired. "Who will try now?" they asked. And they called on the Striped Winds, the Dark, the Blue, the Yellow, the White and Glossy, and these five now agreed to go up. And after they had labored for four days they returned, saying: "We are tired out. Some places are dry, other boggy, but the whole surface looks better than before." And now five of the Winds which we have here and which at times blow very hard, namely the Dark, Blue, Yellow, White and Glossy Winds went up. And when they returned they reported that it was muddy only in spots, but they were very tired. They had passed over some parts, omitting others. Yet they had seen several lakes which have now disappeared and were once considered holy.

The world was then much smaller than it is now, so that one was able to look over a greater level. It was not very wide. The Badger and Gray Squirrel were then sent up to investigate. There were spots which were hardened enough to support them. There were also stones there over which they walked. And since the stones were quite soft, they left their footprints in them—which can still be seen near Navajo Mountain.

6

The Emergence

First Man now made four ladders, one of jet, the second of turquoise, the third of abalone, the other of white shell. Each consisted of two poles and four rungs. And he placed them in zigzag position with the white shell ladder pointing east.

And they ascended the jet ladder, First Man taking up the rear (guard). And after they were up he drew the ladder up behind him, repeating the same after they had finished the turquoise, abalone, and white shell ladders. "These shall not again be made of these jewels, but when the people ever make them (a painting of them) they shall use cornmeal." Therefore the *haneełnéehee* also includes this painting. And to use the prayer (of the directions?) effectively one must know it, and similarly (how) to make this painting. But when the prayer of *haneełnéehee* has proven ineffective there is another prayer, of the Blessing Rite, which begins here and is used in connection with this prayer. This indicates that the Blessing Rite must be used with every chantway and is therefore superior and essential to them. But in the Blessing Rite these ladders must be made of cornmeal and in accordance with ritual prescription. Moreover, if one word of the prayer of the Blessing Rite is missed,[52] it is worthless and destroys the whole effect.

Now, from the point of their emergence to the east there were two lakes which they called Lakes-spread-out. Between these two lakes there was a bank of earth on which the people camped. Some put up near the edge of the lakes *(tábąąhí)*; others were trying to build houses of mud (the Mud People, *hashtł'ishnii)*; the *ta'neeszahnii* were making houses of wood; others camped below an extending rock *(tsé nahabił-nii)*; others made reddish banks *(deeshchíinii)*. And they gave them these names, though they did not live far distant from one another.

After something like four days they noticed that one of their number was missing, and after inquiring of everyone without result, they decided to search for him. But after four days of search they had not found him and somebody suggested to look into the hole from

---

[52]This, however, is not true of all *hózhǫ́ǫ́jí* prayers. The informant probably explained that the Blessing Rite is essential to every chant or ceremonial known to the Navajo, and must accompany them at one stage or another.

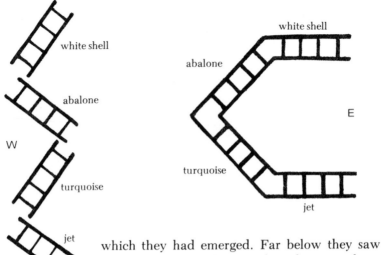

which they had emerged. Far below they saw someone sitting. "Are you he whom we have missed?" they called to him. "I am," he replied. "Up there where you are there will be people inhabiting that world, and when they die they shall come down here." Therefore, when we die we return to this place—(something) which the Americans do not believe.

And the two looking down are also the cause of persons dreaming that they are here in the land of ghosts where these dreams originate. But when they were about to leave, the person below called to them: "From time to time I'll return for dishes, pots and edibles. And if evil spells visit the people, I am the cause of these." It is therefore believed that when pots break, or millstones, ladle, griddlestones, and the like (break), they return to the place where our ghosts move (about) again. And returning, the two related that they had found the missing one and had spoken to him and that they had found him combing his hair. They described his features and told what he had said that "when the people of the earth die they will come there," and "that from time to time he would reappear and come for dishes, and for baking stones, pots, and so forth." Thus this happened.

And the chiefs again spoke: "What shall we do? Shall we live in this manner forever? There is no sun, no moon, nothing to give us light." And the held council for four days about the sun and the moon. "It isn't well that the earth should be so small and that the winds remain here in one place. There should also be a sky." They thus figured ahead for the future how the life of the people on earth might be regulated,

Editor's Note: Traditional Navajos with whom I have conversed about eschatological beliefs do not expect to return to that realm below, either. Instead, they anticipate to travel northward after death, to an afterworld in that direction. The present statement represents a Navajo attempt to adapt to Pueblo anthropogony, eschatology, and cosmology. Navajo eschatology, in general, did not become as Pueblo-ized as their cosmology.

because since he who had disappeared is the beginning (the first) of the dead ones, they realized that it would be so in the future also. And again they held council for four days, making eight in all. And when the chiefs also spoke of the manner in which the earth should be arranged for the people, to cover it with plants, trees, and shrubs, each offered what he had in his possession. "I have seeds of this," said one. "I have that seed; I (have) many of that (kind of) seed," and so on.

Now First Man and First Woman, (the other) First Man and First Woman, and First-Made and Last-Made, and First Boy and First Girl, and First Scolder (Coyote) attended these meetings. They had taken all their evil with them, as also all the things of which we spoke previously (future mountains, sun, moon, etc.) And First Man finally said to them: "Do you really wish for these things of which you speak?" "Indeed," they said, "but we haven't these things with us. We brought nothing with us from below. Could you not make them for us?" "I know, my Grandchildren," said First Man, "yet I think I can make all the things you speak of."

Now he and his companions were witches and ate jet, turquoise, abalone, white shell as food, as we saw before. "I can do many things, my Grandchildren," he said. He was the origin of all evil. "Let us make a hogan," he said. And he produced the five stones which he had, as previously shown, for the making of the hogan. The jet wand he planted south, the abalone north, turquoise west, white shell east, leaving a wand of mixed colors for the additional (doorway) pole.[53] The poles were then raised in the order mentioned—(the) north and south poles first, then west and east, four skeleton poles to support the structure. The additional one he placed to the north of the east pole.

Upon these four poles he blew four times, and the hogan was made. He now sprinkled meal on the four poles and on this occasion also on the fifth, but (he) said that the Earth People of the future should sprinkle only the four. This is done today sunwise, starting at the east, then making the circle to the right. The songs he employed are called *naat'á sin*, chief songs,[54] though some call them *hooghan biyiin*,

[53]The distribution of colors here is so unusual that I am inclined to assume an error in my notes. Ordinarily, we should look for jet in the north, turquoise in the south, abalone in the west, and white shell in the east. This order seems to be followed throughout the whole account. But note the sequel in the colors of the emergence ladder.

[54]The text does not mention songs in connection with the erection of the various hogans thus far built. The chief songs mentioned here are part of the *hózhóójí*, Blessing Rite, which contains quite a number of hogan songs. Meal is sprinkled on the poles at cardinal points usually preceding almost any ceremonial, unaccompanied by song. A new hogan may also be dedicated by devout Navajos in this manner; then later, when any ceremony is held in the new hogan, it is considered dedicatory as well. A special dedication ceremony, therefore, does not seem to be required for the new hogan.

hogan songs, but these originated later with the various chants, all of which take their origin here after the emergence.

The hogan was small, therefore First Man blew toward the west to extend it, then to the east with his back (turned) west. Similarly with his back (turned) south he blew toward the north, then (he) turned to breathe toward the south, thus extending it in every direction. After this the space in the hogan interior was cleaned.

First Man then entered taking his position south of the west pole, First Woman took position north of the west pole. Alternating in this manner their other companions entered, taking position south and north, respectively. First Man, First Woman, First-Made, Last-Made, First Boy, First Girl. First Scolder did not appear. Many other people filed in, filling the south and north sides of the interior to the doorway (which is in the east). Blackgod then took his seat next to First Boy in the back (on the) south (side).

First Man now placed a turquoise in front of him, blew on it and caused it to expand over the floor of the hogan. On this he placed a white shell which, by blowing, he expanded for a second floor. Upon this he placed a small perfect turquoise which was to become the future Sun. To the north of this he placed a similar perfect white shell which was to be the future Moon. Next to the future Sun in the south he placed a perfect jet for the Sky-to-be. Next to the future Moon he set a perfect turquoise for the future Earth.

These he covered with an unwounded buckskin, blew on them so that they increased to the length of a span (the outstretched middle finger to tip of thumb). The future Sun he now covered with a spread of down, the future Moon with a spread of evening twilight, the future Sky with a spread of darkness, the future Earth with a spread of sky-blue. Again he blew on them, increasing them to forearm's length. "This unwounded buckskin (with which he covered them) is to be used for pouches to contain the sacred (mountain) soils," he said. As done at that time, so now the sacred soils are carried in small bags.

Again he raised these covers, breathed four times on them so that they increased in size, measuring from the shoulder socket to the tip of the middle finger. Then he replaced the covers, raised them again and breathed on them four times. Now they had increased in length to measure from his right breast and enable him to put his bent finger around them. The perfect jet (Sky) and perfect turquoise (Earth) were not completely round but eliptical.

He now picked up the first two (turquoise Sun, white shell Moon) and polished them to a smooth and glossy finish. He did the same with the other two jewels (Sky, Earth), although he did not mention their purpose when he polished them. After that was done he sprayed them all with white medicine, with blue and with pink medicines, a mouthful of which he had taken. He next covered up a slender piece of rock crystal, and when he removed its cover it had increased the width of four fingers. This enlarged rock crystal (he) rubbed over the four which made them smooth and glossy like glass.

First Man then rubbed the chin of Sun with a streak of evening twilight (yellow) and his forehead with a streak of dawn. He then rolled a number of small balls of a mixture of turquoise, jet, abalone, white shell, stone mica and *jilgizh*,[55] which eventually became the eyes and mouth of Sun, Moon, Sky and Earth. Next he covered them with dawn, blew four times on it, and this became the time of dawn (awakening) for the eyes. A cover of darkness he treated in the same manner, ordaining this for the time of sleep.

Next he placed dawn white shell on the breast and darkness jet on the back of Sun, Moon, Sky and Earth, holding them in position for some time until they were warmed up in this manner. Therefore, when **dawn appears, we travel; when darkness sets in, we sleep.** Similarly, First Man placed evening twilight abalone on their breasts, and (he placed) skyblue, red-white stone, on their backs warming them up by means of these. The skyblue, red-white stone, indicated winter—when it snows and (when) the cold sets in all around. The evening twilight, abalone, represented summer—when it warms up and (when) plants turn green then yellow (as they) ripen.

As said, the mixture of jewels furnished the eyes. First Man also had winter dew and summer dew in his mouth which he mixed with the eyes. Thus he furnished the eyewater to the Sun and Moon—and our own which oozes from our eyes. The white shell contained in this mixture accounts for *anágai*, the white of the eye. The *jilgizh* which was added to the mixture causes the pupil of the eye with which we see. Next he spread a cover of dawn, evening twilight, skyblue, and darkness over them, breathed on them from east, south, west, north, and from above downward. They had become hardened and glossy.

Jewels used to be their food. Therefore, First Man produced a white shell Wind which was the White Wind, an abalone Wind which was the Yellow Wind, a turquoise Wind which was the Blue Wind, a jet Wind which was the Black Wind, a red-white stone Wind which was the Spotted Wind. These he placed at his right front beyond Sun and Sky.

Ahead of Moon and Earth, at his left front, First Man placed nine winds. (These were) White, Yellow, Blue, Dark, Spotted, and Left-handed Winds, the Wind-that-turns-sunward, the Wind-that-turns-sunwise, and Striped Wind.

[55]*Jilgizh* is the name of Flash Lightning, but here evidently it has another meaning.

With the first five Winds he blew on the Sun from the east, south, west, north, and from above. He repeated this breathing also on the Moon, the Sky, and Earth. By thus breathing into them they received life and bristled, as it were. The other nine Winds mentioned are for us (on Earth). First Man now stood up, blew on the Sky and the Earth which increased their length the width of four fingers. And their heads lay in the same direction, towards the east.

When Blackgod had entered, he carried a sack made of a fawn's hide. At this point other people entered the hogan. The four chiefs, Wolf (and) Mountain Lion, (another) Wolf (and) Mountain Lion, seated themselves next to Blackgod. Of the following, the women were seated on the north, the men on the south side of (the) west pole next to those already seated, namely: Woman Chief, Dawn Man and Dawn Woman, Darkness Man and Darkness Woman, Skyblue Man and Skyblue Woman, Evening Twilight Man and Woman. Others, too numerous to mention, took places along the south and north (of the) interior. Then First Scolder took his place at the doorway.

At his left front (north) First Man placed a prayerstick in the space between the Winds and the Sun, Moon, Sky, and Earth. Another he placed to the right of the first (south). At four points, out along the western half from the center of the hogan, he placed a white shell, a turquoise, an abalone shell, and a jet (for the sacred mountains).

"What now?" they asked Blackgod. "Alright," he replied, then stepped over to where the sky lay. He then placed various stars in position: *hastiin sik'aii*, a large irregular square in Corvus, in the east. Then, coming west in this order: Big Snake and Bear constellations, Thunder and part of (our) Scorpio. Aside of this Ursa Major and Cassiopoea, then Orion, Aldebaran in Taurus, and the cluster under Canis Major, and the igniter stars which are (five) large stars at various points. Parts left over they collected and placed next to the south prayerstick. Blackgod also blew across the Sky and made the Milky Way.

The attending people now placed seeds of trees—of spruce, oak, pinon, and so on—and of various plants near the Earth as well as game (animals) of various description, all of which was to be used in dressing the Earth. The Moon and Sun really belonged to the other (to) the Sky on the south side.

When Blackgod was about to resume his seat, First Scolder stepped over to that side saying: "My Grandchildren, what are you doing? You said nothing to me about this." "Can't you see what we have done?" Blackgod asked him in reply. Now Blackgod was in the habit of placing his starbag below his foot and sitting on this. And before Blackgod was able to arrange himself, Coyote had snatched the starbag and had blown its contents across the Sky, saying: "That looks better!" Therefore, at present there are many stars without names and only those named by Blackgod are known. One star was left in the bag. This (one) Coyote jerked out saying: "This will be my star," and placed it in the southern skies. Therefore it is called "No-month" or "Coyote's star." The mixture left over from Blackgod's distributions, which the people, as said, had placed near the south prayerstick, in time became the genitalia of men. A similar mixture near the opposite prayerstick in time became the genitalia of woman.

First Man also placed twelve wands which were to be winter, and twelve which were to be summer. First Scolder now went on guessing. "The Sky," he said, "looks well, so does the Earth look well, and the Sun and the Moon. And this north prayerstick, well, I know what it is. The lower half is black and represents the Earth, the upper half is blue and represents the Sky. The upper half of this south prayerstick is yellow, the lower white (is) to represent whitening of vegetation and the season when it goes to wood (whitening—that is, ripening in autumn or late summer). It sprouts in the spring, ripens white and yellow in autumn. The black on it represents the return of winter, the blue (represents) the return of summer.[56] The yellow represents the new Moon, the white the (various) months," he said.

"Now you put twelve months on the south and twelve months on the north side. You do not know what you are talking about. The time is too long, twelve here and twelve there, that will never do. I know more about it than you do. Listen to me then! Twelve months for winter is too much, and twelve for summer is equally too much. Instead, put six here and six there," he said.

"Where white and yellow meet, on the south prayerstick," he continued, "we will call ghąąjí'—October.[57] Some will get this right, some wrong in counting," he said. So they put six on the south side and six on the north. "So it should be," he said. "This then will be called October, the next one 'Slim Wind'—November, the next 'Big Wind'— December, then January, then February, then March. These are winter months. Over there, April, May, June, July, August, September are the summer months."

The disagreement in counting the months began with the month of October and continues ever so, because Coyote placed it "where back meets back, or the yellow and white meet." The months on the north

[56]As the notes read, it appears that this prayerstick showed yellow, white, black, and blue for the four seasons of the year. The next sentence seems to imply only two colors.

[57]The meaning of ghąąjí is interpreted by the informant as "backs to(ward)," that is, where yellow and white meet.

side were placed on the Earth and are therefore Earth (summer) months; the others were placed on the Sky and are therefore Sky (winter) months. The one set (of six months) is warm because here (on Earth) it is warm; the others are cold because (they are) placed upwards.

As mentioned before, jewels were placed at four points for the Mountains-to-be. The white shell is *sisnajini*, turquoise (is) Mount Taylor, abalone (is) San Francisco Peaks, jet (is) Perrin's Peak. Between the second and third (mountain) ranges a remnant of white shell was placed for Mountain Woman. Close (to it) Water Woman was placed, represented by a mixture of river clay and hardened water foam (iron ore?). West of these two, four colored flints were placed. Black flint became a sandhill crane which therefore eats flint. Blue flint became brown crane and bittern and curlew. Yellow flint became ducks, dark and blue, and the mudhen. White flint became snowy egret, jacksnipe. And because these were placed on Earth, we see them in summer.

On the opposite, (the sky-)side, birds were placed for the cold. Kingbird, chickadee, snowbird, and *naak'eni* (owl). Their feet are of ice, therefore they were assigned to winter. Kingbird (*chishiisháshii*) has twelve, sometimes six, notches in its tongue. If one loses his way, therefore, he kills this bird and consults (reads) its tongue. On the earth-side, next to the water birds, varicolored flint was placed for the woodpeckers (yellow hammer) whose color is speckled. On the sky-side the woodpecker (sap sucker) was added and he, too, is spotted for winter. The feathers of these are used in the medicine pouch.

The Coyote had little to say but observed everything. First Man and all menfolk sang one hundred and two songs of Sun during this time, alternating with the one hundred and two Mountain songs which were being sung by First Woman and the womenfolk. Thus, First Man would sing a Sun song, then call to the women for help, and these would sing a Mountain song. And these were Blessing Rite songs exclusively. Ceremonies, therefore, must be concluded with Blessing Rite songs to complete them.

On the earth-side First Man now placed the Dark, Blue, Yellow, White, Speckled, Spotted, Twisted, and Striped Winds, eight all told. On the sky-side he placed the Dark, Blue, Yellow, White, Speckled, Spotted, Twisted, and Striped Thunders, eight all told. Next to the Black Thunder, towards the center, he added Dark Cloud, Dark Mist, He-rains and She-rains. Close to Mountain Woman, on the earth-side, he set a jet which was to be Dark Mountain; next to this he set a turquoise to be Blue Mountain; next to this he set an abalone shell to be Yellow Mountain, and then a white shell to be White Mountain.

On the top of Dark Mountain he placed a jet which became White

(-back) Eagle. On top of Blue Mountain he placed a turqoise which became Yellow-bill (American Eagle). On top of Yellow Mountain he placed an abalone shell which became a Bird-Hawk. The white shell on top of White Mountain became White Eagle, Red-shouldered Hawk, Turkey Buzzard, and various kinds of hawks. Therefore, the Hawk People rest on peaks and mountains. Next to Water Woman, First Man placed two kinds of waves *(naalyéhé)* which were to become Spruce Hill and Mountain-around-which-moving-was-done.

He now covered the whole with a cover of dawn from the east, evening twilight from the west, skyblue from the south, and darkness from the north side. Then he breathed four times on it from east, west, south, and north—after which he removed the covers. It showed a large number of things moving on both the Earth and Sky sides. The mountains had grown to some extent.

Again he covered them up as before, breathed on them four times, they removed the cover. By this time they had grown the size of a finger joint but did not breathe. Four times he repeated this process until they were sufficiently large. He then picked up the nine winds from the earth-side and breathed with them on the two prayersticks, on the mountains, and on all things that lay on Earth and Sky, then on all assembled people. That accounts for good winds (spirits) in some people and bad in others who, owing to these bad winds, have very little sense.

After that all things breathed and stood up, but still winked with their eyes. The various things were then dressed. *Sisnajini* Mountain was dressed in white shell, Mount Taylor in turquoise, San Francisco Peaks in abalone, Perrin's Peak in jet, Mountain Woman in vegetation, Water Woman in water foam, Spruce Mountain in soft goods, Moving-around-the-mountain in jewels. The Crane People were dressed with Dark, Blue, Yellow, and White Winds which supplied their travel means in flying. Woodpecker and companions were similarly dressed in flints. The Cranes were also sprayed with water iron-ore and dark, blue, yellow, white, and pink moss. Therefore they have their houses of water moss (scum) in water.

The Kingbird, Snowbird, Chickadee and Owl *(naak'e'ni)* were dressed with ice and Woodpecker with spotted ice. Their beaks were all made of dark agate which accounts for their hardness. Dark, Blue, Yellow, White, and Varicolored Clouds were made of similarly colored mirage. Dark Cloud was dressed with Collected Waters and He-rain, Dark Mist was dressed with Water's Child and She-rain. Therefore we can observe the dark mirage in the small black clouds which gradually increase, and similarly the blue and other colored mirages in clouds of these colors. And the Dark and other colored Thunders are supposed to enter these clouds and therefore thunder is heard at times in these various clouds.

The months of winter were dressed with ice, therefore all waters freeze up in these months. The prayerstick of the south was used in dressing the summer months, that of the north (was) exchanged for dressing the winter months.

Now the genitalia of man remained on Sky, the genitalia of woman on Earth. The Winds placed on Earth belonged to all people who used these as their travel means.

The Sun of turquoise was bordered by a fourfold band of dark, white, yellow, and red sun(light) ray. The east side of the disc was fringed with twelve dawn cords in white, the south side was fringed with twelve skyblue cords in blue, the west side with twelve evening twilight cords in yellow, the north side with twelve darkness cords in black. These fringes passed through the disc, east to west, west to east, south to north, north to south. They terminate in a rainbow bar, one at each direction. The outer half of this bar is red to represent reflected sunred, the inner half blue to represent rainbow. They indicate the travel means of the Sun. Two horns of turquoise were provided, each tasselled with a live feather. Two red feathers were placed between the fingers, indicated (now) by red butts and black tips of the feather.

The Moon of white shell was dressed identically, excepting the horns which were made of white shell and the pairs of feathers between fingers which showed white butts and black tips.

The genitalia of man and woman were dressed in the same manner as had been done in the lower world, using the vomit of Wolf, Mountain Lion, Badger, and Buzzard, and the pubic hair. Coyote then remarked that something is missing. "It can not remain always the same. Some will die, some too should come to life. There should be births. As there is a time for plants and animals to die and revive, so it should also be with men and women. Let the months on this side be for the death while those on that side shall be for life when all things grow anew. Let them give birth and increase! If there be no births, you must continuously create these things again. Let humans get old, let them die. But let the women also beget children," he said as, with his own hair, he furnished the pubic hair of man and woman.

First Man now placed Dawn in the east, Skyblue in the south, Evening Twilight in the west, Darkness in the north. By this time there were still twenty-four songs to be sung, twelve on the men's, twelve on the women's side.

"My Grandchildren, my Youths!" he said. "Who will take these two? We require two persons to carry the Sun and the Moon." In the meantime First Scolder had gone among the people and, by means of sunray and sunlight had drawn their voices out of the good-looking men. And the created things were all breathing but did not move. "Who then will move these?" First Man asked. A youth called *yooɫgai iináyisí* (White Shell?), who had a fine voice, was selected. He stepped before the Sun to shout. But as Coyote had stolen his voice, nothing but a hoarse grunt was heard and he returned to his place.

One-who-moves-with-sunray was tried (selected) next but merely grunted *yée*. Another youth called That-which-lies-within-white-mountain also took his turn, but an indistinct *jéé* was all he could utter. Then Traveller-on-earth was tried out with the same result and he, too, returned to his place in shame.

"What now?" Everybody seemed to be hoarse. First Scolder then proffered his services. "I'll yell, I know I can do it," he said. And he stood in the east and gave one long shout which he repeated in the south, west, and north. And sure enough, all things moved. His yell had moved all things. In this manner the Sun and Moon were made. The Sky was called Sky Man, the Earth was called Earth Woman, made as man and wife. The prayerstick of Sky should always be black they told Sky Man, that of Earth Woman should always be blue, they told her.

"What will you be called?" October month was asked. "I'll be called October," he said. "And you?" "My name will be November." And so on for each winter and for each summer month.

"What will you be called?" "I'll be called *sisnajini.*" "And I Mount Taylor, and I San Francisco Peaks, and I Perrin's Peak. And I (will be called) Mountain Woman, Water Woman, Spruce Hill," and so on.

The same was asked of Kingbird and his partners. The Dark and other colored Clouds, Mists, Thunders, He-rains and She-rains said that they would live together in the clouds. The Eagle People mentioned that they would travel by sunray, sunlight, zigzag lightning, and the like.

"What shall we call you?" they asked First Scolder. "Oh, call me *sisnajini.*" "But that is (already) somebody's name." Well, then Mount Taylor," he said. "That name, too, belongs to somebody." "They are sacred names," First Man said. "You'll be called *mạii* (Roamer) and done with it." "But I am not a roamer," he objected. "Well then, be called First Scolder," he said. "Oh, no. I never get angry. Why should I have that name?" said Coyote. "Oh well then, we'll call you White-coyote-howling-in-the-dawn," First Man said. "Alright," said Coyote, well pleased.

They told Kingbird: "Go north and live there. You need no shoes because the cold will not hurt you." He and his companions agreed. Therefore the cold comes from that direction.

To the crane[58] he said: "You will go south with the return of winter and come north again with the return of summer." By this time eight songs for each side still remained to be sung.

"Now that is done," said First Man. "I can not do all for you, so you had all better think of yourselves." "All right," they said. And Big Trotter said: "I shall be called Wolf."[59] Then follows a list of quadrupeds, water fowls, and flying and creeping animals who repeated that they wish to be called so-and-so. They then discussed the carriers of Sun and Moon, four times they asked and discussed this point.

Now of the peoples mentioned, one and all have their sacrifices, or at least (each has his) special prayerstick; each described his preferences.

"My prayerstick," said Wolf, "shall be white, my sacrifice shall be white shell with tobacco." Mountain Lion asked for a yellow prayerstick, abalone, and tobacco for a sacrifice. Badger specified a black prayerstick with a little white on it, a jet, and smoke for sacrifice.

Big Skunk desired a black prayerstick spotted white and a white tip on it; Spotted Skunk desired it spotted all over as did also the small Spotted Skunk. All three asked for jet and tobacco with their sacrifice. The Bear specified a dark prayerstick with jet and tobacco.

The Porcupine specified a perforated jewel of jet and turquoise tied to (the) prayerstick in addition to a smoke. White Weasel desired a white prayerstick with white shell as his sacrifice and tobacco. Yellow Weasel substituted yellow and abalone. The Locust said: "Jewels are my sacrifice, two white shell, two abalone shell, a red abalone, and some iron ore, that's all." Gopher, and Rock Squirrel, and Ground Squirrel specified a yellow prayerstick, abalone as their sacrifice, and tobacco. Field Rat Man and Field Rat Woman desired a blue prayerstick, turquoise for their sacrifice, and tobacco. Gray Pine Squirrel (desired) a blue prayerstick, turquoise and tobacco; Black Pine Squirrel a black prayerstick, jet, and tobacco.

Kangaroo Mouse desired no prayerstick but abalone for his sacrifice and promised to help with penny royal. The Small Field Rat also refused a prayerstick but asked for abalone and promised to help with slim penny royal. The Common Mouse asked for white shell sacrifice. The Jumping Mouse and the Furrowing Mouse desired nothing. "I'll not injure anyone," said the former, while the latter remarked: "I do not walk on the ground but merely make furrows below ground."

---

[58] In the preceding paragraphs every being, months, birds, clouds, etc., were individually asked for their preferences. I have shortened the text in this detail and have mentioned one crane, for instance, instead of repeating each variety. The list of prayersticks is given in full.

[59] He uses *ma'iitsoh* instead of *naatł'ée'iitsoh*. It means "big trotter."

The Field Mouse said: "My prayerstick is yellow, my sacrifice abalone, and I prepare my smoke in a pipe lit by a rock crystal." It seems he and the Bear met one day. The Bear asked him: "Where do you come from?" The Field Mouse replied: "And where do you come from?" "Oh, I come from around here," Bear said. "Ah," said Field Mouse, "are you the one they call *shash?*" But the Bear got angry and raised his left paw to strike. The Field Mouse, however, quickly disappeared into a rock crevice. From this place of safety he again asked: "Does it hurt you to be called *shash?*" And Bear answered him: "Don't say that. I do not like to be called *shash.*" But Field Mouse slipped out and, running along, shouted: "You are very quick-tempered, *shash.*" "Yes," the Bear replied, "I am." "So *shash* is really quick-tempered, is he?" And the Bear took after him and again raised his paw to strike, but Field Mouse disappeared in a cleft in the rock. After a while he ran out behind the Bear and set fire to his fur. The Bear plunged into the water from the east, south, west, and north but was unable to extinguish it. Bear then sat down in front of Field Mouse, pleading: "Please extinguish this fire. I'll give you four of my songs if you will extinguish this fire and give me back my fur." Therefore if you have some fur of the Field Mouse on your person, the Bear will not touch you, they say. Neither will your dreams be bad if you carry this fur.

Field Mouse then picked up four sacred waters, and with a frosted sage branch,[60] taken from east, south, west, and north of the brush, he extinguished the fire. Thus he has four songs and therefore he asked for so large a sacrifice.

The Small Lizard asked for a blue prayerstick, turquoise, and tobacco. The Sandhill Crane has no prayerstick. But since the Cranes are used in the (medicine) pouch, they said they would be of help in this manner.

The prayerstick of Brown Crane must be a span long. His sacrifice is turquoise with tobacco. The prayerstick of Bittern is of the same length, but white and accompanied by white shell sacrifice and tobacco. Another Crane called *hoz* has a black prayerstick four fingertips in length, jet and tobacco to go with it. The (Twig Bill) or Curlew prayerstick is yellow, four fingertips long, with abalone sacrifice, and tobacco. Blue Heron's prayerstick is also yellow but a span in length, (with) abalone sacrifice and tobacco. Snowy Egret has a white prayerstick spanned from the bent first joint of the index finger to the tip of the thumb, with white shell for sacrifice, tobacco.

The prayersticks of the Ducks are all the width of three fingers and of corresponding color. The Black Duck asked for a black prayerstick,

---

[60]That is, branches white with frost, which are called *dáhts'os* "high-up plume."

jet sacrifice, and tobacco. The Blue Duck (asked for) blue stick turquoise and tobacco. The Yellow Duck (asked for) yellow prayerstick,
abalone, and tobacco. The Mudhen (asked for) a dark prayerstick, jet,
and tobacco.

The Large Jacksnipe desired four black rings around the neck of his
white prayerstick, in addition to white shell for sacrifice, and tobacco.
The Small Jacksnipe desired two black rings instead. The Turtle Dove
asked for a white prayerstick the width of three fingers, white shell,
and tobacco. The Small Turtle Dove desired a blue prayerstick of the
same length, and turquoise with tobacco.

The prayersticks of the Eagle People are all the width of three
fingers and tobacco is required. The White-back Eagle desired a black
prayerstick with four white rings at the bottom, and jet sacrifice.
Yellow-bill Eagle asked for a white prayerstick with four black rings,
and white shell. Yellow-tail asked for a yellow prayerstick with four
black rings, and abalone. White Eagle asked for a white prayerstick
trimmed with four black rings, and white shell. Prairie Falcon specified white with four rings, and white shell. Big Hawk specified a blue
prayerstick with four black rings, and turquoise. Black Hawk (specified) black with white rings, and jet. The Goshawk (asked for a) blue
(prayerstick) with black rings and turquoise. Sparrow Hawk (asked
for a) yellow (prayerstick) with black rings, and abalone. Marsh Hawk
(asked for a) white (prayerstick) with black rings, and white shell.

The prayerstick of Turkey Buzzard is a reddish brown with four
red marks at its butt, the width of three fingers. As a sacrifice he
desired jet, abalone, and iron ore, with tobacco. The prayerstick of
Crow is black, sacrifice is jet, with tobacco.

"A dark big reed must be my prayerstick, my Grandchildren,"
said Big Snake. Jet is his sacrifice, with tobacco. Endless Snake has no
prayerstick, "but I wish to appear in sandpainting, and this shall be
my prayerstick." He usually furnishes the border around sandpaintings.

The prayersticks of other snakes are the width of three fingers.
That of Bullsnake is made of reed and painted yellow. Abalone is his
sacrifice, with tobacco. That of Arrowsnake is blue with three yellow
and three red stripes, his sacrifice turquoise, and tobacco. That of
Flying Snake is yellow, abalone is his sacrifice, and tobacco. That of
Rattlesnake is black, (his sacrifice is) jet, and tobacco. (The prayerstick) of Stubby Rattler is white, white shell is his sacrifice, and tobacco.

The prayerstick of Blue Lizard is blue with two black rings added
to its butt. (His) sacrifice (is) of turquoise, with tobacco. The prayerstick of Green Lizard is identical, but a nice turquoise must be his
sacrifice, and some tobacco. Horned Toad requires a white prayerstick

with three black arrowpoints on his stomach and three on his back and one tied around his neck. (He requires) white shell for his sacrifice, and tobacco. Gray Lizard has a yellow prayerstick the width of three fingers. "Reflected sunred must be put in my sides," he said, "abalone is my sacrifice, and I smoke."

Toad Man was sitting there panting. "What are you panting for? Your butt must be worn down. What will you do for yourself?" they asked him. He answered: "I live in a house of moss. My prayerstick shall be white with four little black specks on both sides. White shell and abalone shall be my sacrifice, and I want tobacco." "Well," they said, "that fellow has no buttocks and sits with his legs spread out." "That's just the way I am, my Grandchildren," he said good-naturedly. "And what a belly," another remarked. "Yes, that's the way I am," he said. "Look at those feet. There are no joints," he thought, "and his toes are wide apart." "That's true," the Toad said, "just so am I shaped." "And his mouth is wide and large, and his neck is continually bulging out," one said. "Yes, my Grandchildren," he answered, "That's just the way I am."

Green Frog also was there and when asked he said: "Oh, let my prayerstick be blue, my sacrifice turquoise, and I want tobacco."

Water Snake desired a mouse-colored prayerstick, jet for his sacrifice, and tobacco. The Turkey specified a dark prayerstick, for sacrifice jet, red-white stone, abalone, turquoise, and white shell. Meadow rue he desired for tobacco (táájí iiłchíín).

Night Hawk was an old fellow with a wide mouth, and half asleep. His prayerstick is black, his sacrifice jet, and a smoke. Beaver Man has a yellow prayerstick, abalone he desired, and tobacco. Otter has a black prayerstick which it rubbed with iron ore to produce a gloss. Jet is his sacrifice, and tobacco.

Just then some strangers came in, a White, Blue, Yellow, and Black Screech Owl. They desired prayersticks as long as the second joint of the little finger. The White one desired a white prayerstick with white shell for sacrifice, and tobacco. The Blue one said he would be in the south and desired a blue prayerstick, with turquoise and tobacco. The Yellow one (desired) a yellow prayerstick, with abalone and tobacco. The Black Screech Owl (desired) a black prayerstick and jet, with tobacco.

The Black, Blue, Yellow, and White Winds asked for prayersticks to suit their colors. The black (prayerstick) should be wound with a white cord, sunwise four times, the blue (one) wound four times with yellow cord sunwise, the yellow one with blue cord sunwise four times, and the white (one) with black cord four times sunwise. Their sacrifice according to color (is) jet, turquoise, abalone, white shell, and tobacco.

In a similar manner the black prayerstick for Black Thunder should show a four-angle line in white, the blue one of Blue Thunder marked four yellow straight lines, the yellow one with a black four-angle line, and the white one of White Thunder marked with four black straight lines. The length of the sticks (should) be the width of three fingers. The sacrifice according to color (is) jet, turquoise, abalone, white shell, with tobacco.

The prayerstick of Sky is to be dark in color, as long as the width of three fingers, (including) a sacrifice of jet and tobacco. That of Earth (is) blue, with turquoise for sacrifice, and tobacco. The big reed prayerstick of Sun is to be painted blue, with turquoise for sacrifice, and with tobacco. The big reed prayerstick of Moon is to be painted white, with white shell for sacrifice, and tobacco.

The prayerstick of Pricking Vagina is to be dark in color, with jet for sacrifice and turquoise, white shell, abalone, red-white stone, iron ore, harebell pollen, flag pollen, ordinary pollen, and small bird feathers; also tobacco.

The prayersticks are at present colored as described. Mountain or wild tobacco (unless otherwise specified) is inserted by means of an owl feather and is lit with rock crystal. When a pregnant woman, for instance, has seen one of these animals, its prayerstick is forthwith made for her benefit. The feathers of small birds, like the Bluebird or Canary, are inserted into the hollow of the stick or reed, then the tobacco as already said, and pollen over the tobacco. The rock crystal is then motioned to the Sun and held to the tobacco as if lighting it. The prayerstick is then deposited (in ritually prescribed places) where the supernaturals (the gods) presumably find and smoke them.

Thus it is seen that all people that stood on the Earth (at) that time had their own name. After this all had happened, First Man placed in position pieces of jet, turquoise, abalone, white shell, red-white stone, red abalone, water iron ore, water pollen, dark water, blue water, yellow water, white water, glittering water. Next he assembled rainbow, stubby rainbow, sunray, and sunlight in his left hand, passed them to his mouth and chewed on them.

Then he stepped to the Sun and sputtered over it four times in the east, south, west, and north. Then he walked over to the Sky and breathed over it from east, south, west, and north. This put Dark Cloud and Mist, He-rain and She-rain, Zigzag and Straight Lightning, Rain and Sunray, and the Stars in firm position and made them stationary.

Going over to the earth-side he breathed four times around it, sunwise. Then four times straight over it from east to west. "The four sunwise breaths," he said, "are to be the oceans. The first of the straight breaths represent springs, the second streams, the third lakes

and pools, the fourth rain and dew which will fall and make vegetation grow." And so it really is today. This breathing also made the
Mountains firm and solid.

He next placed two objects in position which were similar to a
broom. Then he placed a dark body in the east, a blue body in the
south, a white body in the west, a yellow body in the north, a pink
body in the center. These were to be supports for the Earth and Sky.
The two broom-like objects were to be Black Mountain and the other
mountains round about (male and female).

Now there are thirty-two trails for the travels of the Sun (although
in the description given of the Sun, only twelve fringes on each side are
mentioned to represent these thirty-two trails). When they had discussed for some time who should carry them, they selected the two
Gourd Children for the task, the elder to carry the Sun, the younger
to carry the Moon. Both had their reeds with them, as they had extracted these supernaturally out of the waters.

On the north side in the rear part of the hogan, First Man laid
a spread of turquoise, next to this, south, one of white shell. With his
head in the west the elder lay down on the turquoise spread, the
younger (lay down) on the white shell spread with his head also (in the)
west. The first was covered with skyblue, the second with dawn. First
Man stood between them. He now blew over them four times toward
the west, then uncovered them to find two fine-looking young men
before him.

This time he covered the elder with abalone and jet, then with
evening twilight and the younger with darkness. Their heads were
towards the east. Again he blew four times over them, uncovered them
and found them even comelier than before. (Other versions state that
this was repeated four times. This version mentions only two repeti-
tions.) First Man then rubbed evening twilight over their chin, skyblue
over their nose, darkness across their eyes, dawn across their forehead,
and the young men were dressed.

First Man now tied a large Sun plume on the heads of both and one
on their left side. Then he blew on them four times. They were therefore dressed alike and, after he had blown on them, one took the Sun,
the other the Moon disc. And raising the discs a trifle, First Man placed
sunray and sunlight crosswise below them, with sunray uppermost.
The Kingbird, and others dressed in ice, now departed for Perrin's
Peak. The genitalia of man and woman united and crossed over to the
side of the Earth. And the prayerstick on the side of Sky crossed over
to the prayerstick of the side of Earth. All the rest remained firm in
their positions.

But here the Sun Carrier spoke: "My prayerstick will be of tall
reed. I shall travel with the large plume which is tied to my head and

my side. But every time I make the journey east and west, one of the
Earth People shall die. That is my pay." And the Moon Carrier added:
"We shall not return from our journey unless one of them will die.
That shall be our pay," he said. "And I," said the Sun Carrier, "shall
change my color at times." "I shall do likewise," said Moon Carrier.
Therefore the Navajo say that the Sun dies and the Moon dies, but the
ones standing within them never die.[61]

First Man now picked up each of the jewels previously mentioned.
He placed the turquoise over their hearts and both Sun and Moon
Carrier inhaled its breath. This same performance he and they repeated with the white shell, abalone, jet, red-white stone, water iron
ore, water pollen, flag pollen, and iron ore. "You first," he said to Sun
Carrier. But he turned to Moon Carrier and said: "Night Carrier, who
lies on light, my Nephew!" "Now you," First Man said to Moon Carrier. But he turned to Sun Carrier saying: "Carrier of the day, (whose)
light lies (on) the ground, my Nephew!"

With his reed in his mouth, and whistling with it, the elder boy
stepped over to the Sun. The younger, too, walked sunwise to the
moon. But when they tried to put their arms below them, they found it
impossible. First Man then suggested that they hold their reeds in their
hands. And he breathed on them four times so that (the reed) of the
first became a turquoise, that of the other a white shell, and with these
they now stood before the Sun and Moon. First Man then blew from
below the Sun and Moon at the cardinal points which raised them
a trifle.

But now First Man drew a red streak mixed with gray, with a
yellow line above them, across the eastern portion of earth and sky.
"Whatever I think or say shall be done from these," he said. "The
lower red and gray represents smallpox, whooping cough and all other
diseases. The yellow line above them signifies the passing of these
diseases whenever that line appears above the other two."

When the Sun Carrier attempted to lift the sun, it sent forth a
ripping noise as though it would burst asunder. "No," said First Man,
"that will never do." So he placed white shell, turquoise, abalone, jet,
black cloud, and black mist on it, which quieted it down. And putting
a small piece of said jewels into his mouth he turned towards *sisnajini*
Mountain.

And out of the white shell, from the sun, (came) a white sunray
like a bridle rein (and) lit with its white shell tip (the) top of *sisnajini*.
As it struck this mountain the voice of Talking-god was heard. Therefore, he stands within it. Out of the turquoise a bridle rein-like blue

[61]Reference is made here to solar and lunar eclipses.

sunray shot over from the Sun to Mount Taylor, its tip of turquoise resting on the summit. As it reached the summit of this mountain the voice of Calling-god within it was heard.

And out of the abalone a bridle rein-like yellow sunray shot from the Sun to the top of San Francisco Peaks. As its abalone tip struck the summit the voice of Talking-god was heard within. Out of the jet a bridle rein-like black sunray shot from the Sun to the top of Perrin's Peak. As its jet tip struck the summit the voice of Calling-god was heard.

The sunray and sunlight beams which had been laid crosswise over the Sun were now stretching like rubber. First Man then placed the Sun and Moon on their left shoulders—not on the right, because he had to eat with his hand—then told them to walk to the spot where these had previously lain. They therefore stood, carrying them, on the spread mentioned originally.

Meanwhile the *zai-zai* of the heat, working inside of the Sun and Moon, could be heard. But the covers on either side of jet, white shell, and so on, and the dark cloud and mist covers, prevented them from burning up things. First Man now raised Sky in the east with a wand of jet, in the south with a wand of turquoise, in the west with a wand of abalone, in the north with a wand of white shell, and turned it over on(to) Earth so that it rested on the uprights or supports mentioned previously.[62] That done, the Sky rested on these pillars. He then blew on each of the five pillars, east, south, west, north, and center, and both Sky and Earth seemed to be swaying as if carried on waves.

With a jet, turquoise, abalone, and white shell cane he poked into the top of Mount Taylor, saying: "Here shall be the opening in the Sky." He then returned and stood in position behind the six summer months. At his left stood the Sun Carrier and next to him, the Moon Carrier.

First Man then blew a jet to the east jet (pillar) on the Earth, a turquoise to the turquoise in (the) south, an abalone to the abalone in the west, a white shell to the white shell in the north. That caused the Earth to stretch and expand, and the Sky to raise and likewise expand. He then blew with a rainbow in the four directions and with the rainbow he blew the Sun to the east out into the ocean. The Moon followed. This distance would be about a mile according to those standards. He again withdrew the rainbows by inhaling them. He repeated this operation four times in the four (directions) so that Earth and Sky had expanded to proportions equivalent to about eight miles.

[62]The five sky supports or pillars are meant. Five similar ones were provided for earth pillars.

He then blew Dawn towards the east. Therefore there we have the return of Dawn. The Sun then rose. He began his journey, but as the Earth was small it trembled and people were scorched with the heat. "This will not do, my Grandchildren, we shall roast," First Man said.

Again he blew in the four directions, extending the dimensions of Earth and Sky to the edges of the ocean. Again Dawn appeared and the Sun rose. This time it was better so that he removed one of the Dark Clouds. But when the Sun had reached the zenith the heat was terrible. So again he expanded the Earth in the four directions so that it extended over the surface of the oceans. Again the Dawn appeared and the Sun rose. He removed another Dark Cloud, but at noon it was still too warm. A fourth time he blew and now Earth and Sky had reached their present dimensions and distances. Again the Dawn appeared, the Sun rose (and) journeyed on till sunset just as it does now. So he again blew in all directions and made them firm. "Now we have other work to be done," the people said. "We have seeds to plant." But First Man said: "Wait, do not hurry."

Now when First Man had placed turquoise and white shell, and so on, over the heart of Sun, and the latter had inhaled their breath (so that they became his property), and of these he built his home over there. He breathed and made his home of turquoise. In the east of it four turquoise chambers were produced, in the south four of abalone, four of white shell in the west and four of jet in the north. Each chamber was provided with doors of the corresponding jewels. Likewise by breathing he produced corresponding stools for seats but added a red-white stone stool for the center of the chambers. He then planted pillars of dark flint in the east, of blue flint in (the) south, of yellow flint (in the) west, of serrated flint in the north. He also made twelve doll-like gourds of flints already mentioned, excepting that those of the north were varicolored. These he hung up at the cardinal points and they served him as rattles. All this while the Winds were reporting to First Man what the Sun Carrier was doing.

7

The Planting of Seeds

First Man then said: "Now you may go ahead and see what you can do for yourselves." So the White-tipped Pine Squirrel planted four seeds, two each of pine and tall cedar. Black Pine Squirrel planted two seeds of spruce, two of wide (blue) spruce. The Red-striped Pine Squirrel (planted) seeds of small spruce and common spruce. The Ground Squirrel had seeds of piñon and oak, the Rock Squirrel (had) seeds of juniper and scrub-oak (of the valleys). The Bear furnished seeds of "bear-food," serviceberry, sour berry, wild rose, and red bush. The Grizzly, Black Bear, Cinnamon Bear, White and Pinto Bear all helped in planting these.

Gopher had wild potato. Kangaroo Mouse planted *Croton texensis* and box-thorn, the Small Field Mouse added a creeping plant. The Bombardier Beetle planted four-o'clocks.

The Sand Lizard planted *tsábįįd*, a crucifer; Horned Toad planted *ni'hazés (?)*. The Small Lizard furnished blue moss; the Gray Lizard (had) yellow moss. Snake furnished (gray) greasewood and black greasewood. Spider planted *Chenopodium*. Beaver planted quaking aspen. Otter planted slender cottonwood and willow tree. Water Snake planted blue willow and weeping willow.

Toad Man planted sage and wide-leafed beeweed. Green Frog (planted) slim-leafed sage and slender-leafed tobacco. Tadpole planted duckweed. Fish planted watercress. Water Strider planted another kind of watercress.

Sandhill Crane planted "crane-food." The Duck furnished big flag, Snowy Egret (had) round flag, Curlew (had) tassel grass, and Jacksnipe planted reed. Turtle Dove planted bog rush. Deer planted *Frasera speciosa* and *nábįįh*. Antelope (planted) milkweed. The mother of the Gourd Children planted big reed at Taos and wild gourd (which is the male gourd)—also the big reed at Oraibi and the common gourd (which is the female gourd) for the pouch of the Shootingway Chant.

Field Rat Man planted yucca, cactus, yucca gloriosa; Field Rat Woman planted horned and slim yucca, horned and braided cactus. *Hosh ná'ołáałii (?)* planted twisting heart cactus. Dark Medicine planted locoweed (?); Blue Medicine planted poisonous marsh plant; Yellow Medicine planted spurge and jimsonweed; White Medicine planted the poisonous *shílátsoh*.

(143)

Mariposa Lily Boy planted death camass and slim mariposa; Mariposa Lily Girl planted mariposa lily. One called Out-of-blue-earth planted stone parsley, *Fernla multifida* and *Cynopterus glomeratus.* He, called Out-of-yellow-earth, planted *tsíidikaal (?)* and onion. *Tsénásí* planted the stones. *Tsinásí* (planted) the trees of all kinds. Plodding Spider and Tarantuala planted creeping vines (grape) and *tábaah łitso (?)*.

All these things were planted and now may be found everywhere. In this manner Earth, Sky, Stars, Sun, Moon, Months, Waters, Winds, Thunders, Cloud, and so forth, all were made, as well as the two organs for (producing) birth. "All these shall last twelve growths after which they will be destroyed," they said. Up to our generation there are ten, two more (growths) are yet to come.

They now proposed to eat. Salt Man and Salt Woman brought salt, Kangaroo Mouse brought in box-thorn, Small Field Mouse (brought) a creeping vine, Gopher (brought in) the wild potato. The Small Ground Squirrel had his blue (cedar) berries; Field Rat Man brought cactus; Field Rat Woman brought juniper which had been chewed a little. When Wolf saw this he grew angry and said to them: "Why do you bring these dirty things in here when there are plenty of good things? Get out of here and your trash with you!"

Salt Woman was much offended by this, and the others also. Therefore people nowadays also take offense. Accordingly, Salt Woman picked up her salt and walked out without saying a word. Kangaroo Mouse held up his box-thorn saying: "This will always be eaten with white clay." Therefore white clay is now mixed with it. Small Field Mouse held up his vine and said: "Hereafter this must be washed well and its foam must be removed before it can be eaten." Gopher said: "These will be in the ground and they must be dug out. And these potatoes must be prepared with white clay. And when about to eat them people will say 'here comes gopher.'" Field Rat said: "This cactus will be nice to behold and tempting to eat, but I shall make them difficult to obtain. I'll just put a few spines on them." Therefore cactus must be freed of their spines with much labor. Field Rat Woman also carried her juniper away. "This will have berries which will be my food more than theirs." Therefore one does not eat juniper berries very frequently.

Many others would have entered, but because Wolf was out of humor, they would not venture in. It also explains why men and women get angered over food, or when they (the women) are ordered to prepare it for visitors. Blueberries are identical with juniper. If boiled and dried and ground, they are very sweet. Singers at times eat the food here mentioned to refresh their memories.

Some of the Shootingway songs begin here, such as Sun songs, Earth songs, and so on, which are songs of the Blessing Rite as well.

Salt Woman, as said, picked up her salt and walked to a meadow near the present Wheatfields. They followed her. Suddenly she said: "If you can lift me, I shall return." But they did not succeed, so she proceeded to the salt lakes near Long H Ranch. Here again they begged her to return. "All right," she said. "Pick me up." But they could not. Therefore salt is found there.

From here she went to (Zuni) Salt Lake where they again made an effort to pick her up. Therefore Salt Woman lives there. On the east side of Salt Lake is the male mountain, on the west side of it the female mountain, on the summit of which jewels are offered in sacrifice which the Navajo accompany with the invocation: "My (Maternal) Grandmother, pour out water for me." They then proceeded to the east side butte from which sacred water flows, of which they drank. Therefore all people of Earth, Navajos and other Indians, use salt for their food.

The Flying People now held council about their homes. These were the White Eagle, Bald-headed Eagle, Yellow Bill, Yellow-tail Hawk, Gray and Sparrow Hawk, and Falcons, as well as Buzzard, Magpie, Snipe and Jacksnipe, Cranes and Egrets. "You might dwell in the Sky openings and occupy the first, second, third, and fourth stories of it," they were told. "For your travelling means you may use the White and other Winds, Rainbow, Sunlight, and Sunray. You may travel back and forth, and when Earth People come into being you may travel among them and return to your homes from here." "All right," they said. Therefore at the sound of the Winds these people can be seen among us.

"What about us?" the Thunder and Wind People asked. "Your homes will be up there also," they were told, as many as there were, the Blue, Yellow, White, Black, Spotted, Left-handed, Striped and other Winds and Thunders. "You will travel with Dark Cloud and Mist, Sunray, and Sunlight to the sky homes and back among the people here," they were told. We see these people whenever Dark Clouds appear and Lightning comes down to strike.

And the Arrowsnakes, the Flying Snakes, Bull Snakes, and Rattlers, the Big Snake, and Endless Snake are in the east because they chose this for their homes. Thus some of the good and bad people had left not without, however, mentioning again that their sacrifices should be made of jewels, pollen, and so forth, as already stated. Therefore the Dark Clouds, the Dark Mist, and the rest combine, and this produces rain which moistens the Earth. That causes plants to grow and furnishes drink to the animals.

The Kingbird was dressed in dark ice, Snowbird in blue ice, Chickadee in yellow ice, Sap Sucker in white ice, Woodpecker in vari-colored ice. And when they asked where to go, they were told: "You may live in the north where it is cold and there is much ice, but (you) may return here." Therefore we see them among us in winter and with the ice. The various kinds of ice may be seen, but spotted ice will not be seen, they say.

The Sun lives in the east. The Mirage People—dark, blue, yellow, white, pink—went to the south. Therefore it is always warm there. The Haze People went north. Therefore the cold comes from there, although at times also a warm wave or two. "And where shall we live?" asked Gray and Black Squirrel, Badger, Mountain Lion, Bear, and so on. "You may live in the country at large," they were told. "All right," they replied. "I," said Bear, "shall make my home in the mountains." "I shall live in trees," said Squirrel. "I shall travel at night," one said, "and I in the daytime," said another. "We in the ground," and "we above ground," some said. We therefore find quadrupeds on earth.

The Beaver, Otter, Tortoise, and Box Turtle said: "We shall live underwater, but (we) will be of use to people in the future." Therefore the Beaver and Otter are serviceable for dress, the turtle shell for medicine cups. The Black, Blue, and White Ducks, too, the Mudhen and Snipes also selected the water for their homes. The Brown Crane, Snowy Egret, Blue Heron, Curlew, and Sandhill Crane said that they belonged both to the land and water as well as above. The Sandhill Crane said he would be seen in spring and fall. Therefore they go north and south.

The peoples of the upper regions (Eagle, Thunder, Wind People) built houses of white shell, turquoise, jet, striped and spotted houses. The house of White Thunder was white, of Black Thunder was black, and so on for the houses of the others in various colors. The Winds made their houses similarly, corresponding to their color. The house of Bald-headed Eagle had colors blending, lower half to represent dark-ness, upper half white for dawn. The houses in the east were dark, (in the) south blue, (in the) west yellow, (and) white in the north. Here the people lived, youths, old women, and men, and children. The Thun-der and Wind People also occupy houses there. We see the Eagle People at times, but never the Wind and Thunder People. The White-headed Eagle seems to be fine at a distance; at close range when killed, he is ugly like a Turkey Buzzard. Yellow Hawk and White Eagle, on the other hand, are pretty birds.

White and Gray Hawks are not used. The Big Hawk is used in feathering arrows; the Sparrow Hawk, like the Buzzard, is useless. All these birds have their clothes which they don to visit us and hang up again on their return, after which they are humans like ourselves. The Thunder People and Wind People of every direction, the Dark Clouds and Dark Mist, too, have clothes which they don and remove like ourselves. These four peoples then live up there in the Sky homes of four openings, and beyond that there is only space (nothing).

The Mirage People—Dark, Blue, Yellow, White, and Pink Mirage People—live in their underground homes in the south. The Haze People of the same colors also live in the ground in their northern homes. And because First Man had breathed the various winds into all these people, some of them are good, others evil. Therefore we find good and bad people, bright and stupid persons.

As for First Made and Last Made, they were blown to the east by First Man and live in the (west) corner[63] of the Sun's home. On account of these two it is said that Sun and Moon die (eclipse). The second First Man has his home in the west corner of Sky, the second First Woman has her home in the west corner of Earth.

Four guards lay at each side of his (the Sun's) door, facing each other—Mountain Lion and Big Snake, Bear and Thunder. In the front of his home red abalone shell was made, which was converted into water, which is called Equal-standing-waters (or Waters-in-each-direction).[64] The jewels—jet, turquoise, abalone, white shell, red-white stone— he held over the four corners, then placed them in the four waters where they became water animals. The jet (became) a water horse, the turquoise a water monster, the abalone a turtle, the white shell a monster fish, the mixed (red) stone a box turtle. Of these he made spies and pets.

Before he left, First Man said: "I am thinking of something yet to be done (concerning First Boy, First Girl, and First Scolder)." First Woman, too, said: "I, too, have the same thought."

First Man then laid out a spread of darkness on which he placed a jet basket, a spread of skyblue on which he placed a turquoise basket, a spread of evening twilight on which he placed an abalone basket, a spread of dawn on which he placed a white shell[65] basket. These baskets all were as large as one's thumbnail.

Over his extended left hand he blew a rainbow, a stubby rainbow, reflected sunred, sunray, and a sunbeam. Then he placed in his left hand a white shell, a turquoise, an abalone, a jet, a red-white stone,

[63]The corner (ntsitł'ah) is usually the space in the west side of the hogan. As the Sun's home, the Sky and Earth are conceived similarly, the account speaks of this corner as the home of specific beings.

[64]The word ahídaaz'á can also mean "meeting of points," which seeems to be the sense of the text.

[65]My notes place white shell in the third position. Now this seems questionable.

iron ore and harebell pollen, flag pollen and ordinary pollen. He then held his hand toward San Francisco Peaks-to-be and moved it sunwise toward the east, and (he) blew the rainbows and sunlights (five of them) in that direction towards the other side of the ocean. In time these came to be various peoples, the Pueblos, Comanches, Utes, and others we do not see. And some of these had houses of the corresponding jewels which he held in his hand when he blew.

8

Big God Travelling at Hot Spring

CHANGING WOMAN

First Man, First Woman, First Boy, First Girl, First Scolder, these five left for the top of Spruce Mountain, and they were witches. They were poor when they left and wanted everything while they lived at Spruce Mountain. When the Sun arose they noticed that its light was bluish, yellow, and red. "This is bad," they said. But at dawn one day they heard the cry of a child on the summit of Spruce Mountain. "What can this mean?" First Man said to First Woman. This baby was to be the Changing Woman with whom the Blessing Rite begins here.

When First Man searched the place he was unable to find the child. And all day they discussed the matter. The same was repeated on three following days. Both slept little as they studied over the possible origin of this child. Towards dawn he again heard the cry of the child. Immediately he arose, went over in that direction and found a child with its head lying west. He picked it up and carried it home. And First Woman called it *shich'é'é*, my Daughter, and First Man also called her *sitsi'*, my Daughter. She took good care of it and within four days it was well grown. When speaking to her they would say: *Asdzá nádleehí* (Changing Woman)," and she would respond: "*Yá*, (what?)."

In four additional days she was quite a girl, and four more days saw her large and sensible. She and First Woman even had a quarrel. And First Boy called her *shilah*, my Sister. First Girl called her "my Younger Sister." First Scolder refrained from taking sides with either party. "You are witches," she told them. "You bewitch people. You call me Daughter, but I am not your daughter and have none of those (evil) things in me." And the five took jewels, made a mush of them, ate them, and started from Spruce Mountain towards the east, saying: "May it happen as our thought is." They left her in anger.[66]

---

[66]There is evidently some confusion in the account which follows. I am inserting the record as it was taken years ago. The account of the puberty ceremony is fragmentary.

(149)

The next two paragraphs—between asterisks—are a digression into Blessingway mythology. After this brief sample the informant broke off and continued with the *hatáálk'ehjí*, the "side of singing way." The Blessingway version continues below, on page 154.

*   *   *

When her first menses had come, she spoke of her flow of blood saying: "*kinsisdá* (my period is on)." And this happened when she was twelve years of age. Mothers, therefore, at present use this expression when their daughters arrive at this period. "How shall it be done, I wonder," said First Man. Now there were two old women, one an ugly one called Shaking-the-dew, the Marsh Wren Woman, the other (was) the good-looking Bridled Titmouse (?). "Go to these," he said to First Woman, "and ask them to come."

They lived in the neighborhood and soon appeared. "Yuh!" they said, "you told us to come." "Yes," said First Man, "she announced *kinsisdá*."

*   *   *

At dawn again the cry of a child was heard in the east, four times.[67] The lower rest boards were made of rainbow slung under with zigzag and straight lightning. The lace cords were sunray, the footrest (was) reflected sunray. It was learned that Earth happened to be its mother, Sky its father, and that Darkness Man and Dawn Woman had picked it up. These two brought the child to the home of Mountain Woman and Water Woman. (The five—First Man and the others were not present here, but the scene is on the same Spruce Mountain. The girl is not identical with Changing Woman.)

Four days afterward it was large enough to walk and speak. (This was done supernaturally, as those present were all supernaturals—gods.) After four more days she was a young girl who, in four additional days, was a full grown maiden of twelve years. Her father, the Sky, presented her with a jet basket; her mother, the Earth (presented her) with a turquoise basket. Dawn Man gave her a white bead basket; Darkness Woman (gave her) an abalone basket.

During the day they left the virgin at the hogan and went their ways. About noon she left home to gather wood and come to a small wooded ridge in the south. She made wood there; that is, she tied her bundle of wood with earth cord and with sky cord. She crossed these

---

[67]This introduction is not a continuation of the myth proper, although portions of the account, told farther on about the birth and childhood of the Slayers, are very similar.

on her back after the manner of carrying water and bent to raise the bundle. When she felt its weight, she remarked: "It is too heavy for me," undid the bundle, removed some of the wood and re-tied it. She tried again.

Now the Sun was pressing down on her bundle when she tried to raise (it) but she did not know this. He, too, owned four jewel baskets like her own. "How can this be?" she soliloquized. "It ought not be an overweight. I have often carried more wood than this." Again she discarded some of the wood and tried again but could not raise it. "Ch'įįdiitahdę́ę́' chizh, wood from ghostland," she swore and untied the bundle, then tried again. But again she failed and swore. "Is a ghost or a snake holding this? Snake, snake," she was mumbling as she discarded more wood and retied it. And when she was about to raise the bundle and (she) glanced about, she saw a man standing there.

"What is the use of swearing with nobody around?" he said questioningly. She hung her head and said nothing. But when she finally looked up she found that he was fine and beautiful. She smiled at him and he at her in return. Therefore, when persons bent on doing wrong meet, they smile at each other. It was noon then and he slept with her. After she awoke she looked about but saw nobody. She now felt something dropping down her clothes and picked up a beautiful turquoise the size of a finger joint which she slipped into her belt. She now had no trouble packing her bundle and walked off unconcerned, as evil women usually do.

It happened, however, that her actions had been observed. She returned at dusk and sat musing over the events of the past day when to the south the people playing moccasin-game could be heard. Now one sang: "My wood aside he did to me without spreading my legs." When she heard this she knew that she had been seen. And she cried and was ashamed. Therefore a woman or girl, committing fornication without the knowledge of her parents, cries whenever these learn of her offense. She went to sleep and waking up she thought of the turquoise. But hunt as much as she would, it could not be found. (There was no puberty ceremony for this woman.)

When the Sun rose again she found that there was no water. None but the two women, Marsh Wren and Titmouse, were there and those she despised. She used a blue and dark water jug for carrying water and a dark bead basket and blue bead basket (bowl) for cups. At noon she picked up the blue ones and went to the water. This was at a place called waterfall under a curbed rock ledge (over which the water trickled). At the bottom there was a small pool with white clay in it. And the splash of the trickling water as it came over the rock into the pool was distinctly heard. That accounts for the name "trickling or splashing water."

In filling her pots she was in the habit of filling the pots on a small stone. She would then wash her hands, face, and body in the pool. As she was doing this now, she observed the trickling water and looked up. Lewd women in passion, therefore, have the habit of washing their hands, face, body, and privates. Looking thus at the water she was tempted to *copulam habere cum agua*. At once she stretched herself below the fall of water and permitted this to flow into her. She then arose and dressed and now felt a piece of white shell near her belt which was not perforated and as large as one's thumbnail. This again she placed within her belt.

She returned to the hogan with the water, and that evening again recalled the events of the day. And again some moccasin-gamblers sang out: "From trickling water my shadow, come stand here and freeze." When she heard this she cried and realized again that she had been seen. Again she went to sleep and forgot the white shell until she woke at dawn. But now her search was in vain.

Four days after this her abdomen bulged and she found herself pregnant. Indications of this were more evident after the lapse of four more days. It appears that the turquoise and white shell which she had lost had impregnated her. Thus, eight days had passed and the Marsh Wren Woman and Titmouse Woman, whom she hated, visited her. A pregnant woman, therefore, is said to be cranky. After four days again had passed, about dawn she was visibly approaching labor and felt ill. She therefore asked the two women to come and assist her as she was about to give birth. To this they agreed and told her to go ahead, that they would presently follow. For this reason if there are women-folk in the vicinity of a woman in labor, they are called upon to assist.

The Marsh Wren Woman came from the south, Titmouse Woman from the north. "What shall we do, my Grandchild?" they asked her. At once Marsh Wren told Titmouse Woman to bring her some white clay. She went as far as jagged rocks—three miles—and brought some bluish-black clay. For this reason the baby to be born was black. In the Black Rock rincon she found birth (?) clay which she spread out in the hogan. While she labored, Talking-god-who-stands-in-dawn stood at the doorway. "I shall help also, my Grandchildren," he said. "Al-right," they told him.

He then blew dawn four times upon the palms of his hands, then (he) placed them on the girl's abdomen, sang four songs and left. When daylight appeared she gave birth. The Titmouse Woman dried the baby, Marsh Wren Woman cut the navel and tied it with dew cord. The afterbirth was carried out by Titmouse Woman. Marsh Wren Woman bathed the child in collected water and spring water (Water Child). Therefore Marsh Wren is called Shaken-in-dew. The mother of the child gave Marsh Wren a blanket of darkness in which the baby was wrapped.

Again the mother labored. "What is the matter?" Marsh Wren asked. "You still seem to be with child." "Yes, it seems so," she answered. Titmouse Woman now cleaned out the premises and asked Marsh Wren Woman to bring in clean soil. At once she left for red adobe buttes from where she brought red earth croppings, a brownish-red clay, which she spread out.

Another baby was born. This time Marsh Wren Woman dried it while Titmouse Woman cut the navel and tied it with sagebrush (?) fiber. Marsh Wren Woman bathed it in collected dews, wherefore it is called *tó bá jíshchíní*.[68] She also removed the afterbirth. This one was born during the night. And these two were to slay the *yé'iitsoh* later on. For the second boy the mother chose dawn into which Titmouse Woman placed it, then laid it next to the first one.

"Dig out a hole for me," the mother said to Marsh Wren Woman. They procured piñon and juniper, then dug the pit as ordered. Therefore, *naayéé' neezgháni* has a rattle made of piñon which is blackened (and a hand long), while *tó bá jíshchíní* has one of juniper which is reddened. The boys were then placed in the dugout which was covered with a stone slab and dirt, leaving no traces of them. She did this because many gray, scrubby *yé'iitsoh* would prowl about the hogan. They carried head bags with stone axe and arrows in them. These were slung over their backs as they went about in search of humans, whom they devoured.

About noon one of these scrubby *yé'iitsoh* happened about, searched the neighborhood and left. At night she nursed the children and replaced them. Early in the morning she nursed them again and replaced them for the day out of fear of the *yé'iitsoh*. Four days she repeated this. They were large enough by that time to crawl about, so she put them to sleep with her but replaced them in the morning. They had left some tracks in front of the hogan which one of the *yé'iitsoh* was quick to detect. "Oho! these are children's tracks. Any children here?" he asked. "No," she said. "I should like very much to have children around. So to satisfy myself I made some tracks in the sand, this way." And with the bottom of her closed fist she made a fair imitation. "Sho! Isn't that wonderful!" he said. But under his breath he swore at his ill luck.

After four more days the boys were quite large and well built, but they had no sense. "Make us an arrow and a bow, Mother," they said

[68]This is the informant's version. The name is usually interpreted to mean Born for Water.

one night. "But how shall I make you a bow and arrow? I have nothing
to make them with." Still she made them a bow of flash lightning and
two arrows each of zigzag lightning. They were very poor bows and
arrows. In time they were quite accustomed to seek their hiding place
at dawn. Before sun-up, Kingbird and Chickadee would come around.
At these they would string their bows even though they called them
shináli. And when the birds saw the boys take aim at them, they would
say, "my grandson is angry."

   Eight days after their birth they were quite large but showed no
sense at all. They would constantly fight and wrestle, strike and kick
one another. Then one night as they sat before their mother, they
asked her questions. "Mother, who is our father?" "Ah," she said, "you
have no father. Who would be your father anyway?" And they struck
each other again repeating this. "But have we no father? Tell us, my
Mother," they said. "My Children, you have no father," she repeated.
And they fought again, each saying to the other, "you have no father,
you have no father." When it was late they retired.

   And at dawn they stepped out and saw the Kingbird and Chickadee again. And Marsh Wren and Titmouse Woman, too, were there.
They greeted the boys and mentioned that they had washed them at
their birth. But the boys shot their arrows at them and had them
dodging sideways. And whenever the yé'iitsoh inquired, their mother
deceived them. This was the ninth day. And again they asked their
mother. "Bunch cactus is your father," she told them, "and prickly
pear, and braided cactus. Therefore your hair is dirty and scrubby."
And again they would strike one another and with each blow say:
"Bunch cactus is your father," and "prickly pear is yours."

                          *   *   *

   The account which follows here is a better version of the birth of
Changing Woman. After a day's hesitation, the informant decided to
break off the preceding account and to give instead the Blessing Rite
version of events. The following narrative, therefore, continues the
account which was interrupted earlier, on page 150.

   When First Man and his four companions—First Woman, First
Boy, First Girl, and First Scolder—were leaving for Spruce Mountain,
First Man fancied that he saw something. They were travelling along
about noon when First Man remarked: "I thought I had seen a person,
but probably not. I thought it was a tree sticking up with a large head.
Perhaps this is an evil omen." "That seems to be bothering you some,"
First Woman remarked to him. "Who knows? Something may happen.

It appears that way to me," he answered. Therefore, whenever a person uses this expression as here, it is taken for granted that his intent is evil.

They reached the top of Spruce Mountain, the appearance of which seemed satisfactory and inviting. While they had regard for holy things, First Scolder had no regard for anything. First Man then planted a white mirage one finger joint in length at the east, a blue one of the same size in the south, a yellow one in the west, one of various colors in the north, and one of rock crystal in the center. With these he made a hogan for them. Here they had lived four days when, in the morning, they heard the cry of a child.

First Man mentioned it, but First Woman said: "What are you talking about? You always have something in your head." Nothing more was said that day. But going out at dawn the next day they both heard the cry. After a discussion of the matter, both went in search of footprints but found none. This worried them and the cheeks of First Man were drawn, his lips parched. "Why should you worry?" First Scolder said to them. "Have you no eyes? If a child cries, surely there should be some tracks." "But we have searched everywhere and found nothing," they said.

The following morning again the cry was heard. When heard on the first day the cry seemed to be distant, on the second day somewhat closer, today still closer. First Man approached rapidly but the cry seemed to cease as he approached, and again he searched in vain. This worried them so that they even neglected food. "Whose child is this?" he mused, "I have made Dawn, Earth, Sky, and know that it can not be born of them." So he worried through the night.

Again at dawn the cry of the child was heard and this time at close range. And quickly taking rainbow, stubby rainbow, reflected sunred, and dawn, he rolled these into a ball which he blew in the direction of the cry. And sure enough when he reached the place, he found a baby lying there. Below it coming out of the east he noticed a dawn cord, below it from the south a skyblue cord, from the west an evening twilight cord, and below it from the north a cord of darkness. These seemed to rock the child so that it cried. It was a girl he found, resting on dawn and darkness. With rainbow and stubby rainbow slung below it he raised the child. And because it lay on dawn and darkness, he inferred that it must be the child of Dawn Man and Darkness Woman. And he carried it to his home.

"Whose child is this?" said First Woman[69] who was very happy. "Dawn is her father, Darkness her mother," she said. Therefore

---

[69]The narrative does not allude to First Woman as the wife of First Man.

womenfolk rejoice when a child is born in the neighborhood. After four days the child had grown sufficiently to be able to speak. In the folds of her right ear they noticed that a Small White Wind had been placed, and Dark Wind in her left ear, but (they) were ignorant of the fact that these Little Winds had been placed there from within the Dawn and the Darkness (her father and mother).

And whenever she addressed First Man and First Woman as "my Father, my Mother" or addressed First Boy and First Girl as "my Older Brother, my Older Sister," she was told from her earfolds that these were not her father, mother, brother and sister. And while First Man, and First Woman knew her parents, they were not aware that these were keeping the child informed in this manner.

After four days had again passed, the girl was well grown. She was not very tall and strong, but middle-sized. Her fingernails and toenails and her eyewhites shone brilliantly, and First Man more and more realized how different she was from other children. The girl herself knew her parents, but for once it had escaped First Man and First Woman that the girl knew. After eight days the child would not eat their food. Supernaturally she was fed with Dawn pollen and white corn pollen from the east, with Evening Twilight pollen and yellow corn pollen from the west, with Skyblue pollen and blue corn pollen from the south, with Darkness pollen and varicolored corn pollen from the north. This she ate and, whenever she was hungry, she would step outside, call to these directions and food was brought to her. Thus she could refuse the food set before her by First Man and First Woman. Still when they called her *asdzą́ nádleehí*, she responded *yá*, what?

After four additional days had passed she was fully grown. She was very sensible. Her eyes, her fingernails, her whole bearing impressed them as very superior to their own. At daylight of the twelfth morning she announced: "*kinsisdá* (my periods are on)." First Woman at once visited Marsh Wren Woman and Bridled Titmouse Woman asking them to assist. The two women stood outside. (This is the beginning of the puberty ceremony for maidens in their first menses.)

First Man spread out sheets of dark cloud, dark mist, darkness and dawn, then placed a turquoise and white shell upon them. The white shell he rubbed between his hands but did not inhale its breath because something seemed to withhold him. The same he repeated with the turquoise. He then held both toward the Sun, who sent sunray and sunlight upon them. Then again he rubbed the jewels between his hands. He then pressed the body of *asdzą́ nádleehí* with the white shell and with the turquoise, just as the "straightening" of the body is done today. Incidentally, too, these were the nuptials between Sun and Changing Woman, who became his. Today if one desires a girl in marriage, he asks someone to intercede for him. Here the blessing *(hózhǫ́ǫ́jí)* begins and *hózhǫ́ǫ́jí* songs for the chants of any description must be borrowed from this rite.[70]

As he pressed her body, it became white shell and turquoise. The two women mentioned were not evil. Marsh Wren Woman then placed collected water and spring water on the spreads, then washed the body of *asdzą́ nádleehí* with these, then rubbed and pressed it into fine shape. In the east she collected dews and pollens of flowers which she sprinkled on the girl's body—likewise dews and pollens of flowers from the south, west, and north. First Man then rolled up the spreads and laid them aside.

Next she was clothed in moccasins and shoestrings of white shell. Her legs were wrapped in white shell leggings, a white shell skirt around the waist, her sleeves were fringed, wristlets of white shell, and earbands (and) headband all were of white shell, turquoise, abalone, and jet. White shell was placed as a pendant below her eyes. For four consecutive mornings he ran east and back, south and back, west and back, north and back. "In days to come they shall not do what I have done," she said, "but they shall only run towards the east and return." Neither was she bathed afterwards again, and her jewels she had not received from First Man.

On the third day (fourth night) was *bijį́* (closing night). And the Holy Ones heard of it and said: "My song will be sanctified there and my ceremony also shall be sanctified there." Dawn, Darkness, Sky-blue, Evening Twilight People, Talking-god and Calling-god, Hunch-eye, White Corn Boy, Yellow Corn Girl, Pollen Boy, Cornbeetle Girl, all good and holy people gathered there. Dawn brought white corn-meal, Evening Twilight (brought) yellow cornmeal with which they sprinkled her body. Today, too, after a ceremonial bath the body is dried with white and yellow cornmeal. At the *bijį́* the people from *sisnajini*, Mount Taylor, San Francisco Peaks, and Perrin's Peak were there. Also those from Mountain Woman and Water Woman, Spruce Mountain and Moving-around-the-mountain.

The ceremony was begun with twelve hogan songs which at present are also sung at *hózhǫ́ǫ́jí*. (If one is forgotten, the ceremony is discontinued.) Twelve songs followed this. Talking-god then swept the hogan and began:

Asdzą́ nádleehí biyáázh nishłį́igo naashá—Changing Woman's
    Child I am, as such I go about
Shihooghan nitsítł'ahgi dootł'izhii k'ét'ááshchį́igo íí'á—My hogan
    in its rear (portion) turquoise in shape of prayerstick stands

---

[70]This Blessing part of such chants is either called *doo iigháázh*, "no sleep," or *bihózhǫ́ǫ́jí*, "its blessing side." This is part of every chantway.

Shihooghan ya'atniigi yootgai k'ét'áashchíjgo íi'á—My hogan in its
   center white shell in shape of prayerstick stands
Shihooghan honishhahgi diichití k'ét'áashchíjgo íi'á—My hogan
   near its fireplace abalone in shape of prayerstick stands
Shihooghan bá hástł'ahgi báashzhinii k'ét'áashchíjgo íi'á—My
   hogan in its (side) corners jet in shape of prayerstick stands
Shihooghan ch'é'etiingi tséghádińdínii k'ét'áashchíjgo íi'á—My
   hogan at doorway rock crystal prayerstick shaped stands
Shihooghan binaadi ch'il ahéénáánálch'ozh—My hogan in its
   surroundings plants round about stand (the broom)
Shihooghan binaadi tsin ahééní'á—My hogan in its surroundings
   wood stands about (four hogan posts)
Shihooghan binaadi tsé ahééní'á—My hogan in its surroundings
   stones lie about (millstones)
Shihooghan binaadi dził ahééní'á—My hogan in its surroundings
   mountains are set about (four sacred mountains)
Shihooghan biyi'déé' tó adaazłį—My hogan from within waters
   flow away
Shihooghan binaadi hashch'éétti'í (bił) ahééh nízin—My hogan its
   surroundings Talking-god appreciates
Shihooghan binaadi hashchéoghan (yił) ahééh nízin—My hogan
   around it Calling-god appreciates
Shihooghan binaadi naadą́'ałgai ashkii (yił) ahééh nízin—My
   hogan around White Corn Boy appreciates
Shihooghan binaadi naadą́'ałtsoi at'ééd (yił) ahééh nízin—My
   hogan around Yellow Corn Girl appreciates
Shihooghan binaadi tádídíín ashkii (yił) ahééh nízin—My hogan
   around Pollen Boy appreciates
Shihooghan binaadi anitł'ánii at'ééd (yił) ahééh nízin—My hogan
   around Cornbeetle Girl appreciates
Są'ah naagháí nishłįįgo naashá—Long life I bring I go about
Bik'eh hózhǫ́ nishłįįgo naashá—Happiness as one who is I go about
Shitsijį' hózhǫ́ǫgo naashá—Before me it being pleasant I go about
Shikéédéé' hózhǫ́ǫgo naashá—Behind me it being pleasant I go
   about
Shiyaagi hózhǫ́ǫgo naashá—Below me it being pleasant I go about
Shik'igi hózhǫ́ǫgo naashá—Above me it being pleasant I go about
Shinaa t'áá ałtso hózhǫ́ǫgo naashá—My around(ness) all it being
   pleasant I go about
Shizaad hahózhǫ́ǫgo naashá—My speech going forth nicely I go
   about
Są'ah naagháí bik'eh hózhóón nishłįįgo naashá—Long-life Happi-
   ness I so being go about
Shihii álílee naashá—I especially supernaturally go about.

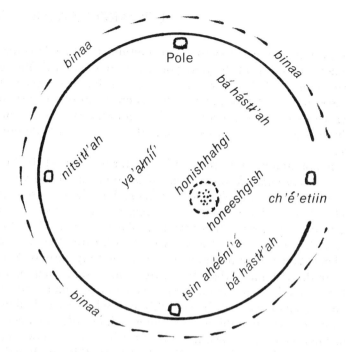

Ceremonial names of hogan parts, places, and song

And in his song Talking-god mentioned other names for the poles and other parts of the hogan than those which First Man had given. The singing then continued all night, some (were) singing two and more songs. No chantway songs were allowed, only Blessing songs so that these are superior and the former are always subordinated to the latter.

Toward morning First Woman was told to make soap suds which she did by spitting into her hands. With the suds *asdzá̧ nádleehí* washed her head, and with the water dripping from her hair she ran again east, south, west, and north. After that they sang the song of twelve words. And when she returned from running, she combed her hair with two songs. They now put white clay from *naasilá* into a white shell basket, then with a rainray they spotted her legs, trunk, and arms white. These two (sets of) songs (for the race and white clay) alone are now used at the puberty rites for girls. At other no-sleep ceremonies others songs are employed. But those mentioned here they sang over this virgin.

She now had become a matured woman. That day she did not sleep. Four days after this ceremony First Woman said to her: "Why do you refuse to eat when I cook for you?" "Oh," the girl said, "I am not hungry." "Well," said the other, "I have been cooking for you every day, but you do not seem to appreciate anything (that is) done for you. And when people speak to you, you seem to resent it." But *asdzą́ nádleehí* replied: "If I do not care to eat, you should not try to force me. I need not eat if I do not care to. There is no reason for you to quarrel with me on this account." "Oh," said First Woman, "I merely thought it was not the proper thing that you should despise my cooking."

"I am not asking you to cook and work for me and get tired on my account," *asdzą́ nádleehí* answered. "If anybody speaks to you," the other replied, "immediately you talk back. You show no respect for anybody." "Well, if your mind is in accord with your speech, I am willing to do as you say, otherwise not," she answered. First Woman then said: "I raised you, I cleansed you, I took care of you." "Oh no you did not. You are not my mother, you are not my parents. You had nothing to do with me. Others took care of me!" said *asdzą́ nádleehí*.

This angered them. At once First Woman put blue and yellow jewels into a pot of water and stirred this mess while it was boiling. All this while she was mumbling something, while *asdzą́ nádleehí* was cooking her own meal at the other side of the hogan. "I know who you are," she again addressed them. "Your bellies are filled with evil. You are witches, bean-shooters, evil-wishers who tell people they will die, just to frighten them. Just go your way and I'll go my own." This speech angered them so much that they did not notice that the food they were eating was hot and steaming. It happened that this food was all sorts of evil, smallpox and chicken pox, whooping cough and similar diseases.

And First Man spoke: "I hope that my thoughts are always fulfilled. May it always be as I think. Let the red and yellow in the east always bring on these diseases." And *asdzą́ nádleehí* replied: "May they all return upon your head. My power will prevent your evil, my streaks shall appear to also prevent your evil influence in due season." They then left in anger and fury and went to *niyá nikéháaghał* where all these evils exist.

She then gathered white corn, yellow, blue, and varicolored corn, put these with seeds and other edibles into a bundle and left for the west. "My ceremonies will be greater than theirs," she said. "They will help my people more than theirs can injure them." And with these various plants and herbs she took with her Dark Cloud, Dark Mist, Dark Thunder, and so on. Therefore, all good rain (female rain) and good edibles come from the west and from her.

She walked supernaturally to the west on rainbow, stubby rainbow, reflected sunred, and sunray. Her house is there over the horizon, on the surface of the ocean at a level spot. Her house was made exactly like that of the Sun by Sky Man, Earth Woman, Dawn Man, Darkness

Woman, Evening Twilight Man, and Skyblue Woman. Sun made his
own house but these persons made her house because she was the child
of Dawn and Darkness. The chambers, doors, and other details mentioned for the Sun's house were duplicated here. The only difference is
a *ná'ol dah naa'eeł*, floating object (?), in the rear of her home, which
is a medicine.[71]

The door guards are identical, but while there are four water
bodies in front of Sun's residence in the east, her house in the west has
four rainbows extending out from one central point.

The Water Monsters, Water Horses, and so forth, are the same as
in the east. Four white shells, and four canes each of turquoise, aba-

Her cane

lone, and jet were made for her. These are pointed at the bottom,
tapered up to proper thickness and provided with a grip for the hand.
This woman committed no adulteries with others, as is related of other
women. When she arrived in the west, the six persons mentioned
received her with all respect, called her Daughter and Relative, while
no mention was made of the people she had just left. They told her that
they had made this home for her.

WHITE SHELL WOMAN

She now threw down a turquoise which changed into a turquoise
stool, and a white shell which changed into a white shell stool. She
entered the four chambers in the east, from which she returned dressed
completely in white shell. She entered the four chambers in the south
from which she returned dressed completely in turquoise. She entered
the four chambers in the west and returned dressed in abalone. She
entered the chambers in the north and emerged dressed completely in
jet. She then reversed the order, entering north, west, south, and east
from which she appeared dressed in white shell. Therefore she is called
White Shell Woman, but in prayer she is addressed both Changing
Woman *(asdzą́ nádleehí)* and White Shell Woman, and he four canes
are also mentioned in prayer. Her house also changes color—white,
blue, yellow, and at times black. As said, her house was made by
others, the Sun built his own house.

---

[71]No further details of this are added in the narrative.

The six people left (to) *asdzą́ nádleehí* (the) creation of man and domestic animals in the same supernatural way. As for the flints, they were identical in both homes, and there were jet, turquoise, abalone, and red-white stone rattles in her house, just like those in the Sun's home. And when each of these rattled in turn, the little one of the Winds and the Child of Darkness, which had been set in her earfolds, whispered to her that the Sun was coming. The doors in the east, south, west, and north creaked as Sun entered. The Sun Carrier wrapped his disc in dark cloud and dark mist then hung it up.

He sat on the turquoise stool. There were also two beds, one of turquoise in the south, another of white shell in the north. The Sun Carrier slept in the turquoise, she in the white shell bed, and this was their marriage. So it is done among better people today, they are married properly. She is not the woman of infamy, as many say. Four days after this, a fine young man entered the house of the Sun and greeted him: "My (Maternal) Uncle," and Sun returned the greeting, as they were brothers. This was the Moon Carrier.[72] Four days after the visit of the Sun she was pregnant with child, and twelve days after this she gave birth to twins, a boy and a girl. The boy was called Who-stands-in-turquoise, the girl (was called) Who-stands-in-white-shell. The Sun made a turquoise bow and arrow for the boy and one of white shell for the girl. They eventually founded the Male Branch of Shootingway with these arrows.

The Moon Carrier called the children *shináli*, "my (Son's) Grandchildren." He made dolls of black and blue flints which he called "my Sons-in-law," because they represented the blue and white children in the west. Twelve days after the birth of these children *asdzą́ nádleehí* made the people of the earth.

From the epidermis of her chest, which she rolled in her hand, she formed the *kiyaa'áanii* (High House People), from that of her back the *honágháahnii* (Who-walk-around-one People), from that of her right armpit the *tó dích'ii'nii* (Bitter Water People), of her left armpit the *tótsohnii* (Big Water People), which are the first four Navajo clans.[73] For each she made a cane. She then made a collection of jet, turquoise, white shell, red-white stone, river clay, water foam, water specular iron ore, water pollen, which she rolled until her skin peeled with it. This ball she placed on an abalone shell (?) next to the four others. At this point *begochidí* or *begołgai, begołtsoi, begoshzhiní* (all names for the Moon Carrier) placed night's fire (?) in the same row with the

---

[72]According to this account the gourd children, who were appointed to be sun and moon carriers, were twins. The address "my Uncle" would imply that the relationship between the two is at least a generation apart.

[73]Informant was a *kiyaa'áanii*.

others. The order would be from her left to right starting at "a" (and moving) to "e" ("d" and "e" are treated as one). These she covered with

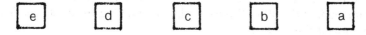

a sheet of turquoise, white shell, abalone, and red-white stone, then (she) sang the Woman's Songs after which she uncovered them.

She then spread a sheet of turquoise (see "a") on which she placed turquoise and white shell; then on a sheet of white shell (see "b") she put jet and abalone. On the first sheet (see "a") she placed the two people made of the epidermis of her breast and back. On the second (see "b") she placed the two people made from epidermis of her armpits. On a third sheet of abalone (see "c") she placed jet, turquoise, white shell, abalone, red-white stone, (together) with the ball mentioned above, as these were to become horses of the color of the jewels—sheep, hogs, and chickens. On the fourth (sheet) she again placed black, blue, yellow, white, and pink mirage to become various White People. And for these on (the) fifth cover (see "e") she placed dark, blue, yellow, and white mirage to be their horses. Therefore the horses of mirage are larger than those given to the Navajos (see "c"), who never received any of these large horses.

Begochidí, however, objected to abalone and red-white stone on the third spread (see "c") and asked them to be added to the fifth one (see "e"). Instead, two other mirage stones, dark and spotted, were added to the fifth for cattle and hogs, respectively.

The first ball from her breast was kneaded with blue medicine and dew, the ball from her back with white medicine and dew. The ball from her right armpit was kneaded with yellow medicine and dew, the one from her left armpit with pink medicine and dew. For the third sheet (see "c") she kneaded dark cloud with jet, blue mist with turquoise, yellow mist with abalone, white mist with white shell, varicolored clouds with what was to be sheep, pink cloud with goats-to-be. For the fourth (see "d") she kneaded dark mirage with jet, blue mirage with turquoise, yellow mirage with abalone, white mirage with white shell, pink mirage with red-white stone.

For the fifth sheet (see "e") she kneaded dark mirage with dark tall medicine, blue mirage with blue tall medicine, yellow mirage with yellow tall medicine, white mirage with white tall medicine, then (mixed) dark mirage with dark tall medicine, then spotted mirage with spotted tall medicine.

In kneading on sheets "a" and "b", the first and second balls representing her epidermis were kept separate; those on the other three spreads ("c, d, e") were each kneaded into one lump.

She then covered the whole with spreads of white shell, turquoise, dark cloud, and dark mist, making a quadruple cover. She then sang four songs for each ball on "a" and "b"—making sixteen songs—and four for each of the other three ("c, d, e")—making twelve songs. Then she removed the covers.

She then covered them with two spreads of sunray and sunlight, then replaced the first four covers again. Again she sang four times four songs for the first four balls "a" and "b", and as before four apiece for the other three ("c, d, e"). Then (she) uncovered them. The first two ("a" and "b") she formed like humans, of the third ("c") she made dark, blue, yellow, and white horses, goats, and sheep. The fourth ("d") she again shaped into figures of men—white, blue, yellow, and pink. Horse figures also—dark, blue, yellow, white—and (she shaped) cattle and hogs of "e". Those on "d" were to be the horses of the men, while those on the third sheet ("c") were to be the horses and animals for the first two spreads of "a" and "b".

Of the remnants of the third spread ("c") she formed burros and mules. Similarly of remnants of the fifth spread ("e") she formed burros, mules, goats, and sheep. Again she covered them with dark cloud, dark mist, rainbow, stubby rainbow, (and) with dark, blue, white, yellow, and pink mirage. For the three spreads ("a, b, c") she sang four horse songs, for the other two ("d, e") also four. When she removed the covers, the people as well as animals had become large and smooth. Again she covered them with sunray, sunlight, white dew, and yellow dew to moisten them. For the first three ("a, b, c") she sang four songs, for the two ("d, e") also four, and when she removed the covers they all seemed quite alive.

Into the first man on the first spread ("a") she placed a blue wind, into the second a white wind. In the first of the second spread ("b") she placed a yellow wind, in the second a dark wind. (This accounts for four people.) On the third spread ("c") a dark wind glittered as it was forced into the (soft) jet horse, similarly a blue wind (glittered as it was forced) into the turquoise horse, a white wind (as it was forced) into the white shell horse, a yellow wind (as it was forced) into the abalone horse, a varicolored wind (as it was forced) into the mule and burro, and likewise the wind glittered which was forced into the mirage sheep and goats.

On the fourth spread ("d") the dark wind glittered as it was forced into the jet man figure, the blue wind glittered as it was forced into the turquoise man figure, the white wind (as it was forced) into white shell, the yellow wind (as it was forced) into abalone, and the glittering or pink wind (as it was) forced into the red-white stone figures.

On the fifth spread ("e") the dark wind glittered as it was forced into the dark mirage figure (of horse), similarly the blue wind (as it was forced) into blue mirage, white wind into white mirage, yellow wind into yellow mirage, a dark wind into the added dark mirage figures of sheep, goats, chickens, and a spotted wind (glittered as it was forced) into the spotted mirage figures of cattle and hogs.

The parts of all man figures ("a, b, d") were made of these materials. Our toe and fingernails of abalone shell, our bone of white shell, our flesh of red-white stone, our hair of darkness, our skull of dawn, our brains of white shell, our white of the eye of white shell, our tears of collected (sky) waters, our pupils of shaken-off stone mica and rock crystal, our ear (lobes) of red-white stone, white shell oval beads make us hear. Our nose was made of abalone, our esophagus (?) of white shell in strips, our teeth were made of white shell, a straight lightning furnished our tongue, a rainbow our arms, plants of all kinds furnished our pubic hair and skin pores *(nihichin)*.[74]

For the animals these materials were used: Their feet were made of striped mirage, red arrowpoint and dark mirage were used for their soles. Their tails were made of drooping rain, their ears of plants of all kinds, their bodies of dark cloud, their moving power (or legs) of zigzag lightning, their eyes of big star, their teeth of white shell, their lips of big bead, their tongue of straight lightning, their man hair of *tsíighá bi'eezh (?)* material. Black, blue, yellow, white and glittering winds were given them to tell them things. With sunray and sunlight glittering in color they eat, they say. All horses and other animals ("c, e") were prepared (dressed) in this manner.

She then stepped to the west side. White and yellow water, greasy in appearance, she put on the human figures and the white became our marrow, the yellow greasy water our sinews. She next covered all, "a" through "e", with a sheet of dawn, darkness, skyblue, and evening twilight. She then stepped over the two ("a, b") east to west, south to north, and *begochidi* did likewise over the three ("c, d, e"). She then threw the sheets back—east, south, west, north—on the two ("a, b") and *begochidi* did likewise on the three ("c, d, e").

The Sun now filled his jet pipe with tobacco which he lit with rock crystal, then blew the smoke over them from east, south, west, north, and down from above. He repeated the same smoke with a turquoise, white shell and abalone pipe. The people then sat upright. And those of the first two spreads ("a, b") spoke the language of Changing Woman while those of the fourth spread ("d") could not speak it. So she took a dark bow about three feet in length with a bowstring of rainbow. On this she placed the people of "d" and the animals of "e", and shot them up four times. And far up the sound of *mal, mal* could

---

[74]Skin pores, or rather the dirt which settles in them.

be heard. Then she blew four times on them and they landed beyond the ocean.

One of these people became the god whom the Americans worship; the others were (the Anglo-)Americans. The others were the cliff dwellers, Pueblos, Mexicans, and other (ancestral) Holy People whom she shot up, then (she) blew after them. Of these some were male, some female, so that they gave birth in time. The animals likewise increased.

A turquoise-perfect-shell was given to the *kiyaa'áanii* (clan) with a turquoise cane. A white-perfect-shell was given to the *honágháahnii* (clan) with a white shell cane. The *tó dích'ii'nii* and *tótsoh* clans received no perfect shells but received canes—the former an abalone (cane and) the latter a cane of jet.

Talking-god then placed next to the four people the following: white corn, yellow corn, russet (?) corn, round corn (female), male corn, blue (corn, with) striped, gray, (and) varicolored corn, plants and herbs, pollen, collected and spring water, which he sanctified with four songs. All people were made to look alike, and thus dressed they sat up and smoked. But Talking-god was jealous of the presents (perfect shells and canes) given to the people. Therefore, at present, also people get jealous of others who receive gifts.

From First Man and First Woman, *asdzą́ nádleehí* had obtained (sacred) mountain soil of which she distributed among them. But she kneaded this with medicine taken from the *ná'ol* at her house, making small packages of it for them. Therefore this was the finest kind of medicine. She then added small particles of jewels, of jet, turquoise, abalone, red abalone, (and) red-white stone. She called them her children and promised them corn of all colors and plant seeds so that these all originate with White Shell Woman. When, therefore, corn will not grow and ripen, women too will not give birth and (this) is an omen of the distraction or cessation of the Earth. The jet and other jewels horses she kept, and the Navajos never received these.

The *kiis'áanii* (Pueblos) were made of turquoise, therefore this jewel is more plentiful among them. The Navajos, however, obtained their jewels directly from her. Therefore, all of this (portion of the account) is *hózhǫ́ǫ́jí* (Blessing side) of (the Upward-moving) chantway (and) there is nothing (included) as the *hózhǫ́ǫ́jí* begins with the ceremony over Changing Woman and continues with her own performances at her home (as described in this section). The happenings in the home of the Sun are considered as belonging to Chantways (*hatáalk'ih*). Thus, dark clouds, dark mist and other pleasant phenomena, and all plants originate from her.

From Walled Adobe she brought a Mountain Lion for us, the *kiyaa'áanii*. From the place called the Fourth-chamber-of-dark-mountain she brought a bear which she presented to the *honághááh-nii*. These, therefore, are their pets. Other animals which were made pets[75] were a Big Snake from Pair-of-rocks-set-upon-another, a porcupine from (Twin) Mountain Buttes, and a weasel from Big Adobe Incline. And because the people possessed the said medicine and jewels, these animals were charmed to remain with them.

[75]The account does not state that pet animals were given to the *tó dích'íi'nii* and *tótsohnii* clans. Perhaps this is implied.

Editor's Note: This paragraph appears to be the end of the digression into Blessingway mythology. Apparently, this digression resulted when the informant felt the necessity to explain the exact relationship between the Woman who conceived from Sun and Dripping Water and Changing Woman.

9

The Journey

In the east there was a Dawn Mountain to which Talking-god led them saying: "I and Calling-god will accompany you on your journey." But he said this because he much desired to acquire their perfect shells. All day, therefore, they travelled on this Dawn Mountain accompanied by Talking-god and Calling-god. In the evening they slept but on the following morning they mounted a Darkness Mountain on which they again travelled all day. On two successive days they travelled on Sky-blue Mountain and Evening Twilight Mountain, respectively.

About noon they reached the top of San Francisco Peaks. Here Talking-god drove away the Winds, Dark Cloud, and Dark Mist, then went into hiding. Following this, the heat became unbearable. "We are suffering with thirst," they called out aloud. And when Talking-god appeared, they said to him: "This heat is about killing us, my Granduncle." "What can be done," he replied. "It seems we must bear with it." "Even so, you came with us, therefore we thought you might be able to help," they again said to him. "Yes," he said, "we could help, if we only had the wherewithal to do so." The two (Talking-god and Calling-god) knew well enough! They again begged them and pleaded four times with them but were refused.

They then produced the turquoise-perfect-shell and passed this from the left foot of Calling-god around his forehead down to the right toe, then repeated the same motion with the white-perfect-shell on the right foot of Talking-god. Both inhaled the breath of the gifts four times. Then Talking-god sang the rain songs and at once the Sky was darkened with Dark Clouds. Zigzag and Straight Lightnings shot out, and it rained, and they drank.

Talking-god and Calling-god then spoke: "This is the last time that you have seen the *diyin* (Holy Ones), and you shall not see them again." And since then they have not been seen in *hózhǫ́ǫ́jí* (in the Blessing Rite). "Now you may continue your journey. And if at any time you are told that some person has seen the *diyin*, you will know that it is not true." But they said to the gods: "We are about to start on our journey and much desire your help for it." And Talking-god assured them: "True, we will not be seen again. But when you hear the twitter and chatter of small birds, you will know that we are nearby.

(169)

And when you call on us, make our prayerstick and offer (us) jewels of jet, abalone, white shell, turquoise, red abalone, and collected and spring water." When the people looked again, the two had disappeared and the perfect shells with them, and none have been seen since then.

On the top of San Francisco Peaks they placed a sacrifice of jewels at a spring. This was the first sacrifice and they sang six songs and ate a meal. They then sang another song, said a prayer and began their journey. The Bear and quadrupeds walked, the Big Snake had to be carried. They reached Awatobi (táala hooghan) where they found Pueblos. They were numerous and had their hair banged in front. They inspected one another and found that they were not alike, neither could they understand their speech.

They remained here four days then continued on to Bear Spring (present Fort Wingate). On the other side of this there was a ledge of white rock under which they built houses and stayed twelve days. The houses can still be seen (kin naagai—House-white-across-or-horizontally).

Mountain Lion and Weasel hunted for them, Big Snake did nothing, Bear remained at the doorway where he prayed and sang for them, the Porcupine cleaned their heads and picked their lice. After twelve days of camp they journeyed on to Bear Spring at which place the Bear scratched for water, which accounts for the name of the spring. As water was flowing from the spring they tarried there a long time then journeyed on to tóyéé', where there is a large cave under a rock below which they found water. When they spoke, the echo of their voices resounded so that one of them remarked doo ládó' hóyéé', isn't this frightening (which accounts for the place name). And they put their hands into the white clay and pressed the prints of their hands on the wall. And these handprints and the smoke of their fires can still be seen because they lived there a long time.

From here they moved to tséní tóhí. On a high rock mesa there was a depression, or rock basin, holding water. Therefore its name is Water-in-rock, near which they had camped. Big Snake was getting too heavy for them so they had dropped him before reaching this place. He lives under a white rock there. In the neighborhood there is a stretch of about an eighth of a mile long, covered with a poisonous weed called "Big Snake food" (tł'iistsohdą́ą́') which kills horses and sheep that eat it.

From there they journeyed to baa bík'aa'í where they found a cave with water. Again the echo of their voices resounded. The smoke of their campfires may still be seen there. (The journey is hózhǫ́ǫ́jí line.) After living there some time they went to Red-grass-hill-rim (southwest of Chinle).

Here they found tall Medicine (People) of various sizes. That night they heard voices and in the morning the tall Medicine People paid them a visit. One spoke in their own tongue and said: "I am a *kiyaa'-áanii*." At once they made friends and became affiliated with this clan. Together they camped here for four days, and (they) constantly greeted each other with "My Friend, my Brother" and other terms of relationship. They then told them: "Just a little farther on there are some people called *hashtł'ishnii* (Mud People), and farther on the *tó áhání* (Water-is-close).

When they came to these, the *honágháahnii* found that the *hashtł'ishnii* and *tó áhání* spoke their tongue. They called each other Brother and Friend, and thus these two were affiliated with the *honágháahnii*. From here they proceeded to a large body of water at the shores of which they found the *tábąąhí* (Shore People). The *honágháahnii* again called them "my Relatives," thus affiliating them.

To the north were ledges of red rock where people had built houses. These Holy People, therefore, were called *tséńjíkiní* (Red-rock-houses). A number of these rock houses were yellow which accounts for *tséńdziłtsooí* (Yellow-rock-houses). These were Holy People, and when these two clans disappear, the Navajos will disappear with them. The visitors to their homes addressed them Brother, Sister, and Daughter, as their speech was one. While the tall Medicine People eventually married those of *honágháahnii*, the latter do not intermarry with the newly-found clans.

They then reached a place called *táchí* where tobacco grew. Hence the Tobacco People of this place are called *táchii'nii* (Red-water People). The White-shell People found at *deeshchíí'* were called *deeshchíí'nii*, Riddle or Red-clay (Red-chalk) People. From there they moved to a body of water where these Water People were called *tł'ááshchíí* (Red-bottom) and *tsé nahabiłnii (?)*. They were also informed that the *tsi'naajinii* lived in a level place and (that) these were relatives of the *tł'ááshchíí* clan.

The *kiyaa'áanii* wore a fluffy bear-fur cap with two horns, and they found a place where the Bear People lived who wore similar caps. At *téhoogai* (White Valley) the *téhoogai* live who wear "a similar headgear," they said. They also found here the Corn People with long necks, and the Turkey People, who all became affiliated with the *kiyaa'áanii*.

At *dziłt'áád* (Face or Front-of-mountain) two streams ran out from the east, side by side, which accounts for the name of the people living here, *tó aheedłiinii* (Side-by-side-streams People). On the other side there was also a stream and its people were called *bįįh bitoodnii*, the Deer-spring People. These also belonged to the *kiyaa'áanii*.

The *kiyaa'áanii, honágháahnii, tó dích'íi'nii, tótsohnii* clans now held council what to do with the medicine (they) received from *asdzą́ nádleehí*, as they were afraid to lose it. They decided to cache it somewhere, take a small portion with them for the (time being), then return for a new supply. They sang four songs, then brought it to Tobacco-pipe-into-stream-flows *(nát'ostse' biihílį)* where it still is. They deposited it here by means of rainbow and stubby rainbow. And if the Sun and Lightnings are seen not to shine upon it, it is an omen that the *hózhǫ́ójí* is not practiced as it should be, or that additions have been made to it. And as they looked back in departing, they saw the (jewel) medicines grow. And it was ordained there and then that, if a mistake were ever made in the *hózhǫ́ójí*, some songs had to be sung near this place and that then the rainbows could be seen. This is not done frequently, and when the songs are sung correctly it is said that the rainbows can be seen to rest on the spot.

Meanwhile a change had come upon the Bear, Porcupine, and the other two pets, and they were found to be quick-tempered. They would sulk about, strike children, and speak very little. One night enemies sneaked up on them, but the Bear fought them off single-handedly while the Mountain Lion slept as the rest did. This accounts for the meanness of the Bear today. During the attack one of the men had said to Mountain Lion: "My Pet, we are sorely pressed, will you not help us?" In a bound Mountain Lion was through the smokehole, swept around the enemy, tore them to pieces or bit off their arms as he encircled them four times. After that he retired to his former place without a word. After this attack, however, the pets—the Bear, Mountain Lion, Porcupine, Weasel—had become so mean that they dismissed them to the mountains and decided to continue their journey without them. The *kiyaa'áanii*, therefore, will not kill a Bear, the *honágháahnii* are kind to a Mountain Lion and Weasel, and Porcupine furnish quills and medicine pouches. The people had promised that they would ever be good to them. And these enemies who attacked them were Utes.

From there they travelled to *hwiich'a*, Anthill (near Forked Cottonwood). Here they found Pueblo People living in white houses set in the east, blue houses in the south, yellow in the west, and spotted houses in the north. These scarcely spoke to them and when they did, they could not understand their language. They, therefore, travelled on to *tséyaa chahałheeł*, Under-rock-darkness (Chaco Wash), under which they camped. That night they heard people play the moccasin-game with counters, hidden ball, and striker. The animals of the day were lined up against the animals of the night, but at dawn the game was unfinished. The Bear hurried to the mountains, but the Sun struck him before he reached them. Therefore his back is red.

The Day People selected the south side, the Night People the north. For counters each side used 102 sticks in imitation of the 102 songs (?) in the underworld. Therefore, too, the 102 counters represent the age limit of 102 years which no man exceeds. The-youth-folded-in-dawn (Coyote) also was present at the game, which he had not witnessed before. As the game proceeded he jumped from one side to the other, whichever happened to be winning. The wager was for day or night so that, if the Day People won, they had to travel by night; if the Night People should win, they had to travel by day.

The White-headed and American Eagle, all flying and water animals, were present. *Yé'iitsoh*, too, had entered (and) nobody knew from where. At the time he was not wicked and did not devour humans as (he did) later, but (he) said he was the son of the Sun. As the people were out for fun, *yé'iitsoh* had suggested a moccasin-game which started the wager. Horned Toad whispered to his neighbor: "His name is *yé'iitsoh*." So that went the rounds and they poked fun at him. Thus, people sometimes amuse themselves at the expense of others.

All night they played.[76] When Dawn overtook them, all hurried to protect and dress themselves. Yellow-tail Hawk decorated his bill and tail yellow with white spots on his plumage, then flew off. White-headed Eagle, too, covered himself with white clay from shoulders to head. The *nak'e'ni* (Owl) made his bill and breast yellow. Magpie spotted himself black and white. The Skunk drew a white streak from the back of his head to his tail and white on his sides making him pinto (spotted). Badger daubed white spots on his forehead. Wildcat drew white and yellow spots over his whole body. Beaver painted himself yellow then added a coat of white. Otter rubbed himself with tallow then sprinkled white clay over this. Roadrunner produced two blue tail feathers which he stuck in his tail. Therefore his tail is thin and long.

Arrowsnake made himself striped, Bull Snake rolled himself in yellow clay. Bear and Crow, however, were fast asleep. Marsh Wren covered herself with yellow flag and added a long bill. Meadowlark decorated her breast yellow. Locust used earth pollen on himself which made him yellow. Horned Toad decorated himself in arrowpoints and lichen. They had all gone when someone stirred the Bear and Crow. "Get up, they are all gone!" he told them. The Bear quickly jumped up and in his haste he put the wrong shoe on his feet. Even then, as mentioned, he was late and overtaken by the Sun. Crow covered himself with charcoal and is now jet black, although he reached the mountains

---

[76]The account of this first moccasin game is given in greater detail by other informants. The present informant appears to have given only a hint here and there of the proceedings, though he adds a number of details not found elsewhere.

in good time. Though the game was played only on one occasion there, it is still in vogue among the Navajos. When the people searched in the morning, *yé'iitsoh* had disappeared and no tracks of the other players were seen.

That day some strangers visited them who spoke the same language. Asked where they had come from and where they were going, they replied that they were Pueblos from the east in search of food. And these were Coyote Pass (Jemez) People, and Black-house (Black-sheep) People and Blue-house (Salt) People. The Jemez came to the *tábąą diné* (Water-shore People) and shook hands, while the *tó dík'ǫzhí* (Salt Water clan) addressed the *áshįįhí* (Salt People) and Black-sheep People (as) relatives and friends. And all the Pueblo People and Navajos made friends and lived together, as is witnessed by their dwellings throughout the country. And they had black, blue, yellow, and white pots, and planted at Noisy Rocks, Jagged Rock, and so forth. Therefore one usually finds water and springs at such places (ruins).

And in those days they had no horses and sheep but they had elk, deer, buffalo, rabbits, and so on. Some of these *kiis'áanii* (Pueblo) lived in the ground, some had houses on elevations or hills. They carried the water (collected water) in dark pots from holy places in the west, and in blue pots from holy places in the east (spring water). Some Pueblos therefore call themselves Collected Water, others Spring Water (Water's Child). They put white moss and glittering moss into it, and reflected sunred and river clay, then (they) planted this water. Therefore it is found in their ruins. At large ruins this water was put into large pots on the east side and this water sprang forth. This water may be collected at Navajo Mountain, San Francisco Peaks, Perrin's Peak, (at) *sisnajini*, Mount Taylor, Taos, at Streams-side-by-side *(tó ahiidlį́)*, waters in the west and north, San Juan Mountains, and (at) the male and female mountains at (Zuni) Salt Lake. Close to such springs one may find river clay, pollen, water pollen, flag pollen.

Yiidiską́ą́góó nihokáá' diné hodideezlį́į'góó—"shizází yę́ę bito' haideeshnił." Jiníigo hajiiníiłgo, t'áá áko tó hadoona', jiní jiní.

In days to come, Earth-surface People, when they come into being, if (they) say this: "My pueblo of old, its water I shall take out," and if one digs (after) it, at once water comes out, they say. It is said.

In their language they called themselves *shizází*, therefore we say *anaasází*—Cliff or Ruin Dwellers. Therefore, if you dig at such places and repeat the words, "I want to dig up Cliff Dweller water," the water will be found, they say.

10

The Monsters

In time the Navajo clans intermarried and had many children. The Pueblos, too, had clans among themselves. There were Squash and Sparrow Hawk and Elk, Coyote, Badger and White Owl, and so on.[77] The Sun then laid out a spread of dark flint upon which *yé'iitsoh* was placed. The dark male figure (a doll) pressed and straightened his limbs. His body thus became dark flint on which he placed arrow-points, yellow, blue, white and flints of various colors, all with points down. Thus, Black Doll dressed the son of the Sun, *yé'iitsoh*, who also received a zigzag lightning arrow, one of straight lightning, a rainbow and a sunray arrow. Zigzag lightning, rainbow, stubby rainbow, and rainray were his travel means.

The Sun also took one of the young of a Water Monster which became *délgeed*, the Horned or Furrowing Monster. A young of White-headed Eagle from the Sky opening and a White Thunder were brought down and this became *tsé náhálé (?)* a monster eagle. As related, Water Monster in the underworld had given birth to a wild gourd which now became *tsé naagháliı*, Travelling Rock. While *yé'iitsoh* was the Sun's own son, the Horned Monster, Monster Eagle, and Travelling Rock were the Sun's pets.

Now the Sun and Moon Carriers were to receive a dead person for every journey made (across the skies). The marrow of these dead persons they gathered and formed a ball of it. This ghost's marrow they inserted, by means of a glittering sunlight, into earth grease (?) which produced the Snapping Vagina. The *yé'iitsoh*, Horned Monster, Eagle Monster, and Travelling Rock were dressed in dark flint by the Sun and (by) the (lifeless) man figure (doll). From the very center of the Sky the Sun shot *yé'iitsoh* down with a zigzag lightning, that is, he wrapped him in zigzag lightning and let him down on the top of Mount Taylor. The Horned Monster, Monster Eagle, and Travelling Rock,

---

[77]My notes read in this form. The mentioning of Pueblo clans in the previous sentence may possibly imply that clans of these plants and animals are meant. As it stands, one can also interpret that both the Navajos and Pueblos were well supplied with vegetable and meat foods, with awls, etc. However, one can hardly infer that Sparrow Hawk and Coyote were relished menus. It would seem, therefore, that Pueblo clans are meant.

(175)

too, were dropped on Mount Taylor from where Horned Monster was sent on zigzag lightning to Black Lake, (from where) Eagle Monster (was sent) to Winged Rock (Ship Rock), and Travelling Rock (was sent) to Wide Valley.

The Snapping Vagina cohabited with an oblong smooth stone and gave birth to Kicks-off-the-rock-rim. And again she cohabited with this stone and brought forth the Gray *yé'iitsoh*. Then (she cohabited) with dark Big Star and brought forth Who-slay-with-their-eyes. Then (she cohabited) with what lies within a mountain (rope-like) and brought forth Tracking Bear. From cactus *(ná'oołáałii)* Heaped Vagina was born. She next rubbed oblong smooth stone and dark pebble together and cohabited with this combination from which she gave birth to Two-crushing-rocks. Her union with milkweed brought forth twelve Roaming Antelopes. Her union with Singing (?) Reed brought forth Slicing Reeds; with Rainbow she produced Moving-sand-wall. With Tree Root she produced Endless Snake.

All of these monsters began to destroy and devour people. And this Snapping (Biting) Vagina gave birth to all of these. She went everywhere, to the ends of the Earth and Sky, to commit her adulteries with anything and everything. In being evil and wicked nothing similar to her can be found. To worship such a woman seems unreasonable. It is a mistake, therefore, to ascribe her wicked deeds to *asdzą́ nádleehí*, then pay her the homage she receives.

Some Pueblos have stories of a Monster Eagle that swooped down on them when she lived in the ruins. Part of the time they lived "in the dirt" (in underground pits) and when they saw these huge birds approaching they would crawl in to await their departure. Or, if the bird would not leave them, they would light a fire to scare it away.

Big *yé'ii* had his home near Mount Taylor and Hot Spring (Grants). He would strike his victim with his club of dark, blue, yellow, and varicolored flint, then devour him. Horned Monster ran at large over the country. His eyesight was keen and he would swallow his victims without chewing them.

At Ship Rock the Eagle Monster had provided five black flint points and five blue flint points, the former along the east, the latter along the west ridge of the rock. He would drop a captured man on the dark flint points and then eat them. A woman victim would be thrust on the blue flint points so that they would be shattered and be devoured by the two (monster) children below; after that they would go on another raid.

The Travelling Rock would run his victims down four times, carry them home and eat them while reclining for a rest. The Kicker-off-the-rock had his home on a rock shelf beyond which there was a field of sage-arrows (?) from which arrow(-shafts) were made. A single path led to the field. Here he sat with his hair grown into the rock and leaning against it with his right foot resting on his knee. If a passer-by inquired about the arrow-field, he was quite friendly and would explain that they were the finest in the country. But as soon as the person attempted to pass him he kicked them over the precipice where his two children were waiting. There was always a struggle for the eye, ear, liver, and so forth of the victim.

The Gray *yé'iitsoh* carried a headbag and could track any victim down on a dirt road. Over rocks where tracks were not visible he would give out his hiss: *síigo, síigo,* which seemed to charm and paralyze his victims completely. These he would pack in his headbag and roast them in hot ashes. If he wished to have a stew he put the neck in first, then added the rest.

The slayers with their eyes would kill by the charm or stare of their eye. Passers-by would look into their hogan to learn who was there but would at once be attracted closer and closer. All the while these monsters would ask: "What has brought you here, my Grandchildren?" In the end they were killed and devoured.

The Heaped or Overwhelming Vagina would invite her victims to sit beside her then throw her vagina over them and kill them. Tracking Bear followed any footprints until he had run down his victim.

The Hunting or Roaming-twelve-antelopes were in the habit of corralling their victims, then of devouring them piecemeal. Therefore their mouths are black. The Folding or Crushing Rocks were in a beautiful canyon from which an attractive view ahead was afforded. To deceive a man, fresh tracks led on through the canyon and while admiring its beauty, the rocks would suddenly close in on their victim.

The Moving-sand-wall, too, was attractive to behold. Anyone approaching to examine it, however, found himself buried below a rising wave of sand.

Slicing Reeds presented a pretty field with a tempting path leading through it. The path, however, closed in on its victim, who soon was devoured by the reeds.

No-passage-in-rock was a crevice in the rock across which one could jump with little effort. As soon as one made the attempt, the crevice would widen and swallow up the victim.

Endless Snake was flat, long and slim so that one would consider it too great a trouble to walk around the thing. The moment one tried to step across, it would snap up and toss its victim high up into the air and kill it in falling.

11

Slaying of the Monsters

The following morning the boys would not enter their cache until the Sun was well up.[78] They were becoming courageous, and that night again said to their mother: "Tell us, Mother, who is our father?" She now said: "I pity you, my Children, the Sun is your father and your *bináli* (granduncle?) is the Moon. The way to your father is a long one and dangerous because he has many doorguards watching." But they replied: "Your verenda *(sic)* for frightful doorguards! Is Sun really our father?" the elder boy asked. "Yes, it is as I say," she said and repeated the same to the question put by the younger. After that they asked no more.

Neither did they wrestle with each other after this but conversed in an undertone in one part of the hogan, out of hearing distance. From a roll of white shell their mother took living feathers, one which she gave to each saying: "Carry these when you go outside in the morning." They put them on themselves then continued their conversation till late in the evening, until their mother said: "Go to sleep, what have you unimportant boys to talk about anyway?" Yet they continued. Even when later she awoke she heard the elder say: "She has braided cactus, and bunch cactus is your father," and (she heard) the other reply, "Yes, but at the time I did not believe her. Still, now when she says the Sun is your father, I believe it." "Go to sleep," she interrupted them. "Youngsters like you should be snoring and sleeping soundly by this time. Quit your talking."

They then lay down and after a while were quiet. When she awoke again she saw them lying there. But when full dawn had appeared she noticed they were gone. So she walked out to look for them but found no traces. She looked and listened but saw nothing, excepting a single footprint, then another, another, and another. And she realized that one had stepped into the footprints of the other. She

[78]This section is a continuation of the account in the preceding chapter. The story differs chiefly from that of other informants by introducing a woman other than *asdzą́ nádleehí* as the mother of *naayéé' neezghání* and *tó bá jíshchíní*. To get the coherent story of the Monster Slayers, the chapters of *asdzą́ nádleehí* and the "creation of man and animals" should be read separately. The chapter on the "monsters" should be inserted after the growth of the boys.

(179)

noticed, too, that pollen was strewn around the tracks and she found where they had eaten and strewn pollen on their heads.

They must have boarded rainbow and used this as their means of travel. They came to the Sand-wall, but when they approached it, the rainbow bounded back with them so that the sand left them uninjured. They laughed at the futile efforts of the sand as the rainbow protected them by springing back with every strike the sand made at them. This was repeated four times. "Wonder what it is trying to do," they laughingly said. "Suppose we sing a rain song." As soon as they finished the song a cloud appeared, and the rain which followed moistened the sand and packed it so that it could not rise and allowed them to pass over swiftly.

They then arrived at the Slicing Reeds whose leaves were partly black and red. When they would enter they saw them close upon each other and they turned back. They picked up a stick and threw it among the reeds with the result that they sliced it up. They next amused themselves with throwing larger sticks among the reeds and watched them cut them. Now these reeds had no tassels at the time. The boys then sang a song for their living feather, then blew this toward the reeds which took the feather. From this feather was produced the tassel which is white now. The reeds now opened and allowed them to pass through unharmed, because these sacrifices had formed the tassel of the reed.

They went on to the Impassable-rock-crevice. When they reached the stone crevice they stood at its edge, looking. When they feigned to step across, the farther wall receded, which they enjoyed and repeated four times. Again they sang a song which caused the rock wall to remain in position and allowed them to step across unhurt.

They then proceeded on to Endless Snake over which they did not venture. After investigating the surroundings they found that they were fairly enclosed by the snake. They placed a forked stick on its back which it tossed high up in the air. They enjoyed this for some time then feigned to step across by raising their foot. Immediately the snake threw itself upward. After repeating this four times to amuse themselves, they sang a song and were allowed to pass over it uninjured.

They were walking along for some time when suddenly someone shied them. Looking around they saw nothing. Only after the fourth repetition they noticed Field Rat Woman sitting on a bundle of wood which she had gathered. "Where do you come from, my Grandchildren?" she asked. "I never saw Earth People around here." "Oh nothing, we are just roaming about," they said. "No you are not," she said. "Why would Earth People be here?" But after the question and answer had been repeated four times she invited them into her home.

This was small so that they hesitated. "No, my Grandchildren," she said, "it is large enough for you." She then blew on it four times which increased its size.

When they entered they found her living in a blue hogan of four chambers. "Eat first, my Grandchildren," she said. From the east room she produced some chewed cedar which she placed before them. "We do not eat that, my Grandmother," they said. "Yuh!" she exclaimed as she returned it. From the south chamber she now brought them yucca seeds and various cacti. "We do not eat that, my Grandmother." Again she returned these. From the west chamber she now brought coyote dung for them and again they said: "My Grandmother, we do not eat that." Finally from the north room she carried out to them some of the vomitings of Buzzard and of similar birds. "What is that?" they asked. "It stinks, we do not eat that." "What do you eat anyway?" she retorted as she carried it back.

Again she entered her east chamber and now carried out a small basket in which lay a cactus, ripe and yellow. "That we shall eat," they said, although they thought it was very little she offered. Yet as they ate, the same amount remained before them in the basket. "Yuh!" she said again. "You do not seem to be very hungry." And with a sweep of her hand she brought it to her mouth and consumed it in one swallow.

After that they continued their journey. They came to a valley where they found an old woman stooped and bent. "Whence do you come?" she asked them. After repeating the question four times, she invited them into her home saying: "I heard that you were coming." This happened to be Spider Woman whose house was of jet with a tiny opening. "How small," they thought. But she seemed to divine their thought, blew on the opening four times and they entered on a slant, then straight down into four rooms in the east, south, west, and north.

"I heard you started away four days ago," she told them. "That's true," they said. "First you must eat, my Grandchildren," she said as she produced a small white shell from her clothes. This she held where the light shone into the house, held it there until it filled with pollen. That she filled with water and gave them to eat. "We are surely hungry," they assured her yet, despite their efforts, the supply in the dish was undiminished. "You do not seem to eat very much," she remarked as she wiped the dish with her four fingers and swallowed the whole in one sweep. "Your father," she continued, "is very wicked. Take this living feather, it may serve you a purpose in the future." They then left her.

In a place farther on there were four points extending, one gray, the next still grayer, the next more so, the last altogether white. This was *sá ooghą́ą́ł*, old age killing (?), and if anyone passed through the points it implied that he would die of old age. "Old age would kill them." So they sang a song, one apiece to each point, and (they) passed through.

As they proceeded on their journey they met an old man with long legs who called them *shinálí*—my Grandchildren. "Where are you from?" he asked and at once challenged them to a footrace. "No," they said, "you can not run, we will (not) race you." Therefore people now say: "*shinálí*, we will race!" This was Meadowlark. "Stand behind each other, *shinálí*," he told them. And when the younger took position behind the other, they heard a song. (This belongs to the Bead Chant.)

They travelled on again and found an old yellow man lying there. When he moved he seemed to move his body with his neck. He had a horn on his head, back and tail. "*Shinálíké* (my Grandchildren)," he said, "Where are you going?" He, too, challenged them to a footrace but they laughed at him. "I have known that you were coming," he told them. "Your father is terrible, he even kills with his smoke," thus revealing that he knew their destination. His shirt was of evening twilight, his dress of new moon (?). The boys tickled his side which caused him to turn quickly, but they tickled his other side and again he turned. "What are you trying to do?" he said laughingly. Therefore Sphinx(-worm) turns quickly if touched.

The Sphinx then vomited his blue phlegm into the hands of both, saying: "Keep this and it will prevent your father from killing you with his smoke. Put it into the pockets of your ear, where he can not see it." Therefore Sphinx vomits when you touch him. "Your father has two Mountain Lions, two Bears, two Big Snakes, (and) two Thunders as doorguards," he said. "And (he) kills all who visit his home. At the four cross lakes he has spies who notify him in advance. But do not mention that I told you this, *shinálí*. When you reach these places the tension of your rainbows will increase as a warning that you are approaching these places."

Sure enough, as they travelled on their rainbow it became rigid, and placing it upright they stepped into it. Looking to the east they noticed a body of water with moving Water Monsters, Water Horses, White Egrets, Brown Herons, White Nostril Monsters, (and) black, white, yellow, and glittering Monster Fishes, all of which were the pets of the Sun. And he alone saw them coming. They then began to sing and the Wind arose. After four songs the Wind had increased and stirred the water and lashing the waves until they drove the monsters underwater. They were then enabled to jump across the water by means of their rainbow so that the spies of the Sun did not notice them. They landed where the doorguards lay.

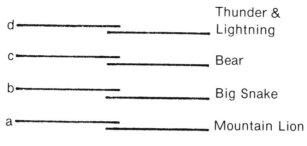

d	Thunder & Lightning
c	Bear
b	Big Snake
a	Mountain Lion

Position of the doorguards

When the boys reached the Mountain Lions, these rose threateningly. But the boys[79] said: "It is I," which quieted them. The first or elder boy stepped on the head of the first Mountain Lion, the younger on the head of the second one, and (they) passed on to the Big Snakes. These, too, arose at once, roared like thunder and their horns grew in height. "What is happening, it is I that is coming?" they spoke and the Snakes lay quiet. They had red spots on their heads. On these the boys stepped to pass on to the Bears. These immediately growled and showed fight. Again they soothed them by saying: "What is the matter, it is we that are here." The older and younger boy were then allowed to step on the heads of the Bears lying face to face and so to pass on. Next they came to Thunder and Zigzag Lightning which were flashing back and forth at the entrance. "We it is who are here," they told them and at once they stepped on their heads and across.

They had reached a door of jet. An opener (knob) of jet extended at the top and center which had to be touched in order to open the door. These the older boy touched and entered. At the time both were filthy and unkempt. They found another door of turquoise with two knobs at top and bottom. These they touched again and entered. An abalone door was provided with two knobs which they touched and entered. Here was a fourth door of white shell with two similar knobs on the left (south) side. When they touched these and entered, they found a middle-aged woman who looked at them, then bowed her head.

In the center stood an upright of dark flint and along the eastern wall hung twelve man figures (dolls) of dark flint, on the south (hung) twelve figures of blue flint, on the west wall (hung) twelve man figures of yellow flint, and on the north wall twelve figures of white flint. Just above these were small round objects in corresponding black, blue, yellow, and varicolored. These were rattles, the lower half (was) white to represent Dawn, the upper (half was) black for Darkness. In the

[79]From another account we learn that the boys were called the "doorguards" by their sacred name, and thus they were allowed to pass.

west part of the room four stools stood side by side of jet, white shell, abalone, and turquoise.

The woman was evidently not pleased, as she said: "From where are you?" "Oh, we're just roaming," they answered. "Roaming, you say?" she asked. "Why yes, of course!" they said. "But what did you come for?" she asked. "Oh, nothing," they said. "For nothing? Why, as a rule, Earth People do not visit here. Why did you come?" she said. "Well," said the older boy, "we were told that our father lives here. Therefore we came to visit him."

At once she produced from the northern part of the room a dark cloud and dark mist, wrapped them (the boys) into these folds, then replaced them on the same shelf. While they lay there they scanned the room again and the elder said: "What sort of a place is this, anyway?" "Whew!" said the younger, "look at that thing, white below, black above. And there is a black flint upright in the center." "Shut up," the woman interrupted them. But the younger continued to whisper: "Look at those man figures, twelve in the east, twelve in the south, west, and north. Wonder what they are?" "Did I not tell you to shut up?" she shouted. "Stop your talk." But again he whispered: "There is a rounded thing also in the east, south, west, and north, the color only differs. There is also a jet, white shell, turquoise, and abalone stool over there." Again she shouted even a little angrier: "Shut up, I tell you, be quiet." "That woman," he continued, "is middle-aged, not very old, but she seems to be angry." "Shut up, I tell you," she shouted and just then the black rattle grated *dja, dja, dja* and the woman said: "Your father started for home." And when the rattle in the south sounded, she said: "He finished some distance of his journey." When the abalone rattle in the west rang, she remarked: "He is pretty close now." At the sound of the red-white stone rattle in the north she concluded: "It's done, he returned."

At that instant the sound of opening the first, second, third, and fourth doors could be heard and the Sun entered. The sun disc he wrapped in dark cloud and mist and placed it on a shelf in the east. "I saw two persons come this way, where are they?" he asked, evidently jealous of her, as it seemed to the woman. "No, there was nobody came this way," she said. "Have I no eyes?" he asked in fury. "I saw somebody come this way, I tell you. Why do you conceal them? Who are they?" "Strange," she said. "Someone always boasts of his honesty. One never commits adultery he insists. And yet here two persons arrived, saying 'where is our father?' Perhaps you know them," she added.

He searched the room, east, south, (and) west, until in the north he discovered the wraps of Dark Cloud and Mist. These he unfolded and

SLAYING OF THE MONSTERS

the two boys lay at his feet, filthy, unkempt, ugly-looking. On the east wall were five peg-like projections of white shell against which he thrust them, thinking to transfix them alive. But due to the living feather which Spider Woman had given them they rebounded at his feet unharmed. "*Sha'áłchíní dó' hóle'*," he said—"if these are my children, let it be so." (The meaning of this expression is doubtful).

Again he thrust them on similar projections of blue flint in the south, on yellow flint in the west, and serrated flint in the north. But each time their living feather enabled them to rebound unhurt. And each time he replied: "*Hóle'.*"

He then touched the dark flint upright on its east, south, west, and north sides, which raised it and uncovered a hole just large enough to hold the boys. This he told the boys to enter, then closed the hole with the dark flint which he now twisted down like a screw. When he removed it they were unharmed, and in surprise again he remarked: "*Sha'áłchíní dó' hóle'.*" Again he told them to enter and gave the upright two twists, three twists the third time, and the fourth time four twists. And seeing them still alive he jerked them out.

The boys were then bid to be seated and the Sun Carrier sat down in front of them. At once he produced a jet tobacco stone (pipe) which he filled with tobacco, then (he) lit it with an igniter of rock crystal that usually hung on the east wall. While he was thus engaged, the boys slipped the Sphinx's vomit from their ear pocket into their mouths. By this time the Sun Carrier handed the burning jet pipe to the elder boy who, after smoking it, perspired heavily but went otherwise unharmed. He then filled a turquoise pipe for the younger. The smoke merely made him perspire freely. "Thanks, my Father, for the smoke," the boys said when they finished. And he in surprise said: "*Sha'áłchíní dó' hóle'.*"

On the west side, next to the Sun Carrier, was a house of white shell in which Moon Carrier lived. He sent his messenger, Darkness Child, to Sun Carrier saying: "Make a sweathouse for them." This was entrusted to Moon Carrier who prepared the sweathouse of darkness and set aside round stones of dark, blue, yellow, white, varicolored, (and) red-white flints for heating. In the south floor he dug a pit which required some time. Sun Carrier was impatient and would send Darkness Child to ask if it were ready. But Moon Carrier sent word to wait. Meanwhile he covered the pit with a curtain of white shell, turquoise, abalone and darkness in the order mentioned. Likewise he hung a curtain of darkness, evening twilight, skyblue, and dawn over the doorway of the sweathouse. He then placed the heated flints mentioned inside. In this manner Moon Carrier had cheated the Sun and instructed the boys about the pit in the south so that they might not be burnt.

When the flints had been heated white, the boys were put inside of the sweathouse. Water stood ready in the dark, blue, yellow, and white water jugs. "Is everything ready?" Sun asked (the) Moon Carrier. "Yes, I fixed it myself." He then raised the door curtains and with the black water jug poured water on the hot flints, which sizzled and popped sending up a cloud of steam. In this manner he would kill his victims. He then waited until the noise ceased, then asked: "Are you warm enough?" "No, not yet," they answered from within. He then emptied the blue water jug and when the noise cease he asked: "How about it? Is that warm enough for you?" "No, we just began to sweat," they answered. He next emptied the yellow water jug and when the noise ceased he inquired: "How now, are you warm enough?" "Yes, we are getting warm," they answered. The white water jug too he emptied on the hot flints. When the noise died away he asked: "Are you quite warm?" "Yes," they answered, "we are pretty warm now."

At once the Moon Carrier removed the doorway curtain of dawn, and it was still white. The sky-blue curtain he found a little warm, the evening twilight curtain was scorched a little, therefore evening twilight is yellow. The darkness curtain (on the inside) had been charred completely, therefore darkness is black. He next removed the jet stone cover from the pit where his son's children lay unharmed. It was burnt a trifle. Next he removed the abalone which had been scorched yellow by the heat, then the turquoise which felt warm, then the white shell which was not affected. All these he slipped into his garments. The boys left the pit and sweathouse covered with sweat. The Sun Carrier again remarked: *"Sha'áłchíní dó' hóle'!"* Then they proceeded to the house.

The Sun Carrier walked first, followed by the boys, (with the) Moon Carrier taking up the rear. His house was half yellow and half blue. In the northern part of the room there were twelve dark man figures, in the southern part twelve blue ones. The two end figures of the northern line ("a, b") were the sons of the Sun Carrier, the other ten man-shaped figures. The two end ones of the southern line ("c, d") were daughters of the Sun. The others between them were woman figures.

He then laid a spread of jet north (see "e") and a spread of turquoise south (see "f"). The Sun Carrier stood toward the north (see "g") facing the spreads. Next to him (stood) the elder boy (see "h"), then the younger (see "i"), then Moon Carrier (see "j"). "My Son," he addressed the elder, "choose of these man-figures in the north whom you prefer to bathe and straighten your body. They are your brothers." And to the younger he said: "Select anyone of these woman-figures in the south to bathe you and straighten your limbs, they are your sisters."

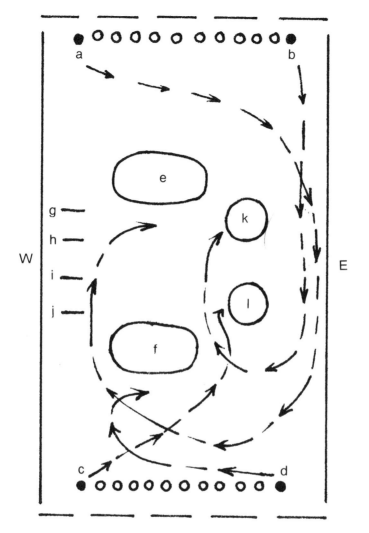

He had hoped secretly that they would select from the center of the two lines. Their mother, however, had placed Little Winds in their earfolds, and these now whispered to them: "choose the end ones in the line, they are his real sons and daughters, the other ten are only figures. "All right," said the elder boy. "The end one at the east ("b"), my brother, shall wash and dress me." While the younger said: "This, my sister in the west (see "c"), shall wash and straighten me." "All right, my Son," the Sun said to the one selected (see "b"), "wash him." He at once arose, made a sunwise circle (as shown by arrows) around the white shell basket to the turquoise basket where he sat facing east. The Sun Carrier then summoned his daughter (see "c") to take position next to him. And she sat facing east before the white shell basket. Both prepared the soap suds.

"Which of these do you select for the shape of your bodies?" Sun Carrier asked again. "Choose the end ones at the northwest (see "a") and the southeast (see "d")," the Winds whispered again. They chose these. Now Sun Carrier sang two songs by which the foam raised over the baskets, and the man and woman figures sang with him. The boys then sat down and were touched with foam on their soles, knees, hips, shoulders, chest, back, and head. After this bath they lay flat on the jet spread (see "e") and that of turquoise (see "f"). The boy at the northwest end (see "a") walked sunwise (as shown by arrows) taking position next to the elder. Their sister from the southeast end (see "d") took position next to the younger boy. They then kneaded their legs and shaped their backs, then shaped their front also, making them not too tall, not too small, but middle-sized and features as beautiful as their own.

The elder they dressed in moccasins, leggings, clothes, headband, and headplume of dark flint. To the younger they furnished these garments in blue flint. A dark flint club was given the older, a blue flint club to the younger boy, and both had four rattles. As Sun Carrier now looked at them they seemed to him as pretty as his other children. "My Children," he called them, and they responded promptly, "My Father." Four times they exchanged this greeting.

Leading them to the east, he opened a jet door for them from which they beheld jet and other jewelled horses. "Have you come for these, my Children?" he asked. "No, not for these, my Father. What can we do with them upon our return?" they replied. He closed that door then opened the turquoise door in the south. Again they beheld game of all kinds, sheep, deer, and elk. "Is this what you desire, my Children?" he asked. "No, not this time, my Father." And again he closed the door and led them to the west white shell door where amounts of white and yellow corn, black corn, and all (kinds of) plants, birds, and rainbow(s) could be seen. "Is this what you desire, my Children?" he asked. "Perhaps you came for this?" "No," they said. "There is no place to raise them, but we shall remember this promise and return for them some other time." This door, too, he closed. Then going north, he opened the abalone door which enclosed plants, pollens, and trees of every description. "Is it perhaps this, my Children?" he asked again. "No, not for these," they said. "Some other time we shall ask for these, my Father." And the door, too, he closed.

"What have you come for?" he asked. "We have come for none of the things you have shown us, my Father," they said. "But our people are disappearing, they are being eaten by *naayéé'* Monsters so that few are left. For these we have come, my Father." The Sun Carrier stood with bowed head. "You certainly are great ones, my Children. It is too bad. You ask for *yé'iitsoh* who is my son. Horned Monster, Monster

Eagle, Travelling Rock have been my pets. But let it be as you desire," he said.

He then made zigzag lightning and straight lightning arrows of which he gave them each two. The elder also received a dark flint and a blue flint club, the younger a yellow and a serrated flint club. He then wrapped them up in dark cloud and dark mist and put them feet first into his pocket. Then (he) started with his disc on his day's journey. When he reached the Sky center, above Mount Taylor, he unfolded the Dark Cloud and Dark Mist, and the elder stood at his right, the younger at his left. He had told them that mountains, lakes, and so on could be seen from above as small stars. But he had changed their appearance so that they now would not recognize one from the other.

He then set them on reflected sunred and made them guess. "From which point did you leave, my Children?" he asked. The Little Wind in their ears immediately whispered: "Tell him from that small gray speck you see there." At once they replied: "We left from the top of Spruce Mountain which is there. The home of our mother is there." Then as rapidly as he questioned they would reply: "That gray spot is Moving-around-the-mountain. Here is *sisnajiní*. This is above Mount Taylor; San Francisco Peaks are there." "It's true, my Children," he would say, not knowing that Little Wind was telling them. "Perrin's Peak is here, Chuska Peak there where that white speck like white shell is. Hot Spring is down there and *yé'iitsoh*, for whom we came to see you, roams there." "It's true," he said a little sadly. "And there is Black Lake where Horned Monster runs, for whom we have come. At the point of Ship Rock lives Monster Eagle, for whom we have also come. In Wide Valley lies Travelling Rock, for which we came. The Rocks-rubbing-together and the One-who-kicks-off-the-rock-precipice lives yonder. Those Who-kill-by-their-eyes live there at Gray Earth. For these we came, my Father. At Wooded Ridge, where you see the trees, lives She-who-overwhelms-with-her-vagina. At White Flat are the twelve Antelope-who-eat-people-alive. And at that Black Ridge yonder is the Maiden-who-turns-into-a-bear. At that Greasy Earth lives the monstrous Snapping Vagina for whom we have come. The Clapping Rocks live at that spot yonder where the outlines of these rocks can be seen against the horizon. We came for that. Yonder is the Sand Wall, full of danger; we also came for that. And for the Slicing Yucca yonder we also came, and for the Impassable Rocks, and the Endless Snake, that streak which is visible from here. For these we have come, my Father, because they have eaten and destroyed our people." "So it is, I see," said the Sun. "Let us start out, my Children."

"How shall it be done?" he asked. "We should like first to go to Hot Spring where *yé'iitsoh* is now singing *sįigo* (is hissing(," they said. "All right," said the Sun. "You may go first. But I must have the red tail feather which he wears for a living headplume. That will be my pay," he said. He then attached a fire brand (?) to their foreheads and called them *naayéé' neezghání*, Slayers of Monsters, because they were to slay these *naayéé'* Monsters. "This fire brand will be a sign for you to kill these enemies (monsters). While it sparkles you will know that you are victorious. Let one therefore do the killing, the other watch the brand. Should he notice that the flame of his fire brand is sparkling, he will know that the other has been conquered. You will kill one of your brothers and my pets. And in days to come, brother will kill brother and his own relatives and his dearest pets." Therefore it happens that a brother at times kills his own brother.

"I'll take the first shot," he continued. And he put them on a zigzag lightning and let them (shot them) down on the east side of Hot Spring (near Grants, New Mexico). *Yé'iitsoh* had been let down to the top of Mount Taylor, not these boys, however. They were standing in gray mirage which made them invisible. Presently they saw *yé'iitsoh* appearing over the ridge of Mount Taylor, scanning the country. He was wearing the red plume, and this alone they saw. Going south he soon again appeared, being visible from the bust up. Appearing in the west they saw him up to the hips. When he appeared in the north his whole body was visible to the ankle so that his feet were not exposed. Though his vision was keen, *yé'iitsoh* had not spied them, and in spite of the songs he sang. Therefore it happens that, in spite of song and witchery, one may overlook an enemy whom he is seeking.

Appearing again in the east he stepped into full view and presently walked to the spring. At the edge of it he stooped to drink when he saw the reflection of the boys in the water. "Are they not fine," he exclaimed. "Which shall I kill?" And the boys (out of the spring he thought) retorted: "Isn't that a big thing coming to water. When shall we strike him?" And hurriedly *yé'iitsoh* drank while *tó bá jíshchíní* raked the water together that he might drink more rapidly, and the giant emptied the spring thinking that the boys were at its bottom. Looking up, he spied them at the edge of the water hole.

The *yé'iitsoh* straightened out. He carried two clubs while the boys had two apiece. He threw his black flint club and the Wind whispered: "Look out!" Their zigzag lightning raised them so that the club passed under their feet. *Naayéé' neezghání* picked it up. This time *yé'iitsoh* threw his blue flint club high and again Wind whispered to them to squat down (so) that the club might pass over them. Again *naayéé' neezghání* picked it up. Next he tried his yellow club and Wind whispered to them to separate so that the club passed between them, and *naayéé' neezghání* picked it up. Finally he threw his dark club with all his force. They now jumped from their zigzag lightning which wrapped itself around the club and this, too, became property of *naayéé' neezghání*.

Yé'iitsoh now was without a weapon. His coat was of flint with points extended downward. The Sun now shot a zigzag lightning at him which encircled *yé'iitsoh* four times, making him powerless to move. And they saw the Sun reach down to remove the red tail feather from the head of his son, and since then there are no more red tail feathers four time struck by Lightning.

The Lightning stunned *yé'iitsoh*, yet, he saw Sun reach for the plume. Lightning thus kills some at times, others it only stuns. Using the club of *yé'iitsoh*, *naayéé' neezghání* now thrust his dark club at his knees which caused the flints there to fall from him. Next *tó bá jíshchíní* threw his blue club striking the hip, which scaled the flint from the body of *yé'iitsoh*. *Naayéé' neezghání* struck him with his yellow club which severed the flint garment from his chest. *Tó bá jíshchíní* next threw his white club striking his forehead, removing the three arrowpoints extending there. Much flint is therefore found in the neighborhood. Shorn of his flint, his naked body was exposed.

Now using their own clubs, *naayéé' neezghání* struck him in the knees with his dark club, throwing *yé'iitsoh* toward the east. Where his feet ploughed the ground the dust was raised and his feet penetrated the mountain. And *tó bá jíshchíní* struck him in the hips, the falling parts raising dust in the south. Similarly the blue club of *naayéé' neezghání* scattered his body parts in the west. And *tó bá jíshchíní* threw his serrated club, striking his head which fell right there. Therefore petrified woods found at one side of the mountains also appear on the opposite side. These are the feet, legs, and body of *yé'iitsoh*.

There was some life left in his head and his tears ran from his eyes. "It is hard when your time comes," said *naayéé neezghání* to him. "But you have done this to others, and my power is greater than yours." And, as though he would assent (in) some way he closed his eyelids. *Naayéé' neezghání* then removed his scalp. Therefore the Navajo scalps. They then collected grasses and herbs and struck by the Lightning, making four circles around the place. *Naayéé' neezghání* carried the scalp, *tó bá jíshchíní* (carried) the lightning-struck herbs. Therefore today herbs are gathered around a tree struck by Lightning and used medicinally. They then continued their journey and returned home. *Naayéé' neezghání* hung the scalp of *yé'iitsoh* outside on a tree, but *tó bá jíshchíní* carried the herbs with him.

"My Aunt, my Grandmother, we have killed *yé'iitsoh*," they said as they entered. "*Yúu!* don't say that. Who could kill *yé'iitsoh*?" Back and forth they repeated this four times, but as she still refused to believe them they said, "Go out and see. His scalp is hanging on the tree." She ran out and soon they could hear her dancing and singing in joy. But when she re-entered she found both in a swoon. At once she mixed herbs in water, poured this over them and revived them. And it was the ghost of *yé'iitsoh* that had caused this.

"You are surely great ones, my Children," she said to them. And when she noticed that they were still indisposed, she sent Little Wind out to get Kingbird and Chickadee to perform for them. And they shot pine arrows and spruce arrows over them to drive away the ghost of *yé'iitsoh*. Therefore a single ceremony may be conducted over two persons at the same time. This part is *hóchǫ́ǫjí* (ghost-side) of *haneełnéehee*. And her dance over the scalp is *anaají ndáá'* (enemy-side group dancing), the War Dance.

They slept. At dawn *naayéé' neezghání* said to *tó bá jíshchíní*: "Remain here as our father instructed us to do." *Tó bá jíshchíní* sat there watching the fire brand, and Wind whispered to him again: "If it is extinguished you shall not see your brother again."

Naayéé' neezghání went out to the plain where Horned Monster roamed. Ascending a hill on the east side he scanned the open space to find a suitable approach for an attack. He repeated the same from south, west, and north, but nothing suitable suggested itself. While still thinking the matter over, Gopher Man approached him saying: "What are you doing, my Grandchild?" "It's just this, that I want to challenge this thing out there, but I walked around everywhere," he said. "Oh," said Gopher, "that's easy. I always go over there to visit him. He doesn't bother me. Stay here till I return."

But when the Gopher failed to return after a long time, *naayéé' neezghání* became restless and suspicious. But presently the Gopher returned with the remark: "All is well. I have dug four trenches, the last one leading directly under his heart from which I have removed the fur." This was fairly well in the afternoon. And the Gopher blew into the furrow which expanded sufficiently to allow *naayéé' neezghání* to walk in them. All this while he was relating to *naayéé' neezghání*: "He awoke with a snort when I touched him. When he noticed me I told him that I had come for some fur for my children, which satisfied him."

When *naayéé' neezghání* reached the spot he could hear the beat of its heart *yid-dog, yid-dog*. At once he shot a zigzag lightning arrow into the exposed spot and immediately fled back. The Horned Monster was up in an instant, looked around, then noticed the opening into which it thrust its horn. This he ran through the first furrow and through the turn at that point to the second furrow, through this again around the bend to the third trench. Here again he tore up the ground, turned and was almost upon *naayéé' neezghání* when, suddenly, he keeled over, kicked the dust so that the earth shook.

Panting heavily, *naayéé' neezghání* stood there afraid to approach the monster lest it were still alive. That explains why some have courage, others lag behind. He still sat there frightened when an old slim fellow walked along. "What is the matter, my Grandchild?" he asked. "I was in that hole when that big thing fell and I am in doubt as to whether it is dead or alive." "I see," said the slim fellow who happened to be Ground Squirrel. "I often go around him," he said. "He pays no attention to me, even if I mount his horns. I shall run over there and give a call from his horn. When you hear this you will know that he is dead."

He sat waiting and waiting. Meanwhile the Ground Squirrel was wallowing in the blood of Horned Monster and had striped his whole body with it. But finally he heard its chirp, *ts'os, ts'os*, and saw him sitting on the horns of the monster. When *naayéé' neezghání* reached the head of the monster he told Ground Squirrel to turn about. With his hand he drew a stripe across his back and pricked his ears for him. "What are you trying to do with me?" asked Ground Squirrel. "Oh, nothing. I am making a good-looking chap of you." "Are you? Do you think I look nice? Of course you do," said *naayéé' neezghání*. Therefore Ground Squirrel is striped with the blood of Horned Monster, and these stripes *naayéé' neezghání* made on him.

Meanwhile they were skinning the animal, when suddenly Kangaroo Mouse began to quarrel by saying: "I want the hide." Gopher, however, objected: "No, my Grandchild, I'll take it." "But it's mine," said Kangaroo Mouse, "I was here before you were." "Even so, it is mine," said Gopher. "It was I who told my grandson where it lay." It is a rule that the hunter who shoots the game gives its hide to his partner in hunting. Gopher and Kangaroo Mouse were thus quarrelling while *naayéé' neezghání* stood by and Ground Squirrel passed remarks such as: "Look at this color, and this big foot. What a nose, and the horn! Isn't he immense? Look at these ribs and bones." The other two almost fought.

Meanwhile *naayéé neezghání* almost swooned from the blood smell. "How about it there," said Ground Squirrel. "Stop your quarrel. Don't you see that your grandson is getting sick?" At once he produced some peppermint, chewed this and pressed *naayéé' neezghání* with it. Kangaroo Mouse also chewed wild onion and pressed his limbs with it. Meanwhile Gopher had continued skinning the monster. Then *naayéé' neezghání* came to. Therefore these two medicines and the lightning-herbs are used for swooning caused by ghosts. The three together then skinned the animal while *naayéé neezghání* stood aside. When they had finished, the quarrel over the hide began again. "What use is there in quarrelling, my Grandchildren," *naayéé' neezghání* spoke. "Perhaps you can divide it among you. You, Gopher, take the front part."

Therefore Gopher has small and brown eyes like Horned Monster. "And you take the rear part." Therefore Kangeroo Mouse has mouse-colored skin. The monster had two large pockets at the sides of his mouth into which he threw his victims. Therefore Gopher puts his food in his cheek pockets.

The Ground Squirrel and his companions had used arrowpoints in removing the hide. When the latter had been divided, Kangaroo Mouse claimed the entrails, and Gopher likewise. "No, my Grand-uncle," said *naayéé' neezghání*, "you take the meat, I have need of the paunch and entrails." They agreed but said, "It is getting late, go home now." "No," he said, "let me show you how to prepare them." "Never mind, you go home," they said, "we know the purpose for which you want them. It is late now, you can return in the morning. *Naayéé' neezghání* therefore left while they prepared the paunch and entrails.

He slept at home but at dawn he started out and arrived at the place where he had left them with their preparations. "Do you have things ready?" he asked. "All is ready, my Grandchild," they said. They had filled the large and small intestines with blood, wrapped his feet with the large intestine and his body and legs with the small intestine, the pancreas they wound around his neck, of the honeycomb stomach they made a mask for him with two eyes of stone mica for vision. All of these were filled with blood and tied on him. "Now I am ready," he said to them. "All right, my Grandchild," they replied as they turned to go home.

He went in the direction of Winged (Ship) Rock. The Eagle Monster saw his approach and immediately swooped down upon him, but missed him. And *naayéé' neezghání* said: "*Atsá náhálé sísí*, Eagle Monster has missed me." But the bird replied: "Your mouth is rotten, I say." And circling around again it swooped down again and repeated twice more, he taunting the Eagle each time, and she wishing him death. At the fourth swoop the Eagle picked him up as he said: "Eagle has picked me up again," to which it answered: "Your mouth is rotten, I tell you." And it carried him away, up (to) where the five points projected, confident that this was but an ordinary victim.

But the Winds carried him slowly down to the points as the Eagle released him. He then slightly pricked the intestines, allowing the blood of Horned Monster to flow over the pointed flints. The Monster Eagle fancied that this was his blood so it sat on its customary perch leaving the prey to its children. When these approached within hearing distance, *naayéé' neezghání* said: "Sht!" and they called back: "My Father, this says 'sht' to us." Without turning in their direction the Eagle answered: "Eat and don't talk." And again when they approached him he sheed them. "He does say 'sht'," they called up to their father. But he replied: "Don't mind that, it is the wounds that make him groan." And he left his perch in search of another victim. *Naayéé' neezghání* now removed the intestines saying: "You big-bellied monsters, you'll eat humans, will you? I'll fix you." From Horned Monster, parts of Shootingway and Beadway begin. At Eagle Monster (the) Eagle-catching (Chantway) takes its beginning.

"You are great ones," he addressed the young eagles, "you have been eating us," he told them. "How do you know when your father returns? Tell me." "When He-rain appears over Butte-lies-on-it, that is a sign that our father is returning," they said. "When She-rain appears there it is our mother." *Naayéé' neezghání* then rubbed his chest and back and looked at the Sun which that day travelled faster. He ascended the peak where the eagles rested. There he built a wall of stone leaving an opening large enough to shoot through it. Then he returned to the young eagles and spent the night with one on either side and they covered him with their wings. In the morning he returned to his eagle trap *(ood)* from which he kept watch on the Butte-lies-on-it. Sure enough, by noon a dark cloud arose over it and He-rain fell presently. At a distance Monster Eagle came soaring, carrying a young man covered with turquoise and white shell. His vain efforts with his swinging arms showed him alive as the eagle dropped him on the five flint points. As soon as the Eagle sat on his perch, *naayéé' neezghání* shot his zigzag arrow into it. It fell down the cliff and the Earth shook as it struck the ground. Shortly after a gentle She-rain appeared and with it the Female Eagle carrying a woman decorated in turquoise and white shell. As it alighted on the peak he shot it with his lightning arrow and its body shook the Earth as if fell below the cliff. Meanwhile the torch of his brother barely flickered and threatened to extinguish. He began to weep, but Wind consoled him and whispered to him not to cry.

And *naayéé' neezghání* started down determined also to kill the youngsters. "Do not kill us, my Granduncle, yet you may do as you like, either death or life. Give us life," they pleaded. He had noticed that the Winged Rock had grown in height in the interval. He then picked up the older of the two, raised it and said: "When the Earth People come into being, you shall be of use to them." Then he released it and it circled higher and higher in four circles from where its cry was heard—*xag, zag*. And this is our present Eagle. The other he carried to a ledge of rock and released him saying: "You shall be a warning in the future, at any rate." And the bird flew away and he heard the call *u-hu* of the Hoot Owl.

And looking over the edge of the cliff for the mountains below, he distinguished them only as tiny specks far away. He became frightened at this continued growth of the rock, the more so as Wind whispered: "Move down. If Winged Rock grows to the Sky you shall not see your people again." At once he drew forth his flint knife and drew a zigzag line on the cliff, using a high pitch of voice as he called *ha-ha-ha!* With his dark arrowpoint he then crossed this line horizontally thus: Giving his call *ha-ha-ha* at a lower pitch, the cliff at once grew lower with him. Even then, after he had examined it four times round about from east to south, west and north, he found no possible place for descent and despaired of ever leaving it.

And he became hungry and thirsty, especially toward noon. His brother's torch was barely red. He recognized from this that *naayéé' neezgháni* was in a plight. But scanning the horizon, the prisoner on the cliff detected two small objects flying in his direction. He watched them closely and saw them alight at the base of the cliff. They were beautiful maidens, light complexioned with black eyes, two turtle dove maidens. It made him forget his plight. "Where are you from?" he called to them. Good natured as they were, they replied: "The question is rather where are you from? What are you doing up here?" Instead of a reply he said (perhaps a little peeved), "I was asking!" "Oh well," they said, "the fact is we were sent to you, we heard you were hungry and thirsty."

So the first maiden produced a yellow earthen bowl and the other four joints of bog rush. From these joints she poured water into the bowl to which the first added meal of green corn. This was given to him to eat. Then another joint was emptied and they gave him to drink and drank with him. And again they filled the bowl with meal and water and encouraged him to eat. "I was hungry," he said, "but I have my fill." "We came for that purpose," they replied. "Your Grandmother has gone to Big-meadow-in-the-rocks, to the house of pine (?) for help," they told as they were leaving. They had come supernaturally and had walked up in the form of maidens but now left him in the form of doves.

The Sun was now still about four fingers above the horizon, but he felt refreshed. And he walked over to the south rim of the cliff and detected a tiny speck approaching it. "Call to her—'my Grandmother, carry me down,'" Wind whispered to him. *"Ch'ééh daane,"* she exclaimed from behind a rock when she heard the call. He called again and again, but she would approach only a small distance each time. "Call to her again," Wind whispered. But he was angry and swore at her. Still Wind insisted: "Call to her again." So he did. Then she stood looking up a while, and shading her eyes she called back: "What?" and again he repeated: "My Grandmother, carry me down. It is I."

"All right," she said. "But turn your back to me. Do not watch me go up." And he heard her approaching as she sang: *Aⱡts'ą́ąhji̇́ tsé bineeshtⱡ'i̇́ tⱡ'ịh tⱡ'ịh*—On-both-sides-rock I am climbing (?), (etc.). But she required a long time to reach the top.

When she did, he beheld an ugly old woman carrying a threadbare headbag on her back. And this was the Bat Woman. While she was singing that song she had inserted dark flint pegs into the cliff without telling him of it. And her ears were wide. At any rate, he was disgusted when he saw her and thought "how can she ever help?" But, as if answering his unexpressed question, she replied: "I am strong, I am strong." Again when he looked at her basket he questioned in his mind how she would pack him in that small basket. And again she answered his thought: "I can pack a whole deer in that, look!" And she blew four times upon it and it increased in size. "Put some stones in it," she said. He gathered four large boulders and put them in the basket. And though the head cord was taut and seemed ready to tear at any moment, she danced about with it as if it had not been weighted at all.

"Now get in, my Grandchild," she said. "But keep your eyes closed whatever may happen." He promised and crawled in and closed his eyes so as to allow him to peep through the lids. Thus he noticed that she had swung the basket in her front and was pulling out the pegs as they went down.[80] After that he closed his eyes completely. But the way down seemed so interminable that he became frightened and fancied her a friend of the Monster Eagle, whom he had just killed. Finally he opened his eyes a little. At once she yelled: "Close your eyes, we are falling." So again he closed them. Then it seemed they were going upward and he fancied that she might take him to the Sky opening. So he opened his eyes wide and saw that just three pegs were left. Immediately she seemed to stumble and lose her hold, then tumbled with him to the ground, breaking the three pegs as they fell. "You certainly have no sense," she said furiously. "What if you had done that halfway up? Little surprise that you get lost way up there." But he laughed which only increased her fury.

"Don't turn your back to her," Wind whispered. "If you do, she will steal the calves of your legs." So when she said: "Let us see where you killed those Eagles," he said: "No, you go ahead." "How can I?" she replied, "I do not know where you killed them." Even so, my Grandmother," he told her, "you take the lead, I can show you." Again she refused, but finally agreed and he followed her. And they found the Eagles swollen to enormous size. "Thanks, my Grandson," she said, "I have no feathers and my children are freezing." And she began to pluck two tail feathers and placed these on top. "It is getting

[80]Other versions give us different details of this descent.

late," she said, "and we must go home." "Yes," he said, "I'll get home quickly. But down in the valley there are many sunflowers. You had better avoid these and stay along the hills." "Yes, my Grandson, I hear," she said. "I always do what people tell me."

She then left and did exactly what he told her not to do. Looking back he saw her going out to the valley and he stopped to see the result. She stumbled a few times and dropped her basket with part of the feathers which immediately turned into various small birds. "There goes my pet, and there, and there, and there," she said. But the birds were flying from the basket so rapidly that she held her hand over the basket to hold the escaping feathers. "There's another fool for you," said *naayéé' neezghání* as he turned on his way home to his brother. There he learned that he had been gone one full day and part (till sunset) of the next day. (The further account is part of the Beadway.) So that he might travel more rapidly he used rainbow, stubby rainbow, reflected sunred and zigzag lightning.

Naayéé' neezghání remained with his brother that night. At dawn he cautioned his brother to be careful, then left for Wide Valley where he arrived at dawn. After studying what might be done about Travelling Rock, he decided to use the torch or fire brand. He held a stone to it and sent its smoke toward the east. At once the Travelling Rock dashed after it. But immediately *naayéé' neezghání* sent its smoke south, then west, and north, never giving it a moment's rest so that, when Travelling Rock returned from the north, he was completely worn out. Trusting on his rainbow and travelling means to make his escape if need be, *naayéé' neezghání* approached the Travelling Rock, poked its ribs and said: "What is the matter with you, old man? You run after human beings, why not run after me?" And even when he punched him twice, Travelling Rock remained silent.

There was a certain spot on the head of Travelling Rock which even the Winds could not reach. Here *naayéé' neezghání* struck him with his club, punched him also in the mouth which was small but which he could open wide. But Travelling Rock was so fagged and stiff from his wild chase that he was scarcely able to move. All the while *naayéé' neezghání* was trying for a vulnerable spot, but his skin seemed too glossy and slick so that the club would glance off. Finally he made a fire with his torch, touched Travelling Rock with it at the east, south, west, and north sides, setting him ablaze. Thus he killed him by fire because his club made no impression on this monster. Therefore rock set on fire bursts asunder. Before sunset he had returned home. (The Hail Chant songs start from Travelling Rock.)

On the following morning he left for the Rubbing Rocks where Kicker-off-the-cliff lived. He waited for daylight, and before approaching he made some noise to attract attention. The monster was able to make his hair grow into the rock and usually sat leaning against the wall with his right foot resting on his knee. Every morning he made fresh tracks to deceive people and these led across a narrow path between himself and the precipice.

Naayéé' neezghání approached him, saying: "You are in a very close place, Old Man." "No," he replied, "there is plenty of space there and many people pass here to get arrow shafts (?)." "Will you let me get some?" *naayéé' neezghání* asked. "Sure," he said, "many others go there and return home with a supply." Meanwhile he placed zigzag lightning below his feet. As soon as he feigned to pass by him, the old man shot out his foot with a vicious kick. But the Lightning had instantly pulled *naayéé' neezghání* out of danger. "Ouch," said the old man. "I have a cramp in my leg, my Grandchild, which often annoys me." *Naayéé' neezghání* feigned again, and the foot shot out just as viciously as before but missed him.

Naayéé' neezghání laughed. "What are you trying to do, Old Man?" he asked him and feigned again and a fourth time. By this time the old man was close to the precipice and as he leaned over, *naayéé' neezghání* struck him in the back of the head precipitating him. After some time the thud of the striking body could be heard below, and the voices of his own two children echoed back as they fought over their father's arms, legs, and body parts. With a rainbow, *naayéé' neezghání* let himself down to them, but as soon as they saw him the children ran into a cave which had served them as a dwelling. To this *naayéé' neezghání* applied his torch and gradually smoked them out. Driven by the smoke they crawled out and pleaded for their life, which he granted them. And these children are now the Horse-fly or Gad-fly, Mosquito, Maggots, and Bottle-flies that eat flesh.

Some of the hair which he had extracted above their ears he had hung in a tree outside. "I killed the Kicker-off-the-cliff," he told his mother as he entered. "*Yúu!*" she exclaimed, "don't say that. Who could kill Kicker-off-the-rock?" But when she saw the hair on the tree she rejoiced and danced. And this is *hastiiniik'eh*—Old Man's Way, a War Dance.

Meanwhile he gave his brother all details of his encounter. Next they went in search of spruce from which they broke limbs pointing east, limbs pointing south, west, and north. Of these *naayéé' neezghání* made twelve hoops tied with zigzag lightning, and *tó bá jíshchíní* added one (hoop) of his own. These hoops were laid one on top of the other, the larger at the bottom, the smaller ones above, so that a cone-shaped fabric resulted in the shape of a dress (see "a"). He carried a bag of salt with him. He then blew a blue, white, red, and glittering wind, and rock crystal into the hoop fabric and slipped the salt into his belt. He then placed a sheet of basic sunred (see "b") over

a curved rainbow (see "c"), stepped
on these and slipped the spruce fabric
over his body. The rainbow and sunred were to provide a means of travel,
the rock crystal (was to provide) light,
and the winds were to carry him.

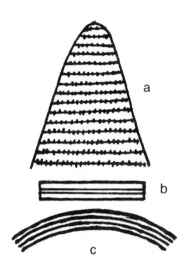

In this apparatus he went out to
challenge Slayers-by-their-eyes. He
travelled in a Sunwise Whirl(wind),
as suddenly a terrible sandstorm arose
which carried him in a bound about a
quarter of a mile away. In this manner he suddenly appeared at their
hogan, divested himself of the spruce
dress, and walked in. Surprised, they
said: "Where did you come from?
We had not expected you now." He
made no reply but kept his eyes on the
fire. Even so he felt the spell of their
eyes coming upon him and quickly emptied the bag of salt on the fire.
Here the salt exploded, filling their eyes. While they were busy rubbing
their smarting eyes, he clubbed them to death, sparing none.

And while he was piling them up, an old man begged him for his
life saying: "My name is Hunger. You can not afford to kill me because
you will want to eat." *Naayéé' neezghání* laughed and spared him.
Therefore, people get hungry and eat.

Another one who was called Poverty Old Man said: "People can
not wear new clothes all the time," so he spared him. Another called
Foam Old Man said: "People will wash themselves at times," so he
spared him also. Louse Man said: "People will get lonesome at times, let
them kill me at such times," to which he agreed. He also found an old
man there called Old Age who pleaded for his life saying: "It will not
do to let people be young always," and he spared him. Likewise
Drowsiness spoke: "People feel better if they can sleep." But he raised
his club to strike because he thought enough had been begging. But he
dozed away (off) with his club in midair. "Wake up," whispered the
Winds, "you can not afford to sleep now." Yet this happened four
times before Wind could fully arouse him. He felt better now, and
therefore he spared Drowsiness. Now, too, people feel better after
sleep.

The Pot Carrier Beetle was quite busy gathering their dishes. "You
have quite a load, my Grandmother," said *naayéé' neezghání*. "Yes,
my Grandson, I thank you for these," she said as she left. And he blew

upon her and her load four times so that today Pot Carrier still carries
these pots on his back.

Naayéé' neezghání then returned home for one night. At dawn he
started out in challenge of the twelve (Hunting) Antelopes. At daylight
he found them and blew a wind in their direction. In an instant they
were up and alert. He now blew the smoke of his torch toward the east
which they followed on a wild chase. As soon as they returned, they
noticed another line of smoke floating south. This, too, they followed
but returned tired and perspiring. Another line of smoke in the west
and north attracted them likewise. By this time they returned staggering and panting, with their tongues hanging far out from thirst.
"You must have had a great race," he said to them, but they made no
reply. "And now I have come to slay you for you have eaten our
people." "Don't do that to us, my Granduncle," they pleaded, "but
spare our lives. What benefit is it to you to kill us? We may be of use
to the people after all, and we promise to slay no more." "All right, I
shall not kill you," he said. And because they had been man-eaters
their tongues are (now) black. Here the corralling, trapping, and
game-burning songs start, which at present are no longer in vogue.
Hunting only is practiced. It was because these antelope would start at
the least breeze or bird that flew up, and would follow when they saw
smoke in the hope of finding food, that he was able to run them down.
He did not kill them and returned home early. But he was nervous and
spent the time walking around with his brother.

They slept. But about midnight he awakened his brother, saying
that he had had a dream. He had seen, he said, how a white column,
as it were, rose in the east and a yellow one from the west. These joined
up above and the two of them were below this. "This must be an evil
omen," he said, "and (it) implies that I should have killed the antelope." "No," said *tó bá jíshchíní*, "if we stood in the center it is a good
omen." Therefore people now relate their dreams. So that happened.

"My Younger Brother, I forgot something," said *naayéé' neezghání*. "What is it?" asked *tó bá jíshchíní*. "I forgot the weeds for the
weed garment," he answered. "I thought of it," said *tó bá jíshchíní*,
"and (I) brought the herbs inside." Of these *naayéé' neezghání* made
five (hoop) wraps on which he blew to increase them to man size. He
had two white shell mixed awls (?) one of which he placed on his right,
the other on his left breast. He then placed sunlight on the east, south,
west, and north sides of the herb dress and entered it. The Wind,
which he now blew on it, carried him to the home of the Overwhelming Vagina. The windstorm outside prevented her from noticing
his approach.

He left the herb dress outside, entered and stood warming himself
by the fire. "It is cold and windy outside," he remarked to her. Therefore we have the expression—it is windy, it is cold. Both he and the
woman had white (deer bone) awls. "Did you come to borrow an
awl?" she asked while handing him one. "No, I have my own," he said
as he produced it. Just then Wind whispered "look out" to him. She
had raised her vagina to crush him but the zigzag lightning, rainbow,
reflected sunred, and straight lightning on which he stood, pulled him
aside in time. Her privates therefore only whirled in the dust, even
(though) she repeated this four times. After that he crushed her head
with his dark flint club. River boulders are said to be part of her head.
Her numerous children, too, were there and he thought of killing these
likewise.

These were bunch cactus, sour cactus, wide cactus, slim yucca,
twisting heart cactus, milkweed—all plants that have spines. But as
they pleaded for their life he spared them, so that they are with us. The
Awl Chant begins here, although now it is no longer existing. He then
left for home and returned late and related his experience to his brother. "Yes, it happened so, I see," is all *tó bá jíshchíní* said. Therefore,
the Navajos (may) use this expression by discussing any (old) thing.

He now assembled the Dark, Blue, Yellow, White and Glittering
Little Winds, Darkness Child (Little Darkness), and Little (Child of)
Dawn, Skyblue, Evening Twilight, and Little Sunlight, which he
carried with him. But a Dark Big-Fly he set in his left ear, a White
Big-Fly in his right ear. He was out to challenge Tracking Bear.

While the Big Flies were guiding him he decided to send the
(children), Little Darkness, Dawn, Skyblue, Evening Twilight, and
Sunlight with the Wind People ahead to Tangled Earth, which was to
be their meeting place. When they met there the Winds and others
reported to him that they had not seen the Bear. He designated Mirage
House as the next meeting place but here, too, they (gave) the same
report. He then told them to meet at Striped Earth, and again they
reported that no tracks had been found of the Bear. They were then
told to meet in the rincon of the Two Ridges, which they did, only to
report that no tracks were visible.

"He is at the lower ridge of Jemez Mountain, I saw him there," said
Sunlight. After discussing the matter, *naayéé' neezghání* dispatched
Big Fly to locate his exact position. That done, Dark Wind took the
form of *naayéé' neezghání* and leaped in front of Tracking Bear then
ran toward the east, the Bear after him. Just when he was about to
grab him, the Wind disappeared under the Bear, which forced him to
return. But here Blue Wind was waiting for him in the form of *naayéé'
neezghání*, whom he chased to the south where Blue Wind disap-

peared below him. The Bear then chased Yellow Wind west, White Wind north, always with the same result.

Big Fly now whispered to *naayéé' neezghání* to get ready in person. At once he entered Glittering Wind and stood facing the Bear. By this time, (the Bear was) panting heavily and rolling about for breath, scarcely able to stand. "Hurry up," *naayéé neezghání* said to him, though the Bear's feet were red and raw with bruises. "Those red spots are his heart, shoot him there," Fly whispered. *Naayéé' neezghání* therefore shot his zigzag and straight-lightning arrows into the palms of his feet, killing him instantly. In (suffering) death he opened his mouth. Owl, Small Bird, and Mountain-top-way Chants begin here.

The head with the open mouth he cut off and threw it east, which became Gaping-bear Mountain. The trunk lying east became Grizzly Bear (Long-back Bear). Its entrails he threw into the water, where all kinds of water animals originated from it. He then cut off the right leg (and) threw it east where Erect Forelegs (synonym for Bear) walked away. The left (leg) he threw south where it turned into the Cinnamon Bear. The right leg he threw west where the Long-body (Grizzly?) walked off. The left leg he threw north from which Wide-feet Bear originated. Returning home he related to his brother what he had done.

At dawn he tackled the Sand Wall which was black in color. Upon his approach a wave of sand arose and he jumped aside. And lighting an arrow with his torch, he shot it into it on east and west side, then on its top, and it caught fire. The sand of it became (so) very fine and is so today.

The following morning he visited the Slicing Reeds to whom he said: "I came to kill you all." Four of them, however, walked out to him saying: "Do not kill us. In days to come we will be of use to the people. They will make prayersticks of us for sacrifice." Thus he spared them. And because they formerly ate people, some reeds have red and black stripes.

When on the following morning he challenged the Impassable Canyon, he carried four fire-clays with him—dark, blue, yellow, and white. And the Stone Wall receded as before when he feigned to step forward. "What do you mean?" he asked. "Oh," said the Rock, "I am (made) that way, I always do that." And four times he feigned a step forward but always received the same answer to his question. He then prepared to set fire to the fire-clays. When they burnt, the monster begged him to extinguish the fire. He did so but moved the wall far out for an open passage through it. Therefore our canyon walls are wide on top. Therefore, too, some places in the Earth are still afire, and stones contain fire because these colored fire-clays became (ignition) flints.

On the following morning he left again and arrived exactly at noon at the Endless Snake. He used his flint club on it, but its body was smooth and slippery and at every stroke it raised its body with equal strength, so that he realized that his club made little impression on its upper side. He therefore tried below. He sent the Dark Wind under the Snake and while the Whirlwind was flapping it up and down he quartered the Snake with his club. "Spare me," said the Snake. "I see that you are more powerful, my Grandchild." Therefore there are many small snakes today. And because the Snake said: "I'll be seen only in summer," we see them only during that season. And some of its parts became rattlers, bullsnakes, and others. The Navajo Windway (Chant) begins here, and the Earthway (Chant begins) at Sand Wall. It is said, too, that the *diné náhódlóonii* (other Navajos) also know of the Slicing Reeds and the Impassable Rock (Canyon).

That night he spent at home. At dawn he prepared to go to Folding Rocks. He entered a dark cloud and placed a rainbow under his feet and travelled in this manner. Or, too, he entered dark mist and placed reflected sunred at his soles and rolled on in this shape. It hailed furiously. A dark and a white mist fell also in such density as to make them impenetrable.

 The rocks were somewhat curved and facing each other in this shape so that a victim was crushed whenever they folded together. *Naayéé' neezghání* in his clouds entered the rocks in hail and storm, while even the Rock Children sought shelter under the (parental) Rocks on both sides. He then stamped his foot. At once the children called through the mist: "Who is walking there?" He promptly answered: "Nobody." Again he stamped his foot and the children on this side called across through the mist: "Is that you walking there?" "No," they called back. But *naayéé' neezghání* spoke: "It is I that is walking, what is it to you?" Instantly the rocks closed at top and bottom. But *naayéé' neezghání* set zigzag and straight lightning crosswise into the opening, which held the Rock apart. And White Thunder went into Zigzag Lightning and Spotted Thunder into Straight Lightning so that the Rocks were torn asunder. The children of the one Rock became deaf-rock (a rock resin), those of the other Rock (became) rainbow-excrement (another rock resin).

The rain ceased. And *naayéé' neezghání* looked about and saw that where Lightning had struck the stones showed the zigzag lines of it, others were blue with moss. Therefore, at times the marks of Lightning can be seen on rocks. He returned home and (for a) long (time) discussed with his brother what could be done to kill the Snapping Vagina. He prepared a red Big Star, a blue, white, and yellow one which he put in his red flint.[81]

He then entered gray mirage, sang a song and hurried over in the mirage cover. On account of the mirage she did not detect his presence. But *naayéé' neezghání* was frightened when he saw lightning shooting from her body in every direction. It was learned that this was due to the opening and closing of her vagina. At once he sent the red Big Star encircling the Sky edges. No sooner had she seen this than she dashed after the Star, but it escaped her. Again she dashed after a blue Star which he dispatched around the horizon, and likewise after a white and yellow Big Star. Worn out from this extended chase she returned and lay under her cover.

"Hurry now," Wind whispered, "she is fatigued and unable to do you harm." At once he poked her with his flint from east, south, west, north, asking: "Are you asleep?" and then drove his club into her open mouth. Therefore, today in a fight Navajos shove their fingers into the mouth and under the lip of their opponent. He then slew her with red Big Star, and with the blue, white, and yellow ones, shattering her to pieces. But while he was so engaged she still whispered: "Let there be a prayerstick of mine, let it often be made." Therefore, there are many prayersticks to this vagina woman and (to) parts of shame.

He returned to his brother. "Are there any more *naayéé'*, monsters, I wonder?" he said to his younger brother. So they dispatched the Big Stars in the four directions, then the Winds, then the black form of Darkness, the form of Skyblue, the form of Evening Twilight, and the form of Dawn. These, however, all reported that there were no more *naayéé'*. "There must still be some others," they said.

---

[81] This *béésh łichíí'*, does not occur in the following description. I am unable to say what is meant.

12
Changing Bear Maiden

The house dwellers (Pueblos) and different tribes, including the *diné nohodlóóni* (other Navajos) were living comfortably. The Tingling Maiden had twelve brothers who were great hunters and brought in sheep-horns containing much marrow. Deer and other game were well supplied in the home of the twelve brothers and their sister. While they were on the hunt, she was alone as usual and one day Coyote visited her.

"Are you alone?" he asked. "Yes," she said, "my brothers are gone." Immediately he made himself useful in carrying wood and water for her, then left again. On a subsequent day he met Badger and said to him: "My Cousin, let us visit that maiden over there." "Why should we do that," said Badger, "when the person is alone and we are unacquainted there." Now there was just one *yé'iitsoh* left, short of stature, whose whereabouts were not generally known.

But Coyote coaxed the Badger so long until he consented to go. It was dark when they reached her home where Coyote took possession of one corner, Badger of the other. "Are you alone?" Coyote asked. "Yes," she said, "my brothers did not return." "Why don't you marry instead of sitting here alone?" Coyote ventured. "What kind of man would you like? What must he do, how must his looks be?" he asked. "Yuh," she exclaimed, "I never thought of that. At any rate, it would not be you." "Even so, you ought to think of it. Somebody should carry wood and water and venison," he said. "I have other things to think of than that," she answered.

Coyote then turned to Badger saying: "Sing, my Cousin. If people don't want to get married, you ought to do something anyway." "Oh, I am not making love to anybody," Badger said. "I have no songs, you sing some." And Coyote at once began: "May the snow be level with the tips of the grass! *Ni-yo-o.*" "That will not do," said Badger. "If you say *ni-yo-o* it spells ill luck. You will chase your game but never reach it. Rather say *gó-la.*" And he sang a song but added *gó-la* for *ni-yo-o.* After that they went to sleep and she slept soon after.

In the morning there was snow. And they went hunting, both Coyote and Badger. Coyote used a moistened stick to drill the rabbits out of their holes. But he succeeded only in getting four ugly-looking rabbits whose fur was almost gone. Badger had four bundles of fine rabbits which he had scratched out. At sunset he was still working under the rocks when Coyote came along. And seeing the four bundles, he took two and replaced them with his scrubby specimens, then rolled a huge boulder over the burrow in which Badger was working and returned well satisfied.

"Clean these rabbits," he told the maiden. "No," she said, "wait until the other returns also." That was the custom. "But look at these fine rabbits," he said. "What can that fellow catch with his little toes? It requires real skill to catch rabbits." Just then Badger entered, threw down his bundles and said: "You certainly are a great one, Old Man. I had much work getting out from under that boulder with which you covered that hole. Besides, you took two of my bundles and put these things there instead." But he (Coyote) paid no attention to this but sat there with his back to the fire. The maiden then cooked the rabbits. Then they ate and went to sleep. They spent the night there then left in the morning.

After four days Coyote visited her again and packed wood for her. "What kind must he be whom you would marry? A hunter or what?" he suddenly asked her. "Oh," she said, "I have made up my mind that he must die four times before I marry him." As soon as he heard this Coyote went outside, hid his vital parts and returned only with his skeleton. "Here I am. Hurry, kill me!" At once she dragged him out, picked up two clubs and beat him to death. To make sure she had killed him, she beat his head and then returned to her hogan.

She had scarcely seated herself when Coyote entered saying: "That's once, come and kill me." She then dragged him to the south and there crushed him with stones, leaving nothing but a mess of him, and then returned. But scarcely was she seated when she heard him say: "That's twice. There are only two more left. Hurry." She then took him west, again crushed him with a rock and scattered the parts in all directions, then returned. Hardly had she entered and Coyote was there. "That's three times. Hurry, kill me." Again she dragged him north, crushed him with stone, mixed the parts with soil and scattered them at large. "There, now stay dead," she said as she started home.

But he returned his vital parts to their proper place, returned to her and said: "The number is complete, here I am." He then stepped outside and motioned to the Sun, and presently the Sun set. He returned inside and asked what more she expected. "Whosoever kills Gray *yé'iitsoh* and in proof brings me his head-bag with his quiver and stone axe, him I shall marry," she said.

That night he did not sleep but lay awake planning what to do. At dawn, however, he ran out to *yé'iitsoh* and found him asleep. "My Cousin," he said as he awakened him, "you sleep too long, therefore people outrun you." While the maiden was asleep he had stolen two thigh bones of deer from her which he carried with him. But *yé'iitsoh* said: "My Cousin, you alone get up early." "Of course I get up early," said Coyote, "but I also have a medicine that makes people run fast. You are too slow, my Cousin, therefore people get away from you. Let me make medicine for you, then none will outrun you." "That's true that you get up early," said *yé'iitsoh*. "Yes, you should get up earlier," Coyote suggested. "And you are fleet, too," *yé'iitsoh* said, "while I am not fleet because these Earth People often get away from me." "Then let me make medicine for you," said Coyote, "after that nothing afoot can outrun you. Stay here awhile and I'll show you how fast you will be." With that he went out east, south, west, and north and defecated at these points. Then he sat in the east and gave his call which was taken up immediately by the feces left there. Then he re-entered and *yé'iitsoh* was much pleased. "Press my legs also," he said, "that I may become as fleet as you are."

"For that we must make a sweathouse. No doubt you have many ugly things in your body which must be removed. Therefore we must take a sweat bath," said Coyote. "Alright," said *yé'iitsoh* and at once set to work while Coyote heated the stones. Inside the sweathouse Coyote carried some herbs and his the stolen thigh bones under them. When the curtains were hung and the stones inside, they divested and Coyote entered, followed by *yé'iitsoh*. "We must sweat first, then go out again," he told *yé'iitsoh*. After sweating they again left the sweathouse and returned, Coyote entering first.

He seated *yé'iitsoh* opposite himself then removed the fur from his leg, laid the deer thigh there and said: "Look I have cut the flesh on my leg to the bone. Put your hand here and feel it," he told him. "*Sho*," said *yé'iitsoh*, "you surely are a great one." But Coyote said: I'll now break the bone, then heal it again and do the same to you." He then broke the deer bone with a stone. "Feel here," he said, "it is broken as you see. It hurts but not much." "Hm," the *yé'iitsoh* mumbled. "Put your hand away now so I may heal it." And when he had done so, laid the broken bone aside, spit on his leg and said: "Get whole again, get whole again. There, feel her," he said. And immediately he slipped the second bone over his leg. "It is healed. How did this happen, my Cousin?" But Coyote repeated the same on the other leg putting the broken parts on the sound bone then removing them for the hands of *yé'iitsoh*. He then said: "Now, I'll run out and show you." And returning from the rounds he made, he said to *yé'iitsoh*: "You will be just as fleet as that, my Cousin." "You are a Holy One," *yé'iitsoh* said. And Coyote (said): "You, too, will be holy, as I am. You must now cut the flesh, then break the bone of your legs, just as I did. I shall then heal them for you."

And again they entered the sweathouse. Here *yé'iitsoh* moaned. "This will hurt a little more when I break the bone," said Coyote as he placed a stone below his leg just under the cut. Then with a second stone he struck the bone, breaking it. "Look out, here is the other. You'll feel better after I heal it." And again he broke the bone of the other leg.

"Spit on it, spit on it quickly, and say 'heal again'," *yé'iitsoh* said. But Coyote dashed for the curtain, raised it and said: "I never heard of a broken bone healing again." He then went to the house of *yé'iitsoh* and said to his wife: "*Yé'iitsoh* sent me for his stone axe, quiver, and head-bag; we are going on a big hunt because I made him fleet of foot." "There they are," she said. And he returned with them to *yé'iitsoh*, who was crying and shouting for help. And he shot his own arrows into him, then crushed his head with the stone axe and left him.[82]

With the quiver and stone axe in the head-bag, he returned to the maiden. She was friendly to him thereafter and accepted him as her husband. In the morning he was carrying wood and water for her but urinated anywhere in the hogan. That continued four days. On the fourth day she whispered to him: "My brothers are coming." He was frightened and she hid him in back of her belongings. The hogan showed filth and ashes everywhere. As a rule they would leave their bundles outside for her to sort the meat and boil what she liked. This time she did not stir. They also noticed the filth and disorder inside, but said nothing.

"Build a fire," one of them suggested after some time. But when the fire started they immediately perceived the smell of Coyote urine, threw the wood aside and angrily said: "Where did you get this wood? Throw it out and bring in some other." But when this was lit and warmed up, the smell became unbearable. And they swore at the Coyote who had done this. Meanwhile he lay behind the bundles. Again they sent out for wood taken from the lower limbs of trees. This, too, had the smell of Coyote urine. Even when they broke them off higher there was no relief. Again they swore at the Coyote who at that instant jumped into their midst and said: "Here I am, my Brothers-in-law." They hung their heads in shame.

Finally the elder said: "It is true, we have a Brother-in-law. Let us move away." And they built a hogan some distance away. In the evening the eldest brother said to the youngest: "Go over carefully and listen to what they say." And he heard Coyote tell her: "Do not believe what your brothers say against me. I have many things to tell you

---

[82]This entire section of the maiden who married Coyote, and the tests she exacted from him, is told in better detail by other informants.

which I have experienced. They will try to influence you but listen to me, not to them." He returned and reported this. Therefore, a mean man will always turn a respectful girl against her own family. And they were sorry and silent and that night slept very little.

On the following morning the elder said: "Let us go on the hunt." At once they made preparations, but soon saw the Coyote come over. "We do not want him to go with us," they said and told him to stay where he was. He came in spite of that and said: "My Brothers-in-law, what are you saying? Why these preparations? I shall go with you." None answered, neither would they look at him. But one remarked: "Let him come, you can not speak (sensibly) to a fellow like that." But Coyote returned to his wife and they hoped he would stay at home.

After they were out some distance, Coyote overtook them and they soon learned that, instead of helping, he scared the game away. And they were angry with him. Still they managed to get eight antelope and four mountain sheep. As one of the boys was carrying his mountain sheep, Coyote said to him four times: "Let me have the marrow of the horn." But the other replied. "If you want some, kill one yourself." But when he began to cut the horn to get at its marrow, the Coyote said: "Turn into bone, turn into bone," and so it really happened.

They then sent him after some water. When he was gone they said: "It is impossible to keep this fellow with us." And this happened at Spruce Circle. After Coyote returned, one of the brothers said to him: "One ought to go home (using the Brother-in-law polite form), his wife is lonesome and one should help at home. Take the venison home and let her cook it." They said this to rid themselves of him. Coyote agreed. Of the two packs of venison they made a small ball which they gave him. "Take this home," they said, "but do not open it until you reach home. There it will become large again. But it is easier to carry in a small package."

He seemed to consent to everything. From that place to their home was no great distance, but he detoured to Red-rock-ledge-canyon where the Spider and Swallow People lived. He had noticed the smoke of their houses in the distance. On entering the canyon he was curious to see how the bundle had been fixed, but when he opened it the (pemmican) increased to a large bundle. When he tried to lift it again he found it too heavy. He then divided it into four bundles, then carried one bundle after the other until he had reached the canyon rim. There he left his bundles and stood watching the people below.

"You Coyote People, what are you doing down there? You are so ugly that your teeth protrude. You try to marry and can't. Look at me. I have married Tingling Maiden." "Don't talk, First Scolder, move on and go elsewhere," they told him. That made him angry: "You ghosts," he said. "Your wives are just as ugly as yourselves." That vexed them. "Get the fleetest runners we have and go after him," they said.

And the Spider People encircled him with a fan-like web without his being aware of it. And when he saw the people rushing at him he taunted them and held his foot out saying: "*Eng, weng*, you can't catch this." When they reached the rim he laughed at them and turned to run. And coming to the first web he merely jumped through it. They had gained on him when he reached the second web, and almost had him when the third web checked him. But he turned and laughed at them. As he was checked by the fourth web they pounced upon him and cut his flesh. And Coyote whined, *wa, wa*, and *wa* again. But one said to him: "Did we ask you to say *wah*? Talk sweeter." And they pounced upon him again until he breathed his last. Therefore Plodding Spiders and Swallows have gray spots on their heads.

After a twelve-day hunt the brothers returned. They did not see Coyote but soon noticed that his wife was angry. Not knowing what had happened, they searched for him without finding a single trace of him. At sundown she asked: "What became of the man that accompanied you?" "We do not know," they answered. "All we know is that, on the day we left here, we sent him home to you with a bundle of venison." "But what has become of him?" she asked. "I suppose you killed him." "No," one of them said, "that fellow is not worth killing. We know nothing of him." She repeated her question time and again.

At dawn on the fourth day, after their return, they heard footsteps pass their hogan and they led to the canyon. Here she inquired of the people whether they had seen the man. "No," they said, "we have not seen him." "But you are the ones that killed him," and she fought them all day long and returned at sunset. On the following morning they heard the same noise, and one remarked: "This is bad. It must be that the worthless fellow whom she married has told her things of which we know nothing. We shall probably all be killed."

While one of them dug a pit in the hogan, the others gathered four stone slabs. After putting food and water into the pit, he told the youngest brother to go down. "If we are killed you will still remain to do something for us," they said. Then they covered the pit with the slabs, one above the other and levelled the ground again. They then left for the east side.

When she returned that evening to look for their tracks she found none. "What has become of my husband. Surely my brothers have killed him," she thought as she lay awake that night. At dawn she again visited the canyon. Her teeth and mouth had lengthened out like that of a Bear. After the brothers had gone east the elder spoke: "It is better that we separated and go in different directions." He turned east but had not gone farther than the Standing-big-spruce when behind him he heard a noise and suddenly his sister, in the shape of a Bear, was upon him and tore him to pieces. She returned to the hogan, and the younger brother could hear her raving above him. "She has turned into a Bear and killed your oldest brother," Wind whispered to him.

On the following morning she ran east again and overtook the second brother at Thick-pine-needles and killed him, then returned. This time the youngest heard her in the form of a woman: "Of my brothers that were, two are dead." And Wind whispered: "She has slain your two brothers." The third brother had gone to Thin-standing-rock where she overtook and killed him under this rock. The rock turned over and the place therefore is called the Rock-which-turned-over. She returned in the form of a Bear and he heard her claws rattle.

On the following morning she left for Round Mountain, on the north side of which there was a cave. Into this the fourth brother had crawled, but she traced and killed him there. Therefore a Bear always hibernates in a north-side den. He heard her return in her natural form and Wind whispered to him the news of his brother's death. She tracked the fifth brother to a place called Bear-food-spreads-out. And while she was killing him she heard the sound of breaking branches behind her. She found the sixth (brother) picking berries there and also killed him. Therefore, in war, the Navajos sometimes kill one or two enemies a day.

She now buried her vitals (heart, lung, and so on) under an oak tree with low thick umbrage, which was known as Oak-is-spread. She returned and he noticed that her breath was not human but the whistling zǫǫ-zǫǫ' of a Bear. She then ran to the place called Much Toadstool where she killed the seventh who had gone in hiding there. "She has killed seven now," Wind whispered when she returned as a woman. That night she killed the eighth at Creeping Darkness and returned at night. At the south side of Forked Mountain she killed the ninth one that morning.

When she returned he noticed that she was a Bear and heard her go to the Swallow People, with whom she fought all day. In the evening he heard her build a fire and extract arrows from her body. At dawn she went to Big Flower Patch. The tenth brother fancied he might evade her in this place, but she found and slew him there. "This is ten she has slain," Wind whispered, yet he dare not cry aloud. At Torn Adobe she killed the eleventh. "She has slain them all," Wind whispered, "but sing now." And while he (the youngest brother) cried, he began to sing as told. "I wonder where my younger brother is," he heard her say as she returned. "He must have died of lice and hunger."

And she travelled east, south, west, north, and returned east, humming to herself: "Where is my younger brother. Let me see. Wherever my excrement stands or falls, there my younger brother must be. Where my urine flows there my younger brother is." And it so happened that her voidings remained erect and her urine would not flow. "Down here he is," she said as she quickly removed the soil of the floor. Soon she struck the stone slabs, one and then another and another. And she greeted him: "Come, my younger brother, you must be dying with hunger and thirst. Come up. Let me kill your lice for you." But Wind whispered: "Do not do as she asks."

"Come, let me help you out," she coaxed. "I shall comb your hair and kill your lice." He took hold of her wrist and she pulled him out. Of the stone slabs she named one Sun, the next Moon, the next Sun, the next Moon. It was just past noon then. Wind whispered: "Do not let her get behind you. If you do she will bite your head off." So he told her: "Sister, let us go outside." "No," she said, "I'll pick your lice here." And four times they exchanged summons and answer. Then she consented. Again Wind whispered: "Watch her shadow."

Accordingly he seated himself so that he could watch the shadow of her head on the ground. And he sat facing north so that their shadows fell east on the ground. As soon as she stooped over him he was thus able to see her snout grow longer, similar to a Bear's snout. "What are you trying to do, my Older Sister?" he asked. "Nothing, my Younger Brother," she answered. "I am trying to kill your lice." Twice more this happened, then Wind whispered: "Be quick. The next time she will bite your head off. Watch for a place where you will see a Ground Squirrel dancing up and down. There she has hidden her heart and vital parts. Be sure not to miss them."

His brothers, too, had given him two zigzag lightning and straight lightning arrows before leaving him. For this reason Navajos groove their arrow shafts with straight and zigzag lightning. These arrows he held between his feet as she was working over him. As soon as he saw her stoop again he picked the arrows up and got to a start just as she was about to grab him. As he ran along he sang two songs, and looking back he noticed that she was gaining on him rapidly. "Look out," Wind whispered and with a leap he bounded over a wide yucca and *yé'ii* yucca which she was forced to encircle, giving him a new lead.

Again when she approached too closely he bounded over horned and slim cactus around which she had to circle. He now saw the oak tree and the Ground Squirrel dancing on leaves. On the run he shot the lightning arrows into the leaves from which a stream of blood flowed. At that instant, too, (when) she fell to the ground a stream of blood gushed from her mouth. "Draw a mark across quickly," Wind whispered. "If the two streams meet she will revive." At once he drew a zigzag line with an arrowpoint in the path of the streams which stopped further flow, and this blood is malpais (rocks) which are close together in the the east (location unknown).

He was panting for breath and whittling a stick with his arrowpoint and he sang two songs. He then cut off her vagina and tossed it up into a tree, and this became a Porcupine. Her left breast he threw away, and piñon nuts originated from it, while acorns sprung from her right breast. One after another he cut legs and arms off, throwing them to the four directions. And looking east he saw a Bear trot away and he called after it: "If ever you do this again I shall cut you up more than this time." But the Bear shook his head and left. And here the Bears start. In the south he saw a White Bear, and though he spoke to it the Bear paid no attention. Therefore, the White Bears of the south are very mean. In the west a somewhat Yellow Bear trotted along, which is the Cinnamon (Bear) of today. And when he spoke to this one, he answered: "All right, my Granduncle." Therefore these are not mean. In the north he saw Spotted Bear going along. It never answered when he addressed it. Therefore these will attack a person even without provocation.

From her trunk (spine) the Long-back Bear originated which are harmless and will only defend themselves if attacked. Her paunch he dragged to the water and left it. Here alkali was produced from it. The aorta (trachea?) he threw to the west where a plant sprung from it, which is used in stomach trouble. The kidneys changed into mushrooms. Her entrails, bladder, and gall he threw out in a lump from which we have sorrel or dock. The intestines he scattered and herbs of various kinds sprang from them which became food of the Bear, for they eat the roots of plants. In this manner he killed his sister.

He then wept for his brothers. He then wrapped lightning around his legs and body and hurried to Standing-big-spruce, where he found the bones of his oldest brother. And Dwarf Boy put lightning below these bones, raised them and sang one song of Owlway, and his brother became whole again. He sent him to a place called Medicine-coiled-over-each-other where he told him to remain until his return. Making the round to all places where his other brothers had been killed, he revived them and sent them to the same spot. At each place he sang the same song and finished this work in one day. The eleventh brother he accompanied to the place. All these brothers now took the name Dwarf Boy.

In the east, south, west, and north, he now gathered medicines (roots). He put these into two baskets, an Earth (Woman) and a Water Woman basket. In the first mixture they bathed themselves, out of the second basket they drank. After this they discussed future plans. And when the elder wanted to speak out as he had done before, the others said: "We will do as our youngest brother says." Therefore, if the oldest among brothers has no sense, a younger one is chosen as spokesman. These boys, therefore, became Medicine and Holy People and the *haneełnéehee* had these medicines.

"We shall go to Mirage-material(-place) and live there," said the youngest. They started out for this place and reached it. It was a sloping canyon into which they looked. They saw a ledge of dark mirage, over this a ledge of blue, then of yellow, and of white mirage on both sides of the canyon. On the north side twelve persons stood whose features and general appearance resembled their own. "Who can these be?" the elder remarked. And the younger brother replied: "Just like ourselves." Yonder in the mirage they had their women, of whom there were many. With these they mingled and exchanged rites and songs, and they found that in language they did not differ. They stayed here four days, among these other Navajos.

13

The Flood

In those days many people appeared. At Awatobi they had a great village. At Wide Ruins, and at Standing Willow, and south of San Francisco Peaks there were House Dwellers and Cliff Dwellers. They were numerous as Red Ants, all the way to Pueblo Bonito and the river. The Navajos lived among them. At Blue House, they claimed, were two Non-sunlight-struck Maidens, and two at Awatobi, and near Allantown, and in the south. The people transported their goods and travelled afoot. There were no enemies to fight. On the south side of San Francisco Peaks there were enemies, but not on its west side. And they exchanged visits, especially after the *naayéé'* had been destroyed. After *yé'iitsoh* had been killed by Coyote, *naayéé' neezghání* visited east and the other points but found no *naayéé'*. Then he sang his song.

The House Dwellers (Pueblos) were getting mean and abusive toward the Navajos because they were proud of themselves. While they had no horses, cattle, sheep, and hogs, there were numerous antelope, deer, elk, rabbits, jackrabbits, and porcupine in the mountains.[83] They had great farms and built fine houses which filled them with pride and meanness. The House Dwellers finally outnumbered the Navajos greatly and imposed upon them more and more. They ventured even to impose upon *naayéé' neezghání*, which set him thinking. The woman (who was) chosen as the future wife of *naayéé' neezghání* took sick. Every means to revive her failed, even the House Dwellers tried but could not help her. The *haaneełnéehee* then was performed over her just as it had been performed in the lower world. Therefore, there is no danger if the singer performs this rite over his own wife, which can not be said for other chants. The *haaneełnéehee* which was held here, with bough enclosure (for nine nights) was more holy because it was actually performed, while in the lower world it was typical only of what was to take place (up) here.

This was the last Bough Circle (Corral) Ceremony of the *haaneełnéehee*, therefore (of) a nine-night ceremony. Here it was ordained that in (the) future it should be of a five-night duration (or less). Today it is so and is held only inside the hogan.

---

[83]This sentence seems to apply to the hunters, the Navajos. The following sentence applies to the agricultural Pueblos.

After this ceremony a council was held. Here they mentioned that the House Dwellers were rubbing their fingers in their eyes and imposing on people otherwise. On the fourth morning after the council, *naayéé' neezghání* and *tó bá jíshchíní* left for their father's home in their usual supernatural way. Without an obstacle or delay they reached (their destination) in four days. "Whence did you come, my Children?" he asked. "From the same place as before, my Father," they said. "And for which purpose?" "We came to see you about something, my Father," they answered. He offered them the jet and turquoise stools.

And they noticed a middle-sized woman who rose, took a white shell cane and went east; (she) then returned much younger than she had been. When she went south and returned, her hair was gray. When she returned from the west she seemed quite old, and her hair was completely white. And when she returned from the north she walked slowly and in a stooped position. And she looked at them, then went north again and returned as a beautiful young maiden. And returning from the west she showed gray hair, from the south she returned as an old woman, and from the east (she returned) decrepit and very aged.

"My Children," the Sun said, "tell me the news." And they related what they had done to *yé'iitsoh*, Eagle Monster, Travelling Rock, and the others. "That I know because I was present," he said. "But why are you here now?" "Well," they said, "when we were here last you opened these doors and showed us horses, cattle, and corn of which you promised to give us. As all is peaceful now, we can plant and use these things. Therefore we are here now." He bowed his head and said nothing. He stood this way for some time then spoke: "My Children, you expect too much. I sacrificed my son and my pets. You are increasing in men and women and children. Now I can not always bestow favors. I shall therefore ask something of you which you must first consider before I can do anything more." "But you promised this," they said. "It's true that you have helped us, but we asked this that we might grow and multiply. Therefore we are here now to receive the things you promised."

"Even so, I have given enough. I see every day how you are multiplying and increasing in wealth. Had you taken the things which I showed you, I should not have helped you in the manner I did. Therefore it seems to me that I have done enough," he said. "Well, if you can not give us all, give us at least some horses. Give us corn which we can plant and such seeds as we can use in our country." And they pleaded four times with him, but he refused. "There is no use of further mention. If you wish, however, to do me a favor, give me their (the House Dwellers') souls. I may then consider the thing."

"Don't say that, my Father. You ought to pity them and not ask their lives of us." "Did I take pity on my son? I never argued the matter with you when you asked it of me. Do this favor now for me and I'll do anything you ask. Why do you hesitate?" "All right," they said. "What can be done about it." "Thanks, my Children," he said. "I promised you jet, turquoise, abalone, white shell horses, but I have no spotted ones. And likewise what is in the south—elk, buffalo, antelope, porcupine, deer, and rabbit—(it) is yours. Likewise in the west, the white, blue, yellow, and black corn, (the) striped and varicolored, (and) the pollen is all yours. And in the north the plants and pollens, the small birds are yours. The rainbow, zigzag lightning, reflected sunred, and sunray in the east, and the various mirage in the south I promised to you, and He-rain and She-rain in the west and Dark Mist and White Mist in the north are yours," he said. "In how many days will it be that you do this?" he asked. "In twelve," they said. "No, let it be in four days," he said, and they agreed. Therefore, appointments are usually set for four days. On that day all House Dwellers, and the Navajos included, were to be slain. So they agreed.

And he opened the doors for them and sang a song. At once a jet horse came to him and he patted its neck and body and collected shaken-off pollen from it and mouth-pollen from its mouth. Similarly he did to the turquoise, abalone, and white shell horses. In the south again he sang a song. A fine buck ran to him from which again he collected the pollens from its body and mouth and also the soil on which it had walked. Like soil from the tracks of antelope, of the fawns of both. He then opened the gates in the west. Here they saw mirage sheep where before they had seen corn. And from these he shook the pollen and mixed eyecrusts. In the north he gathered (pollen) of corn and plants (which were) there, and in a white shell basket he gathered their pollen and dew.

Mixed *ajáájí (?)* and jewels he now put separate on a buckskin. The shaken-off pollens he placed in small bags east and west, the mixed jewels and *ajáájí* (he placed) south and north. "Stand here," he told *naayéé' neezgháni*. He then gave him all the things mentioned. "When the rainbow stands in your door you will know what to do, not before. You gave your consent first, and I gave you these things first." He then sang four songs in which he placed the bundles on their breast, back, shoulders, and head, and told them to go because he had given these to them. After this he sang four additional songs. He then tied the bundles with sunray and sunlight and handed them to the boys. "I shall be there in four days," he said. They returned on rainbow and dismounted at Streams-side-by-side.

In four days the Sun arrived with sticks of pine, spruce, oak, and valley oak in length of the arm to the little finger. The Dark, Blue,

Yellow, White, and Glittering Winds ran in every direction to warn the
people. "This will be an evil day for you, make the best of it." And the
Holy People picked up a man and a woman, each a pair of them. In
the shape of an arrow the Sun then put dark big hail into the pine, blue
big hail into the spruce, white big hail into oak, mixed big hail into
scrub-oak of the valley. These he shot east, south, west, and north. At
once a Whirlwind arose and Thunders, but Sun made two leaps and
disappeared. Then the Winds came up and uprooted trees and stones,
and clouds burst, and it rained and hailed for twelve full days. And the
mountains were covered with water so that none could be seen. Ice
floated everywhere and covered the whole surface.

And the Sun threw off his blankets. And the hot Sun beat down
upon the big hail and the ice which immediately began to melt. To
speak of this in summer is dangerous. Four days this lasted and the
water decreased at a rapid rate. In four more days there was still less
water, and after four additional days all water had disappeared. The
Sun left only the springs and water holes. Therefore on some of the
mountains, the melted dirt (slides) can still be seen.

Crow had been picked up by Dark Wind and Magpie (was picked
up) by the Dawn. And after the flood they were walking side by side,
picking eyes out of the dead bodies. That's all here. And when the
Earth dried again, the Holy People replaced (the dead with) those
whom they had saved, and these are the ones living here now. They
had also picked up birds and animals, male and female, and replaced
them. These we see now.

PART TWO:

UPWARD MOVING
AND EMERGENCE WAY

PRACTICE AND APPLICATION

14

The Ceremonial Performed

AN INVITATION

The *haneełnéehee bihóchǫ́ǫ́jí* is still invoked by present-day Navajos. At the time of recording the legend of this rite in 1908, the singer *gishin biye'* was called on to perform a five-night ceremony in the neighborhood of Saint Michaels, Arizona. Being familiar with the legendary account, as he said, he also suggested that the occasion may be profitably accepted to witness the rite in practice. Accordingly, he made every arrangement at the patient's hogan for my presence during the entire ceremonial.

As the full name of the ceremonial implies, it refers to the *bihóchǫ́ǫ́jí* (ghost-side) influence which induces indisposition, swooning, and danger to life and health. As the legend has brought out, this ghost-side performance does not exclude the blessing aspect *(hózhǫ́ǫ́jí)* altogether. As a matter of fact, Blessingway must be included in *hóchǫ́ǫ́jí* as in other ceremonials.

The occasion for the chantway performance was presented by the birth of twins who were the pride of their family. They called one boy Monster Slayer *(naayéé' neezghání)* and the other Born-for-Water *(tó bá jishchíní)* in honor of these mythic slayers of monsters. The birth of twins is variously mentioned in the legend. Subsequent to having given birth, the mother suffered frequent attacks of swooning and spells of weakness. The cause of these was unknown but was ascribed to the ghost of some person whose death the mother had witnessed some years earlier. The family decided on having the *hóchǫ́ǫ́jí*.

They considered that a new site should be selected for the ceremonial which would be sufficiently distant from this ghost's activity. As soon as the new hogan was ready, the singer was notified. No special dedicatory ceremony was required, the singer said, but small twigs of scrub oak were inserted in the crevices of the hogan at its cardinal points.

A ceremony usually begins in the evening, and its duration is measured by the nights it may require. The ceremony in question required five nights, terminating with the Closing Ceremony *(bijį́)* of the fifth night. The singer advised that the preparatory night would scarcely be of interest, as it required but an hour and a half, and consisted of singing a set of songs. The ceremony proper began on the following morning, shortly after sunrise, with the Fire Ceremony.

At the hogan the patient, the singer, and a few attendants had gathered and were awaiting my arrival. Presently a large bundle of small pieces of firewood was stacked on the south side of the entrance inside the hogan, after which the curtain was drawn and secured, so that nobody might enter or leave while the ceremony was in progress. This done, the singer and the men proceeded to divest themselves of their garments, down to the breechcloth, while the patient and the attending women removed their upper garments to the waistline. I received an invitation to do likewise; as they explained, the fire later on would prove decidedly uncomfortable. I declined, saying that I thought I would be able to stand the heat in my shirt sleeves.

The hogan was hectagon-shaped, possibly eight to ten feet in diameter, with four uprights supporting the superstructure or dirt roof. All told, there were some fifteen to twenty persons present. The men were sitting along the south, the women on the north side of the fire. The fire was built in the usual fireplace, a spot on the floor below the smoke hole through which the smoke could easily escape. Sufficient cedar wood, which causes very little smoke, was stacked at the south side of the entrance curtain to feed the fire. The patient, and the singer to the south of the patient, squatted in the west corner of the hogan and were facing east. As the space was small, the singer had moved his paraphernalia toward the south. Thus, practically the entire west side was being reserved for the patient and the requisites of ritual. A small piece of calico print had been spread between the patient and the singer. On this, native earthen bowls and pots of various sizes had been placed and filled with water. This done, the singer produced a rattle made of hide and intoned several songs. During the course of these he prepared a lotion, or bath, by adding various herbs to the water. In the process of this preparation, one of the attendants gathered up a bullroarer. Its cord he dipped into the bath of herbs and twisted it across his knee to render it more pliable. With this he slipped outside through the curtained entrance, passed around the hogan from the north side to the south, whirling the bullroarer so as to produce a vehement buzzing sound.

Upon re-entering the hogan he passed around the fire "sunwise," south of it, and wrapped the cord around the bullroarer. In this shape he pressed the face of the bullroarer to the soles, the knees, the hands, the breast, the back, the shoulders, and to the top of the patient's head. He then passed with it in front, to the right, and to the left of the patient. He raised it to the smoke hole, toward the sun, breathed toward it and laid it aside. This provided an opportunity to examine it.

They called it "the groaning stick." It is elliptical in shape with a perforation at the bottom, or butt, through which a thong of Bighorn sinew is passed. The wood, they said, is pine riven by lightning which, after being shaped by scraping, is covered with a mixture of yucca pitch and pitch gathered from a lightning-struck tree. The whole body of the stick is then charred with lightning-struck ashes or charcoal.

At its top or "head" the groaning stick has settings of three turquoise stones which represent its eyes and mouth. This side is therefore its face. Just above these settings, but on the back of the stick, I noticed a small setting of abalone, which was its headrest or pillow. To produce a buzzing sound it must be well moistened and rubbed, and for this reason it is dipped into the medicine and rubbed across the knee.

It appears that the songs and the buzzing of the bullroarer were part of the ritual in the preparation of the medicine bath. The singer repeatedly sipped from this preparation and finally handed it to the patient, who swallowed a mouthful of this herb mixture and then bathed her hands, chest, back, face, and knees with it. The remnant she passed along to the audience. By the addition of water the supply was sufficiently increased to permit all of them to bathe themselves as the patient had done.

During this ceremonial procedure the fire had been regularly fed from the stack of wood at the entrance. As stated before, there was nothing distinctive about the fire, except that it was fed more often than usual. But four sticks, called *honeeshgish* (pokers) surrounded it. One was placed east of the fire, another south, one west, and the fourth north of the fire. These pokers are not actually used during the ceremony, but they represent four youthful horned rattlers *(tł'iistso)* that enter from the cardinal points to assist at the ceremony. Accordingly, the ritual prescribes that these pokers should be taken from branches of a piñon tree, one each from a branch pointing east, south, west, and north. These respective positions the pokers must occupy around the fireplace. They may be taken from a single tree, of course, so long as the branches point in the required directions.

The sticks were not colored, not even shaven of their bark. The singer, however, explained that originally these rattlers were beautiful youths whose bodies were formed of these colors and sparkled with them gorgeously: the youth of the east had a body of a beautiful red-white stone, the youth from the south "walked in" turquoise, the one of the west in abalone shell, and the youth from the north in rich black jet. As these materials can not be had in large quantities, this ritual permits the use of piñon sticks as a substitute, with their "heads" or direction of growth pointing toward the fire.

Similarly, the singer continued to explain that they have done away with the fire drill: "As I told you in the legend, the Firegod or Blackgod *(hashch'ééshzhini)* always carried the drill and the igniter to build this fire. We used a flat tinderbox of cottonwood with holes carved into the soft wood, and a slim hardwood igniter which we set into the hole. The fire is produced by whirling the igniter between our hands. But this is a slow and uncertain process, and we now often use matches which are easily carried."

During the bath I also had time to inspect the two rattles which, to distinguish them from claw, hoof, and gourd rattles of other ceremonies, were called "hide rattles," because the body of the rattle required buffalo or rawhide material. "Now that buffalo hide is difficult to obtain," said the singer, "we must substitute rawhide. This we shape while it is moist, and then we sew it at the top or at the side with deer sinew. Feathers that are alive, I mean such as you catch from a flying eagle, either in captivity or in flight, are tied here at each upper corner. At the bottom this collar is a plush of muskrat, sometimes of beaver skin, while the neck or handle of the rattle is wrapped with porcupine quills over plaited rawhide. This tail of a buffalo—at present a cow tail—is wrapped and secured with a sacred buckskin thong, taken from a deer that has not been wounded but killed otherwise." "And the rattling noise," I asked, "how is that produced?" "You insert hard goods, that is, fragments of white shell, abalone, turquoise, red-white stone, and jet. Both rattles are alike and are used when you have another singer to assist you, as you will see when we get further along."

After the bath the singer distributed some herbs among the audience. Of these, a portion was boiled in an earthen pot, while another portion of herbs was placed into a basket and water mixed with them. During this time he sang what was called a Flash Lightning Song. Before the song ended the boiled herb concoction was distributed in various pots.

A number of broad yucca leaves were then handed to the patient who pressed them against her arms, face, breast, and stomach. After each pressing she raised them to the cardinal points in rotation. Some of the assistants now interlocked their yucca leaves which, with tips extending, gave them the appearance of a pointed star. Four of these were made and were called *yéí bitsáanii woltááá* (yucca knot). These were spattered with the herb concoction when the singer sprayed a mouthful on each of them. They were then laid on the right side of each poker.

Thereupon the herbs were removed from the water with which the patient and those present bathed themselves. After the bath was finished, a small heap of sand was levelled smooth, over which two crow feathers were laid with their shafts crossing each other diagonally. A third crow feather was laid across the shafts of the first two. Another mixture of herbs was added to the boiling water, all of which was accompanied by song and rattle.

The patient was now directed to proceed around the north side of the fire to the east, then to step from the eastern yucca knot to the one in the south, from this across the poker to the western one, from this to the northern knot, and then to complete the circle and to return to her place. This procedure was repeated, in turn, by all who were present, except the singer. He explained that this part of the ceremony was called *bikáá' nadinizhał* (step from one on the other).

Upon completing this stepping ceremony, crow feathers were distributed among all who were present; the patient was directed to take one of the three from the sandhill. The herb concoction was then distributed with instructions to drink of it. The patient then inserted the crow feather into her throat and produced emesis. The others drank likewise and irritated their throats with the crow feathers until each had succeeded in vomiting.

Meanwhile the stack of wood was disappearing rapidly. In the course of subsequent songs the men and women repeat the "stepping on the knots" ritual four times. Two men are then designated to jump over the fire. They step on the yucca knot in the east and hop over to the knot in the west and back again. Then they step on the yucca in the south and hop onto the knot in the north and back again. This performance they repeat four times.

Now the patient was directed to stand on the yucca knot in the east. Standing behind her the singer chanted a song, accompanied by the men present. When this was finished, the patient was directed to go to the south knot, while the singer cut or unravelled the east knot with the bullroarer. He handed the yucca leaves to the audience and the people put wood ashes from the fireplace on them. The patient did likewise with the bullroarer when the singer handed it to her. While matching their actions to the words of the song, each blew the ashes toward the smoke hole, that is, toward the sun. In the absence of yucca leaves, the others used their crow feathers. This unravelling proceeded, in the same manner, at each of the knots at the other cardinal points, thus ending with that of the north. All turns in the ceremony must be made "sunwise"—proceeding from the east to the south of the fire and around.

The patient now was allowed to leave the hogan, and she did so after the curtain had been raised with one of the pokers. The vomit in the sand was collected and the sand gathered up in blankets which each one carried out to the north side of the hogan.

A basket with water was now placed before the singer; into it he placed the bullroarer and four large arrow points of various shades. To this he added, from several pouches, a mixture of dried and pulverized herbs. Apparently this he dedicated with song and rattle. Presently he laid the rattle aside, picked up a sprinkler—a bundle of turkey feathers—and he proceeded to sprinkle the patient: her feet and knees, her right and left side, her front and back, and her head. He sprinkled all those present more generally, after them the unravelled yucca leaves, the four corners of the hogan, the fire from each of the cardinal directions, also four times over or through the smoke hole, then his entire paraphernalia, and finally he ended by blessing himself in the same manner.

After this some hot embers were raked from the fireplace, with the used of hands, and placed near the patient. A pouch containing "incense herb" was produced, and a generous pinch of it was sprinkled on the hot coals. These produced a sweet-smelling smoke which the patient inhaled by leaning over them, while the others present eagerly gathered the fumes toward them with their hands. The embers were then extinguished with water and the charcoal thrown through the smoke hole. Thereupon the entire fire was extinguished and the ashes removed.

An attendant carried away the yucca leaves. Following directions, he laid all tips or "growing ends" toward the north. Finally the "pokers" were gathered up and laid aside in the south end of the hogan with their butt ends pointing south. This concluded the Fire Ceremony. After this, all were allowed to leave the hogan to get fresh air, to remove the sweat with sand and to dress themselves again.

Preparations were now made for what proved to be the closing ceremonies of that morning's ritual. A bundle of sumac twigs, about twenty in number and twelve to fifteen inches in length, were brought in. Together with these spruce twigs were laid, side by side, with a supply of gramma grass, sage, watercress, dodgeweed, and other grasses. From his paraphernalia the singer produced cords and deer thongs to which, under his direction, downy eagle feathers were fastened. Two or three attendants were now directed to select four sumac twigs, to cross the ends so as to form a square, and to tie a bundle of spruce and other branchlets at each corner, with the cord, by forming slip knots with the dangling ends feathered, so as to allow the arrangement to be easily unravelled later on.

Of these arrangements there were five in number, one smaller than the other, so that the finished products had a beehive or cone shape. These were called "small hoops" (tsabąs) and the ceremony was called "unravelling of the small hoops."

When these were ready, a mixture of dried herbs and water was prepared. With this mixture the singer dedicated the hoops by spattering it on them, by the accompaniment of song and rattle. This done, he continued the song and directed the patient to remove her moccasins and to assume a sitting position by drawing her feet close in. In this position he passed the largest hoop over her, close to the ground. The next one he passed over her knees, the next one over her breast and shoulders, the next one over her mouth, and the final one over the crown of her head. Dressed in this manner, the patient sat during the singing of two songs. In the course of these songs the singer sputtered her again with the herb mixture, from the front, the sides, the back, and from the top. He now took what was called "the knife of the Slayer of Monsters" (of *naayéé' neezghání*) and of his brother Born-for-Water *(tó bá jishchíní)* into his hand. In this instance this was a large and slightly serrated arrowpoint.

With this knife he unslipped each knot at the corners of each hoop by drawing on the feathered cord. He began with the hoop of the head. The twigs and feathered cords he dropped aside on the floor. As he proceeded with the song, he unravelled each hoop in the order in which they had been placed on the patient, reversing the order from the crown to mouth, to shoulders, to knees and feet. The patient was now allowed to stretch out her feet again.

The singer now gathered up all feathered cords and pressed them against the soles, the instep, the knees, the sides, the chest, the back, the hands, the shoulders, front, back, and top of the head. After each application of pressure he turned the cords up toward the east and the sun, and the patient was directed to breathe over her hands in that same direction. This identical performance was repeated with the twenty twigs of the hoops, after which the spruce and grasses were collected and were passed right and left before the patient. Thereupon the twigs and herbs were gathered up and deposited north of the hogan. There they were sprinkled with corn pollen.

The singer produced a gourd ladle and also asked for small bowls and saucers. These were filled with water and mixed with dried herbs taken from various medicine pouches. These mixtures were then dedicated with song and rattle, in the course of which the singer applied them to the soles, the instep, knees, hands, breast, back, shoulders, mouth, forehead, and crown of the patient. Thereupon the patient was given the medicine to drink from the ladle. With the medicines in the bowl and saucers she bathed her body and face. The singer now sprinkled the patient with pollen in the usual manner—the soles, instep, knees, hands, chest, back, shoulders, mouth, forehead and crown—after which the singer and the patient ate a pinch of pollen. The pollen bag was now passed to the audience. All sprinkled a pinch on their heads and then tasted some.

They spread out a buckskin with its head portion toward the east. On this the patient was seated. The singer handed her the bullroarer and the *azee'* (medicine) to hold in her right hand.

This was a small buckskin of about six by six inches square, containing dust from the sacred mountains of the east, south, west, and north, also clays from other sacred spots. To this was added *aa nahoogáád*, dust gathered in the tracks of animals like deer, bighorn, mountain lion, usually from spots where such animals have taken a dust bath, or spots into which "live" feathers of an eagle or the like have been dusted or shaken. Stone or agate which they call *hadahoniiye'*, mirage stone or *hadahoneestiin*, haze stone of the north, as well as small fetishes representing horses (*ńishchiin*) are included among its contents. The corners are then gathered and wrapped securely with a sacred buckskin thong. The entire preparation is called "medicine," or it may be named "sacred mountain dust" after its essential ingredient.

Holding the pollen bag and some large arrowpoints in his right hand, the singer squatted down before the patient and began reciting a long prayer which the patient had to repeat verbatim. As this must not suffer interruption and a slip of tongue must be carefully avoided, I was able only to catch the initial sentences:

Ch'ól'į́'į́ bitáál áádę́ę́' hashch'éełti'í binii' łigaigo bigish łigaigo shíká nikiníyá....

From the summit of Spruce Mountain, Talking-god, with thy white face, with thy white cane upon me, come thou to my home....

Then in rapid order follow each other: invocations to his blue cane, to his yellow and black cane, to his home in white, blue, yellow and black mist, to his home in the first, second, third, and fourth shelves of the skies—with petitions to remove the spell and to remove all witchcraft. The prayer required approximately a half hour. This was followed by pressing the limbs with the bullroarer, with the sacred mountain dust bundle, with pollen and arrowpoints. Eating and sprinkling pollen concluded the ceremony for that morning.

There was nothing further on the program for that day, also nothing for the second night of the ceremony.

On the morning of the second day, the same Fire Ceremony was repeated, only this time scrub oak twigs, instead of sumac, were used for the five small hoops. This and part of the previous day have been spent in gathering yucca leaves, spruce twigs, and various grasses which the singer required for the subsequent ceremonies. In the late afternoon I was summoned again to witness the continuation.

Suspended from a beam of the hogan I found what appeared to be a conical cover made of spruce twigs, which was called *ch'ó'éé'* (spruce dress). Apparently, this dress consisted of four spruce boughs entwined with wreaths of spruce twigs which had been tied in slip knot fashion with yucca thongs. The wreaths were five in number, they circled from bough to bough and were fastened there. The lower wreath consisted of nine bunches of spruce twigs, the number of which was decreased down to five for the upper wreath. Four yucca thongs were fastened to the butt of the boughs and passed, through the center at the top, to the beam where it was tied to a rope. A bundle of plants, with two turquoise feathers, was secured in the opening at the top of the spruce dress—with yucca thongs.

After a preliminary song, the singer raised the spruce dress and carried it to the north side of the hogan entrance. From this point he stepped across the fire and held the dress over the smoke. The dress was then unravelled and the spruce twigs gathered into blankets and laid aside. The hogan was swept and all rubbish removed. The singer explained that the spruce dress must be made in daytime, that the yucca thongs are ripped with claws—that is, with one of the claws of the claw shoulderband or wristlet—and finally, that the four spruce boughs must be taken from an east, south, west, and north branch of a spruce tree.

Meanwhile some of the attendants were ripping yucca leaves for thongs, while others were preparing a number of bundles of plants made up of grama grass, spruce, dodgeweed, sage, watercress, and like grasses. A number of spruce twigs were tied with yucca thongs and laid aside, while seven bundles of mixed plants were additionally decorated with turkey or crow feathers to which two olivella shells had been tied. These feathered bundles were secured by way of a slip knot with the familiar feathered cords of the hoops of the Fire Ceremony, and also laid aside.

What is called *hóchǫ́ǫ́jí azee'* (witch medicine) was then applied. This consisted of powdered Russian Thistle, wide-leafed spruce, Erio-gonum *(ni' bighánt'i')*, and a liniment made up of horsemint *(azee' ndoo'í'eezhí)*. This mixture was dedicated in the usual manner, with song and rattle and sputtered on the bundles of plants, after which they were laid on a blanket and covered up.

The patient was now called in. She entered sunwise and resumed her seat in the western corner of the hogan where she removed her blanket and moccasins. Four songs were now sung.

In the course of the song that followed, the singer dipped a bundle of plants into the horsemint liniment and began to press it against the right knee of the patient, downward to the foot. He then raised the bundle to the smoke hole and unslipped it while holding it against her right sole. He applied the second bundle in the same manner to the left knee and foot and unslipped it against the left sole. He again dipped the third bundle into the liniment and pressed the weeds against the chest, the right and left arm, and the back of the patient. He paused to raise it to the smoke hole and unslipped the bundle on her chest. The fourth bundle was unravelled in the same manner against her back. The fifth bundle he applied to her right elbow and arm, where he unslipped it also. The sixth was destined for the left arm and hand. The seventh and last bundle he dipped into the liniment as before and pressed it on her forehead, the back, right and left side of her head, and then unslipped it on the top of her head. With a passing motion he then covered the feet, knees, thighs, arms, shoulders, chest, back, and all of the head with the thongs. He raised the entire bundle of plants and permitted them to rain over the patient. Then, as with a whisk broom, he proceeded to brush off the patient with a bundle of crow feathers. He continued this in the immediate surroundings of the patient. Standing before the patient, he made continuous motions as though he was cutting the air with his feathers at the right and left, before, behind, and above the patient. He concluded by brandishing his feathers toward the smoke hole. The attendants removed the plants with instructions to point their growing ends northward.

This was followed by more songs. In the course of these, the "witch medicine" was administered from the gourd ladle. Likewise, the singer applied the horsemint liniment to the feet of the patient. After this the patient herself sipped of it and then applied it to the significant parts of her body as required. Again hot embers were raked from the fireplace for incense, which the patient inhaled and also pressed to the ritually significant parts of her body. After ashes had been placed outside on the four cardinal points of the hogan, the ceremony was suspended for a while.

The several bundles of spruce were then laid in order. Two single bundles with the turkey feathers were fastened to the soles of the patient in such a manner as to point the growing parts upward. On each leg or knee a bundle of spruce, without feathers, was secured in the same manner. Likewise, the wreath of nine spruce bundles, without feathers, was fastened on the stomach. The "shoulderband," with its turkey feather in the center and three spruce twigs on each side, was passed over the left shoulder to below the right arm. This was crossed by a similar shoulderband passing from the right shoulder to the left side. Each arm was now decorated with a feathered bundle of spruce. The top of each hand was decorated with twigs of spruce whose growing tips pointed downward, while the palm of the hand also received a feathered spruce twig. Finally, the wreath was placed on the crown with the feathers in the center. Unfeathered spruce was put at each side of this center.

Meanwhile, two of the attendants had left the hogan. They now reappeared stripped to the breech-cloth. Each was furnished with a miniature war-club, which is an oblong flat stone, the one edge of which is rounded, the other being slightly edged to represent a knife.

These two attendants impersonated the Slayer of Monsters (naayéé' neezgháni) and his inseparable twin brother Born-for-Water (tó bá jishchíní). They stood right and left of the patient. The song probably described the deeds of these two in the legends, because they presently made vigorous passes with their knives cutting to the right and left, before and behind, above and across the patient. With Monster Slayer on the right and Born-for-Water on the left side, each in his turn, first one then the other, cut the yucca strings—of the wreaths on the head, shoulderband, on right arm and hand, the wreath covering the stomach, that of the right leg and foot, then behind the head again, the back, left shoulder, left arm and hand, left leg and foot. Then they pressed the head of the patient in their hands, accompanying their offering with a brief u-u-u-hu, upward or toward the smoke hole.

Thereafter they "cut up" into fragments each bundle of plants associated with the wreaths; these the patient unravelled completely and laid aside. The spruce twigs were then held over the patient, sprinkled with ashes from the fireplace by the two Slayers and then dropped over the patient. They then brushed her completely with the whisk broom of crow feathers. Then they moved along the north side of the fire, from there to the south side of it, where they marched up and down, constantly making their cutting movements with their feather broom. The spruce was now collected in a blanket and carried outside, while the two Slayers each took his leave with a pinch of ashes from the fireplace.

Now the singer took the bundle of crow feathers, dipped them into the ashes and intoned a slow melody during which he repeated the passes with the feathers on all sides of the patient. He ended the song with a light tap of the feathers on his left hand, held toward the smoke hole. In the course of the song that followed, he repeated his sweeping passes along the north side of the hogan toward the south side, and during the third song he passed from the south side of the fire to the north side, ending both songs with a light tap of the feathers on his hand toward the smoke hole. He resumed his position in the southwest corner of the hogan. In the course of the next song the bullroarer was whirled around the hogan outside. After this Monster Slayer entered and pressed the limbs of the patient with both ends of the bullroarer. This performance was repeated during the next song by his brother, Born-for-Water. After each pressing the bullroarer was raised toward the smoke hole and breathed upon. Born-for-Water now applied a mixture of cedar ashes and water to the patient's feet and limbs of the body, after which he bid her drink of it. This was then also passed to the others who were present. They tasted of it and rubbed their hands and face with it. With the remnant the patient was allowed to bathe her limbs. With this activity the two Slayers finished their part.

The bullroarer was now handed to the patient and the others who were present were supplied with crow feathers. These they dipped into the ashes, blowing them toward the smoke hole at a given word during the four songs which were then chanted.

A brief interval was allowed. Clean sand was carried into the hogan in a blanket and spread with a batten stick before the singer in the southwest corner. Colors, to be used in the construction of a sand-painting, were carried in on small trays of pine bark. One tray each was used for white clay, blue cedar ashes, yellow ochre, charcoal, and brown—which was a mixture of charcoal and crushed red sandstone. Apparently there was no prescribed order in which to proceed as, under the direction of the singer, the attendants proceeded almost at random—one with the body, another continuing with the arms, or legs, or neck of the figure, or with whatever was convenient. The colors were slightly "stiffened" with sand, so as to permit them to flow more readily through the fingers. Obviously, the painting required every attention so that for the time being no other ceremonial activities were pursued. Conversation and smoking were therefore freely indulged in.

The painting represents the Monster Slayer. Points or knives make up his "dress" which he supplements by adding knives on his head, shoulders, wristlets, sides, and knees. He darts lightning from his feet, his left hand and head. His right hand holds the rattle. White footprints show his entry from his home in the east. At the cardinal points the sacred mountains of *sisnajinii*, Mount Taylor, San Francisco Peaks, and Perrin's Peak are represented in their respective colors.

The finished painting was sprinkled with pollen by the singer. He also decorated the sacred mountains (each) with a feather. The patient was then called back in and directed to approach the painting sunwise, to step in the "tracks" of the painting, on the figure itself, and there to be seated. Thereupon the patient was sprinkled with pollen which was subsequently passed on to the audience for a pinch. The tracks were then effaced. The bullroarer and the large arrow points were handed to the patient, while the singer recited two songs without rattle accompaniment. He then faced the patient and recited a long prayer with her, addressed to the Slayer of Monsters. This done, the patient pressed her limbs with the pollen bag and the arrow points. The audience tasted of the pollen and finally handed it to the patient who sprinkled the fire and smoke hole and resumed her usual place in the west corner. The feathers were then removed from the mountains with instructions to the assistants to carry and to deposit each in the (proper) cardinal direction—east, south, west, and north. The painting was then destroyed and the sand carried outside in blankets. The ceremony is thus concluded.

ELEVEN BUNDLES ON THE FOURTH NIGHT

On the fourth evening a large number of bundles of plants are prepared with feathered cords. Two of these bundles are decorated with wide-leafed or giant yucca in the shape of horns. In addition, eleven other bundles are made with crow feathers and are tied together with a single knot of yucca thong. An herb tea is prepared which is sputtered over the several bundles. Rattle and song accompany these preparations as well as the ritual that follows.

The singer dips his fingers into the herb mixture and unslips the knots—one (each) after pressing the limbs, the right and left foot, the right and left arms, the shoulders, at the front and on the back, and at the top of the head. Then he passes the strings through his hand over all body parts. He dips the feather broom into the ashes at the four points of the fire and sprinkles the patient with the plants. These he brushes away. The plants are then removed. He administers the herb medicine and the liniment. After this the patient drinks and bathes her body.

Another tea is prepared in which the four arrow points and the bullroarer are immersed. After this has been dedicated, the singer intones a song in the course of which the Slayers decorate the patient as follows: two bundles of plants with their growing parts turned upward, and feathers are tied to the soles, two to the knees, and two around the waist. During the next song another bundle is tied over the left shoulder and under the right arm, another over the right shoulder under the left arm. These together form the shoulderbands. One bundle decorates each wristlet to extend over the palm of the hand, while the eleventh, which shows the two horns of yucca, is secured to the forehead. The arrow points are then given to the Slayers, who pass through the hogan and outside. The next song calls them in again, and they proceed to walk around the patient cutting the air with their knives four times in the east, west, north, and south of the patient. Then they unravel or cut the various bundles, finally also the horned wreath on the head. After this they each press the limbs with the plants, which they then destroy, even to the yucca cord. Then they sprinkle the patient with plants, brush them off again and also brush the upper part of the hogan. The plants are then removed and deposited with a pinch of ashes.

Now the singer resumes his activity with the feather broom and, after dipping the feathers into the ashes at the cardinal points, brushes or taps the patient and subsequently the two sides of the hogan. This is repeated.

The Slayers now touch the bullroarer with medicine, that is, they moisten a finger in an herb mixture and apply it to the eyes and center of the bullroarer. Each brushes the ashes and then leaves. Taking turns, they whirl the bullroarer around the hogan, they re-enter and press the limbs of the patient with the bullroarer. Thereupon the liniment is applied to the limbs, the patient drinks of it and passes it along to the audience. Then the patient bathes her body. After this, the ashes are blown from the feathers through the smoke hole.

On the morning of the last day a bath is performed. Soil of the field is carried into the hogan where a small mound is spread in the west. Water is poured into a basket and four wide-leafed yucca ribs are placed into it, their tips extending toward the cardinal points. In addition, bundles of plants and spruce twigs which have been gathered from branches of the cardinal points, and a cup of ground cornmeal, make up the preparations for the ceremony.

The patient then enters. Her assistants are seated south of the basket. During the subsequent songs these assistants raise the yucca that is in the basket, whirling it in the water for foam. They continue whirling the yucca during several songs and frequently stir the water with their hands. The singer then marks the foam with four different kinds of pollen—white pollen from the east to the center, blue pollen from the south to the center, yellow pollen in the west, and dark pollen in the north. He marks the center "sunwise" with white meal. Then he adds a circle of pollen around the design from point to point. He also prints four crosses at the (cardinal) points on the soil and draws a circle around these with the pollen. In the center of (these circles on) soil, he plants the twigs of spruce and the bundles of plants.

The patient is then told to step on the two crosses in the west and to be seated on the earth. One of the attendants takes a pinch of pollen and foam from the cardinal points in the basket; he applies these to the soles, knees, chest, back, shoulders, and head. After this the patient undoes her hair with the help of her assistants. She then bathes her face, her head and hair in the yucca. The assistants screen her from view with a blanket curtain when she bathes her body. The soil is then removed in a blanket, together with the plants, spruce, and yucca. After the bath, during which the singer continues the songs, an assist-ant rubs the patient with pollen (cornmeal?)—her soles, knees, hands, front, back, cheeks, chin, and head. This the patient completes over her entire body. The rattle is then laid aside and the singer again applies pollen to the limbs of the patient, then east (his front), west (his back), south and north (his sides), and around, then upward over the body and from the mouth upward to the top of the head.

NINE BUNDLES ON THE FIFTH NIGHT

The first of the nine bundles of plants is decorated with olivella shell and a feather, and a slip knot is made to secure it by means of a feathered cord. The patient is seated in her usual place, the west corner of the hogan. Water is poured into the gourd ladle and into saucers, and a mixture of pulverized herbal leaves is added to the water. The rattle accompanies four or five songs, during which the bundles are spattered with the herbal mixture. The singer also dips his fingers into the mixture, picks up a bundle and presses the right leg and foot of the patient, unslipping it at the sole of this foot. The second bunch he repeats on the left leg and foot, unslipping against the left sole. The third song and bundle he applies to the right foot, then to the right breast, the chest and to the right arm, and there unslips the knot. The fourth song and bundle is applied to the patient's left side in the same order. With the fifth bundle he presses the chest right and left and unslips at the front. The sixth is pressed on the back, the right and left arm, and thence to the chest and right arm of the patient and is un-slipped on her back. The front shoulders are next as the seventh bundle is passed right and left and unslipped on the right shoulder. The eighth is pressed against the back and the left shoulder and is unslipped there. With the ninth and olivella shell-feathered bundle he presses the top of the head, its sides right and left, its front and back, and unslips it on the top of the head.

He now passes the feathered cords through his left hand which he holds in turn to the soles, knees, breast, front, back, and head. He gathers the plants in his left hand, taps them slightly with the crow-feathers broom, and allows the plants to shower on the patient. He then removes the plants with the brush. They are then removed to the north (of the hogan) and sprinkled with pollen as they are deposited there.

In the course of another song, the singer applies an internal medicine by way of the gourd ladle. Externally, liniment is applied to the soles, the knees, thighs, shoulders, arms, and head. Of this the patient also sips and with it completes a superficial body bath.

Another herb mixture is now prepared in a bowl as water is poured from each of the cardinal directions. Into this mixture varicolored arrow points are immersed from each of the cardinal directions, one is put in the center. The butt (thong) end of the bullroarer is finally

immersed from the east side of the bowl. The patient is seated on a
spread of calico print, while the two assistants, representing Monster
Slayer and Born-for-Water, await orders. The dress of spruce has been
placed at the right hand of the patient. During the subsequent song the
Slayers cover the patient with the spruce dress. The singer hands them
two of the arrow points and they leave the hogan. The song which
follows invites them to come inside again. They stand before the
covered patient and go through the motion of cutting from all cardinal
directions, from the top on down. After completing this cutting motion
from all sides, they remove the top bundle of plants at the top, then the
several wreaths. They gather the four spruce boughs, and with their
tips they press the limbs of the patient. During the song that follows
they cut up, over the patient, the bundles of plants of the several
wreaths. She unravels them completely and lays them aside. This
done, each Slayer showers an armful over the patient, who is then
brushed with the feather broom. They go outside, and the spruce and
plants are removed.

Several songs follow. With the bullroarer the singer makes four
crosses in the east, south, west, and north of the hogan and immediately erases them. Then he makes four straight lines at the north, west,
south, and east on the body of the patient and erases these also. Incense
is burned which the patient inhales, and the hot embers are thrown out
through the smoke hole. In the course of several more songs, he removes the cover from the patient with the bullroarer and with the
arrow points. Repeatedly he applies the bullroarer to all parts of the
body, starting with the right side and blowing toward the smoke hole
after each of the many applications of pressure. After this the bullroarer is whirled outside by the two Slayers, (then brought in and)
applied again to the patient. The herb tea is applied and passed to the
audience for drinking and bathing. Feathers are distributed, and the
ceremony is concluded with blowing the ashes toward the smoke hole.

American Tribal Religions

Available from the University of Nebraska Press, Lincoln

Volume 1. *Navajo Mountain and Rainbow Bridge Religion,* 1977.
Karl W. Luckert

Volume 2. *Love-Magic and Butterfly People: the Slim Curly Version of the Ajilee and Mothway Myths,* 1978.
Father Berard Haile, O.F.M.

Volume 3. *A Navajo Bringing-Home Ceremony: the Claus Chee Sonny Version of Deerway Ajilee,* 1978.
Karl W. Luckert

Volume 4. *Rainhouse and Ocean: Speeches for the Papago Year,* 1979.
Ruth M. Underhill, Donald M. Bahr, Baptisto Lopez, Jose Pancho, David Lopez

Volume 5. *Waterway: a Navajo Ceremonial Myth Told by Black Mustache Circle,* 1979.
Father Berard Haile, O.F.M.

Volume 6. *Women versus Men, a Conflict of Navajo Emergence — the Curly To Aheedliinii Version,* 1981.
Father Berard Haile, O.F.M.

Volume 7. *The Upward Moving and Emergence Way — the Gishin Biye' Version,* 1981.
Father Berard Haile, O.F.M.